石油科技英语系列教程

丛书主编 ◎ 吴松林　江淑娟

Geologic Exploration of Petroleum

石油地质与勘探

郭玉海　韩福勇　范金宏　张曦 ◎ 编

石油工业出版社

内 容 提 要

本书对石油地质勘探技术、油藏描述、油藏地质结构、地质结构与油气成藏以及石油勘探与开发的相关知识进行了介绍，并配有导读、词汇及词组翻译、重点句子讲解和强化学习等内容。

本书是石油相关专业的英文教材，也适合从事海外石油勘探开发工作的相关人员。

图书在版编目(CIP)数据

石油地质与勘探/郭玉海等编.
北京:石油工业出版社,2014.8
(石油科技英语系列教程)
ISBN 978-7-5183-0275-8

Ⅰ. 石…
Ⅱ. 郭…
Ⅲ. ①石油天然气地质-英语-教材
②油气勘探-英语-教材
Ⅳ. H31

中国版本图书馆 CIP 数据核字(2014)第 143105 号

出版发行:石油工业出版社
(北京安定门外安华里 2 区 1 号 100011)
网 址:http://pip.cnpc.com.cn
编辑部:(010)64251362 发行部:(010)64523620
经 销:全国新华书店
印 刷:北京中石油彩色印刷有限责任公司

2014 年 8 月第 1 版 2014 年 8 月第 1 次印刷
787×1092 毫米 开本:1/16 印张:16
字数:289 千字

定价:42.00 元
(如出现印装质量问题,我社发行部负责调换)

《石油科技英语系列教程》
编　委　会

前　言

全球石油资源分布、生产及消费三者间存在着严重的地区失衡，中东和亚太是失衡最严重的地区，中东地区严重供过于求，亚太地区严重供不应求。因此能源行业出现了全球化发展趋势，能源国际间的交流与合作日益密切。为保证中国能源安全，中国石油石化行业的国际化和本土化发展势在必行。中国油气企业正在积极进行海外业务拓展，了解资源地区的文化背景、经济发展状况、能源开发政策以及掌握其石油地质结构、油气成藏条件、开发和炼制技术等，将有利于我们对资源地区的油气开发和炼制，更有力地支持中国经济的快速发展。

自1993年起，为了解决石油院校和石油职工专业英语教材的严重匮乏的问题，丛书主编陆续出版了系列专业石油英语教科书，积累了一定的编写经验、培训经验和图书项目导向经验。20年过去了，石油行业也发生了巨大的变化，新油气资源不断发现，开采与炼制等技术不断更新，海外合作区域也不断拓宽。为了适应新形势，我们通过不懈的技术努力，在石油工业出版社的大力支持和协调下，开始编写一套更大规模的《石油科技英语系列教程》，既包括石油上、中、下游生产技术，也包括世界主要石油资源国的经济、贸易和文化等，目的是为读者奠定走向世界石油领域的语言基础。

我们深感责任重大，从中国石油大学（北京）、东北大学、东北石油大学、西安石油大学及各油田石油地质研究院、设计院等单位聘请有关专家学者，确定编写提纲，搜集资料。在选材上，注重内容的系统性，争取覆盖本领域主要内容；语言方面，注意遴选突出科技英语语言特点的语段和篇章，并对语言使用方法作详尽解释，以英语基础知识和基本技能的培养为主。为降低学习难度，为每篇课文还配写了汉语译文，以提高学生的石油科技英语阅读、翻译及写作能力。

《石油地质与勘探》分册本着英语语言能力与石油地质勘探专业知识相结合的原则，在编写过程中注意了以下几个方面：注重英语基础知识和基本技能的培养；注重石油地质专业英语知识的介绍；培养和提高学习者的英语阅读和翻译能力;为进一步进行相关专业学习打下基础;为学习者撰写本专业学术论文和进行国际学术交流打下基础。

本书共分为5章,分别对石油地质勘探技术、油藏描述、油藏地质结构、地质结构与油气成藏以及石油勘探与开发的相关知识进行了介绍。在每一节内,为了能够让学习者更好地掌握课文内容,均列出导读、相关专业词汇及词组翻译、重点句子讲解,并强化重点内容相关问题的学习。读者在回答问题的同时,可以巩固对课文的理解,进而掌握相关石油地质专业知识。为降低学习的难度,本书对文化背景中所涉及的专业词汇尽可能地作了详细的介绍。

本书各章节分工如下:范金宏编写第一章及第二章前两节;张曦编写第二章剩余部分及第三章;韩福勇编写第四章;郭玉海编写第五章。全书由郭玉海、韩福勇统稿。

本教材的编写得到了多位同仁的鼎力帮助。由于笔者水平有限,书中内容涉及面广、专业性强,难免出现不当之处,敬请专家和读者批评指正。

丛书主编:吴松林　江淑娟

2014 年 3 月

Contents

Chapter 1 Petroleum Geologic Exploration Technology

1.1 Palacios Field: A 3 – D Case History

Guidance to Reading

In late 1992, *Mitchell Energy shot its first* 3 – *D seismic program in the Texas Gulf Coast. The purpose was to unravel a fault pattern consisting of subtle faults — with throws of* 30 – 100 *ft — that significantly influence oil and gas production from Palacios Field in Matagorda County. The successful* 3 – *D survey allowed us to reconstruct the geologic history of the entire area. This text focuses mainly on three aspects of Palacios Field*: 3 – *D results, geologic history, and the distinctions between* 2 – *D and* 3 – *D survey.*

Text

In late 1992, Mitchell Energy shot its first 3 – D seismic program in the Texas Gulf Coast. The purpose was to **unravel** a **fault** pattern **consisting of** subtle faults — with **throws** of 30 – 100 ft — that significantly influence oil and gas production from Palacios Field in Matagorda County. The successful 3 – D **survey** revealed a fault pattern much different from those **derived from** 2 – D data and allowed us to reconstruct the geologic history of the entire area. Although oil and gas development in this area is very mature (the field was discovered in 1937), there are still many things to learn (even for Mitchell, which has been operating here since 1953)... and 3 – D is the best teaching tool we have.

Palacios Field is in the southwestern part of the county. The **coastal** town of Palacios sits on Tres Palacios Bay just south of the field. Over 230 billion ft^3 of gas and 7million bbl oil and **condensate**, from depths of 7,500 to 15,200ft, have been produced out of this rollover **anticlinal** feature which is downthrown to a large growth fault that we call, with great originality, the Palacios Fault.

The above figure is a **log** of the main producing zones, Frio A – G, which are very fine grain sands **deposited** in shallow water during the Middle **Oligocene**. The primary zones in this study are the F – 1 and G sands.

Mitchell Energy, over the years, purchased more than 200 miles of **seismic** data over the field. Although most were acquired 20 years ago, reprocessing maintained their usefulness for some time. In 1983, an F – 1 structure map was made from these data and well control. This map's fault pattern had a good fit with all of our data. Also, it supported a simple age – old model in the Texas Gulf Coast; i. e., local faults should **run parallel to** the main growth fault (the Palacios Fault in this case) and to the coast. The faults should also run parallel to each other and have similar timing. In other words, the model states that the structure should fall within one stress **regime** that is uniform in time and space. Or as one of our senior vice – presidents said, "Keep it simple, stupid." And why not? The data fit pretty well. Still, there were some **nagging** production **anomalies** that this map could not explain.

In 1990, we once again mapped the F – 1 sand structure. We added more 2 – D data, some of which were recent **40 – fold spec data**. This map is different from the 1983 map but, in general, it matches the simple structural model that we had in 1983 — parallel faults that are also parallel to the Palacios Fault to the north – west. The 1983 and 1990 maps are only two of many maps made over the years; each had its own fault pattern but all followed the idea of simple parallelism.

Even though the faults in the field are small (rarely exceeding 100ft of throw), correctly mapping them is critical when determining **drainage** and predicting **reservoir** quality. The faults are sealing, and deposition of the sands took place **contemporaneously** with the faults' movement. With the 1990 map in hand, we were ready to drill a new development well but we decided that it was in the long – term interest of the field, which we wanted to develop further, to shoot a 3 – D seismic survey to help **pin down** the fault pattern. (Also, the founder of our company, George Mitchell, said we needed to shoot a 3 – D survey over the field and we tend to do what George tells us.) The 7.5 mi^2 survey was acquired by Tide – lines Geophysical at the end of 1992.

3 – D RESULTS

The red event is the top of the F – 1 sand. In the initial stages of processing, we loaded **a brute stack of** the 3 – D volume onto a workstation and viewed an early version of this time slice. When we saw it, we were shocked. We immediately realized, from the time slice, that the fault pattern at Palacios was much different than expected. We had predicted that the 3 – D survey would lead to some minor changes in fault placement, not a gross **realignment** of faults. Some faults strike to the northeast and some to the west. Several **die out** as they extend from the south.

Based on the 3 – D survey, we made a new map of the F – 1 sand in 1993. There are now three distinct fault systems — **designated** red, blue, and orange.

The blue faults are downthrown to the east and run at a 60° – angle to the Palacios Fault. Also, the structural **contours** downthrown to the blue faults are parallel to the strike of the faults. Therefore, the fault system created this depositional structure. The F – 1 sand quality also improves downthrown to these faults.

The red faults are more complicated, but they are all downthrown to the south and run at a 30° – angle to the Palacios Fault. They have similar timing to the blue faults. All but one of the red faults **terminate** upon **intersecting** the blue fault system. Their influence on the quality of the F – 1 sand is less favorable.

The third system of faults is the orange system, seen best on the deeper G sand structure map. This fault system is parallel to the Palacios Fault. It is an older fault system that practically died at an angular **unconformity** that exists between the F and G sands. The unconformity marks the appearance of the *Nod. blan.* paleomarker and is the top of hard **geopressure**. The orange faults are critical to trapping gas in the G Sand.

The crossline, or strike line shows the three fault systems. The red faults and blue faults are clearly different systems with similar timing. The orange system parallels this seismic line and is difficult to see. It is important to note that all 3 – D seismic fault picks were subtle but obvious and exactly matched all fault picks in the wells.

GEOLOGIC HISTORY

We now recognize that the newly discovered complexity of the Palacios Field fault pattern is due to the history of the Palacios Fault and the deposition of **sediment** downthrown to it. Some have observed the fault pattern to be that of a **radial** distribution of faults that might **be associated with** a **diapir**. But there is neither salt nor **shale** diapirism at Palacios Field. The cause of the **divergence** of the fault systems lies in the deeper Lower Frio section.

The first significant deposition began with the Lower Frio *Anomalina bilateralis* and *Tex. miss*, sections. The sand – to – shale ratio is high in the Lower Frio. The shale – prone Middle Frio *Discorbis D and Nod. blan.* sections were deposited next with the growth rate on the Palacios Fault during *Discorbis D* time exceeding 100 – 1. We can demonstrate the presence of only 35 ft of *Discorbis D* upthrown to the fault, whereas nearly 6, 000 ft of section lies downthrown to the fault. The growth rate decreased substantially at the top of the *Nod. blan.* which falls between the F and G sands. The orange faults, parallel to the Palacios Fault, occurred during this time. Stress that caused this faulting was strongly controlled by the Palacios Fault. Also, the growth and movement along the Palacios Fault' s glide plane **tilted** and displaced basinward the sandy Lower Frio. This section, tilted as much as 40°, was relatively incompressible and acted as a **buttress** during Upper Frio deposition.

It was in Upper Frio time that most of the producing Frio sands were deposited with little growth on the Palacios Fault. The red and blue fault systems were activated as slumps by differential compaction on the **flanks** of the sand buttress. Without the 3 – D survey, we would not have been able to reliably reconstruct the geologic history of the area. So why did we not see this fault pattern with the 2 – D data set?

2 – D VERSUS 3 – D

One reason for the difference between the 2 – D maps and the 3 – D map is the inadequacy of the 2 – D seismic coverage. The 2 – D seismic lines are highlighted on the 1990 (before 3 – D) map. We interpreted the fault known as "01" primarily from cuts, some of which were **dubious**, on several 2 – D lines. Green circles highlight key fault intersections that were used to interpret the "01" fault. **As a result of** the 3 – D survey, we discovered the "01" fault cuts were actually the intersections of several different faults with the 2 – D seismic lines. We had mistakenly lined up the seismic cuts as those of a single fault. **In an effort to** keep the fault pattern simple on the 2 – D maps, this mistake was repeated on other faults. Only with the density of data offered by the 3 – D volume could we discern an accurate fault pattern.

Another 2 – D **pitfall** is the inability to image small faults. One of the 40 – fold spec lines we purchased is a dip line that **runs through** the middle of the survey. Its **multiplicity** is twice that of the highest fold of the 3 – D survey, and its trace interval is 82.5ft compared to a bin size of 110 × 110 ft. The 2 – D line's counterpart from the 3 – D volume was explained with the 3 – D fault interpretation. The **horizontal** and **vertical** scales of the two lines are identical. The contrast in the placement and the number of faults is striking. We would never have precisely and accurately interpreted the current fault pattern on the 2 – D line.

An obvious question is: "Did the 3 – D survey help us find new reserves at Palacios Field?" Answer: Probably not. Maps made before the 3 – D survey indicated that fault blocks existed that were undrilled and separated from other wells. Unfortunately, the radial distribution of faults that actually exists showed us that most of the Palacios feature is open to drainage and **pressure depletion** from most of the wells already drilled there. We now feel that there is some limited potential left there, but nothing commercial at current gas prices.

But, although we did not add reserves as a result of the 3 – D survey, we did save money. As previously stated, before we shot the 3 – D survey, we were fully prepared to drill a well based on the old maps. The 3 – D survey **kept us from** following that course of action. The survey's cost was about a third of the cost of a development well so savings were approximately $ 1 million.

Moreover, we have learned that small faults are critical in the field and other fields. We are presently **working on** a nearby 3 – D project where small, previously unmapped faults have created compartments, many of which are undrilled. There we hope to make money, not just save it.

When we **set out to** shoot a 3 – D survey over Palacios Field, we simply wanted to firm up some development locations by confirming our fault pattern. Instead we **ended up with** a much different fault pattern. The reasons are:

(1) Inadequate coverage and improper—or lack of—imaging of subtle faults on 2 – D seismic lines make it impossible to accurately and precisely interpret the correct fault pattern.

(2) A simple fault model can be supported by 2 – D data, but the complexities of the real world can only be understood **with the aid of** 3 – D seismic data.

The senior vice president who said, "Keep it simple, stupid," also said to us, "Think like a rock." For too long, interpreting geophysicists have kept their interpretations too simple, and too wrong, with two – dimensional data. With 3 – D data, we can now understand the true structural and **stratigraphic** nature of our prospects and we can now also formulate significant new ideas about structural and stratigraphic geology **in general** and **on a larger scale** than that of our prospects. Indeed, with 3 – D data, we are now able to truly think like a rock.

Words and Expressions

unravel	解开,阐明,弄清楚
fault	断层
throw	距离
survey	调查,测量,勘察
coastal	沿海的
condensate	冷凝物
anticlinal	背斜的
log	详细记录,航海日志
deposite	沉淀,沉积
Oligocene	渐新世[地质时代中古近纪(Paleogene)的最后一个主要分期,大约开始于3400万年前,终于2300万年前,介于始新世(Eocene)与新近纪的中新世(Miocene)之间]
seismic	地震的
parallel	平行的
regime	(某类现象发生时所需的,或者某类现象起主导作用时的)物理条件/环境
nagging	令人心烦的
anomaly	异常,异常现象
drainage	排水系统
reservoir	储层
contemporaneous	同时发生的,同时期的
realignment	重新排列
designate	标明,指定
contour	等值线

terminate	结束,终结
intersect	相交,交叉
unconformity	不整合面
geopressure	地压
sediment	沉淀物
radial	辐射状的,放射式的
diapir	底辟构造
shale	页岩
divergence	分叉,发散
tilt	倾斜
buttress	扶壁,扶垛,支墩,支撑体
flank	侧边,侧翼
dubious	可疑的
discern	看见,发现
pitfall	缺陷
multiplicity	多样性
horizontal	水平的
vertical	垂直的
depletion	消耗,损耗
stratigraphic	地层学的
Frio	得克萨斯州南部渐新统弗里奥(Frio)组。Frio组是一系列相互穿插的海相与非海相的页岩和砂岩。

Phrases and Expression

consist of	由……组成,构成;
derive from	源自于
run parallel to	与……平行的
pin down	把……固定住,敲定
a stack of	一堆,大量的
die out	逐渐消失
be associated with	与……有关,相关的
as a result of	由于,根据

in an effort to	为了
run through	穿过
kept . . . from doing	使……避免
work on	从事,致力于
set out to do	开始,着手
end up with	以……告终
with the aid of	借助于
in general	总体而言,大体上
on a . . . scale	在……的规模

Proper Name

40 – fold spec data	40 次覆盖专用资料
pressure depletion	压力损耗,压力递减

Language Focus

1. The successful 3 – D survey revealed a fault pattern much different from those derived from 2 – D data and allowed us to reconstruct the geologic history of the entire area.

(参考译文:这次成功的三维地震勘探发现了与依据二维地震资料所做的完全不同的断层组合形式,使我们能重建整个地区的地质发展史。)

本句中 revealed 与 allowed 是并列谓语,而 much different from those derived from 2 – D data 是形容词短语充当 a fault pattern 的后置定语。在这个结构中 derived from 2 – D data 是过去分词短语充当 those 的后置定语。

2. With the 1990 map in hand, we were ready to drill a new development well but we decided that it was in the long – term interest of the field, which we wanted to develop further, to shoot a 3 – D seismic survey to help pin down the fault pattern.

(参考译文:我们曾准备用手头上现有的 1990 年的构造图钻一口新的开发井,但为了油田的长期利益——因为我们想进一步开发它——我们做了一次三维地震测量,这有助于把断层组合敲定下来。)

本句的主干是由 but 连接的并列句结构。But 后面的句子中 that. . . 是宾语从句,该从句由 it 作为不定式 to shoot a 3 – D seismic survey to help pin down the fault pattern 结构的形式主语。句中 which we wanted to develop further 是非限制性定语从句。

3. Unfortunately, the radial distribution of faults that actually exists showed us that most of the Palacios feature is open to drainage and pressure depletion from most of the wells already drilled there.

（参考译文：不幸的是，实际上存在的放射状分布断层向我们指明，多数 Palacios 断层特性是与排液系统相通的，且从这里许多已钻的井来看，油层压力都已在递减。）

本句中 showed 是谓语动词，全句主干为主语 + 谓语 + 双宾语结构。句中 that actually exists 是主语 the radial distribution 的定语从句。Showed 的间接宾语为 us，直接宾语是 that most of the Palacios feature is open to drainage and pressure depletion from most of the wells already drilled there 从句。从句中 already drilled there 是过去分词短语充当 the wells 的后置定语。

4. We are presently working on a nearby 3 – D project where small, previously unmapped faults have created compartments, many of which are undrilled.

（参考译文：目前，我们已在附近做一块三维勘探，上面有许多小的、以前构造图上没有的断层组成封闭断块，许多断块上还未钻过井。）

本句中 We are presently working on a nearby 3 – D project 是主句，where small, previously unmapped faults have created compartments 是地点状语从句，many of which are undrilled 是非限制性定语从句。

5. With 3 – D data, we can now understand the true structural and stratigraphic nature of our prospects and we can now also formulate significant new ideas about structural and stratigraphic geology in general and on a larger scale than that of our prospects.

（参考译文：现在用三维地震资料则可以认识到我们所勘探的真实构造和地层特征，并且我们可以以常规的，并以比原有期待更大的范围去阐述重要而且全新的有关构造地质和地层地质的概念。）

本句主干 we can... and we can... 为 and 连接的并列句。

Reinforced Learning

Ⅰ. Answer the following questions for a comprehension of the text.

1. What is the purpose of the 3 – D seismic program in the Texas Gulf by Mitchell Energy in late 1992?

2. Why were the researchers shocked when they loaded a stack of the 3 – D volume onto a workstation and viewed an early version of this time slice?

3. When were the producing Frio sands deposited on the Palacios Fault.

4. Did the 3 – D survey help us find new reserves at Palacios Field? If not, what is the significance of this survey?

5. In the last paragraph, "think like a rock" appears twice. Do they have the same meaning? If not, what's your interpretation of them?

Ⅱ. Multiple choice: choose the correct one from the alternative answers to give the exact meaning of the words.

1. Police are trying to unravel the mystery of their sudden disappearance.

A. answer B. unfasten C. undo D. undertake

2. They designate Mr. yang as director of the laboratory.

A. sign B. resign C. appoint D. signal

3. He was just able to discern the road in the dark.

A. concern B. see C. discover D. uncertain

4. Mankind have been trying every means to maintain the balance of nature.

A. preserve B. contain C. attain D. captain

5. A week consist of seven days.

A. compose of B. is made up of C. make up of D. constitute

6. Thousands of English words derive from Latin.

A. keep from B. prevent from C. come from D. result from

7. Europe's foreign ministers met this week in an effort to devise an approach to Iran.

A. effect B. attempt C. affection D. efficiency

8. Streets usually intersect at right angles.

A. cross B. interact C. intercept D. interior

9. We interpreted his silence as a refusal.

A. intended B. understand C. initiated D. innovated

10. Ozone – layer depletion above the Arctic is not as extensive as expected because of unusually warm weather.

A. completion B. repetition C. competition D. loss

Ⅲ. Multiple choice: read the four suggested translations and choose the best answer.

1. In other words, the model states that the structure should fall within one stress regime that is uniform in time and space.

A. 政体 B. 范围 C. 统治 D. (物理)状态

2. The purpose was to unravel a fault pattern consisting of subtle faults.

A. 故障 B. 错误 C. 断层 D. 缺点

3. The above figure is a log of the main producing zones, Frio A – G, which are very fine grain sands deposited in shallow water during the Middle Oligocene.

A. 圆木 B. 日志 C. 对数 D. 测井

4. Some have observed the fault pattern to be that of a radial distribution of faults that might be associated with a diapir.

A. 底辟 B. 绝望 C. 维修 D. 灵感

5. But there is neither salt nor shale diapirism at Palacios Field.

A. 鲸鱼 B. 形状 C. 页岩 D. 荫凉

Ⅳ. Put the following sentences into Chinese.

1. In late 1992, Mitchell Energy shot its first 3 – D seismic program in the Texas Gulf Coast.

2. Still, there were some nagging production anomalies that this map could not explain.

3. It was in Upper Frio time that most of the producing Frio sands were deposited with little growth on the Palacios Fault.

4. Without the 3 – D survey, we would not have been able to reliably reconstruct the geologic history of the area.

5. Only with the density of data offered by the 3 – D volume could we discern an accurate fault pattern.

Ⅴ. Put the following paragraphs into Chinese.

1. The application of physics to the study of rocks (geophysics) is very important in petroleum geology. In its broadest application, geophysics makes a major contribution to understanding the earth's crust and, especially through the application of modern plate tectonic theory, the genesis and petroleum potential of sedimentary basins. More specially, physical concepts are required to understand folds, faults, and diapirs, and hence their roles in petroleum entrapment.

2. Seismology is the branch of geology that deals with the movement of waves through the earth. The study of the form and occurrence of earthquake waves recorded by seismographs has been the principal source of knowledge of

the constitution of the interior of the earth. Using a special type of seismograph, or geophone, seismic surveys explore the geological structure in the earth's sedimentary section by recording the ground movements produced by man – made explosions.

1.2 Stewart Field, Finney County, Kansas: Seismic Definition of Thin Channel Reservoirs

Guidance to Reading

Fluvial channel sandstones of Early Pennsylvanian (Morrowan) age comprise regional reservoirs in parts of Colorado, Kansas, Texas, and Oklahoma. In southwestern Kansas, these reservoirs commonly exist at depths of 4000 – 5000*ft* (1200 – 1500*m*) *and have reserves of* 150,000 – 200,000*bbl of oil per well, making them highly economical. Reservoir sandstones form part of transgressive valley – fill sequences deposited within channels incised into underlying Mississippian carbonates. Thickness of the fill varies up to* 60*ft* (18*m*), *is commonly* 10 – 30*ft* (3 – 9*m*), *and displays rapid changes along channel length. As a result, detailed mapping of channel trends is difficult. Stewart field, located in Finney County, Kansas, is a good example of this type of reservoir. Maximum reservoir quality exists in very fine to fine – grained fluvial sandstones reworked by tidal action. Early attempts to extend the field to the east failed because existing two – dimensional seismic and well data did not help workers properly resolve channel orientation. A three – dimensional* (3 – *D*) *seismic survey, shot prior to initiation of waterflood operations, helped* (1) *locate the channel between existing dry holes and* (2) *identify prospective locations that were then successfully drilled. Further extrapolation of the* 3 – *D data resulted in a dry hole that established the limits of interpretation in this area. Stewart field thus provides an important case study regarding the capabilities and limitations of* 3 – *D data in exploring the interwell frontier.*

Text

INTRODUCTION

Lower Pennsylvanian Morrowan channels are productive of oil and gas within the greater Hugoton **embayment** of Texas, Oklahoma, Kansas, and Colorado. Such channels developed within and along the margins of a paleobasin during a major regressive event. Erosional valleys incised into underlying Upper Mississippian limestones were sequentially filled with **fluvial** material, estuarine sands, and marine muds. Oil – productive channels are those containing fluvial sandstones that were either deposited under high – energy conditions or reworked and winnowed by tidal influence.

The distribution of Morrowan channel sandstones is commonly complex, involving crosscutting relationships. Individual channels contain not one but several valley – fill sequences, at different stratigraphic levels and in different stages of preservation. Later sequences are frequently incised into earlier sequences. Not all fill sequences contain reservoir – quality sandstones. In addition, abrupt changes in net sandstone thickness and character occur along the length of most channels. Thus, predicting reservoir occurrence can be difficult using traditional subsurface methods. Channel sandstone thicknesses averaging 25 – 30ft (7.5 – 9m) place distinct limits on the ability of two – dimensional (2 – D) seismic data interpretation to resolve potential reservoirs. Reservoir resolution has been significantly advanced by the recent careful application of three – dimensional (3 – D) seismic data.

Stewart field, located in Finney County, Kansas, provides an excellent case study of such application. Originally drilled and developed as a shallow Mississippian pool in 1956, the field was later expanded by unanticipated discovery in the overlying Morrowan at 4700 – 4800ft (1430 – 1460m) depth. Several wells encountered a thin, oil – productive sandstone (15ft (4m) or less), but operators were unable to locate the thicker part of the relevant sandstone. Finally, a well drilled by Sharon Resources in 1985, the 3 Sherman encountered 36.5 net ft (11m) of reservoir sandstone distributed among three valley – fill sequences. Subsequent acquisition of 2 – D seismic data **resulted in** the drilling of more than 30 producers and only 5 dry holes by 1994. Despite such success, the thickest part of the channel, later shown to have as much as 55 ft (16.6 m) of net sandstone, was not penetrated. Moreover, subtleties in the occurrence of productive and unproductive channel subfacies could not be adequately explained by 2 – D seismic interpretation. The lack of such explanation was recognized as a potential difficulty for unitization and waterflood studies.

A small – scale, 1.5 mi^2 (3.2 km^2) 3 – D seismic survey shot in 1994 proved essential in advancing understanding of the reservoir and suggests the value of related data to the study of thin reservoirs elsewhere. Better delineation of channel boundaries and improved prediction of reservoir occurrence were important results of this survey. **On the basis of** the data acquired, Sharon Resources determined that three dry holes, drilled on the basis of 2 – D seismic anomalies, had narrowly missed probable reservoir sandstone, instead penetrating parts of the channel where siltstone and shale formed the main fill. The dry holes would not have been drilled if the 3 – D data had been available. The $42,000 cost of the 3 – D survey would have saved nearly $0.5 million in drilling expenditures. In addition, future development of Stewart field, including secondary recovery, will benefit strongly from the enhanced ability to locate and characterize Morrowan channel facies.

The following report is a summary of geological and geophysical information relevant to the 3 – D recharacterization of Stewart field. These data are considered to have broad potential significance regarding analyses of thin sandstone reservoirs, especially those with erratic or complex distribution.

REGIONAL SETTING

Stewart field lies in the northeastern part of the Hugoton embayment, along the margin of the giant Hugoton gas – producing complex. It is among a number of areas in southeastern Colorado, western Kansas, and northwestern Oklahoma that produce oil from Lower Pennsylvanian (Morrowan) channels. These channels formed as a result of transgressive – regressive cycles that characterized the Hugoton embayment at this time. The boundary between Mississippian and Pennsylvanian sediments is marked by a regional unconformity and a marked change from limestone to clastic deposition, corresponding to a major regressive event. Coastal onlap patterns indicate a maximum of 6 – 7 transgressive – regressive cycles within the succeeding Morrowan section. The preserved record of these cycles varies with location relative to the limits of the Hugoton embayment and surrounding uplift areas.

The Hugoton embayment during Early Pennsylvanian transgressive episodes was an extensive, northwest – trending oceanic arm bounded by several major uplift provinces. These provinces include the Central Kansas uplift to the northeast; the Transcontinental arch to the north; the Las Animas arch/Ancestral Front Range to the northwest; and the Sierra Grande uplift to the west. All of these areas display evidence of structural activity at this time related to movements **associated with** the early stages of collision between the proto – North American and South American continents (Kluth,1986; Rigo and Kanes,1986). Plate reconstructions suggest the region of southwestern Kansas lay in an equatorial position (Kluth,1986).

During the Morrowan, this region was crossed by southwest – draining stream systems sourced in the Central Kansas uplift. During episodes of sea level highstand, marine waters encroached upon this highland and extended as far north as southern Nebraska. During periods of minimum lowstand, the ocean withdrew almost entirely from the area of southwestern Kansas. At such times, the Central Kansas uplift became a major supplier of detritus. Resulting fluvial systems were typified by low gradients over the exposed marine shelf and by intense seasonal discharge, which aided both rapid incision and later **aggradation** (Krystinik and Blakeney,1990). These fluvial systems debouched into the Anadarko basin, where they fed deltaic complexes (Swanson,1979).

Initial Morrowan **regression** produced an erosional surface with progressively older Mississippian deposits exposed northward. Early channels incised into carbonates that included the St. Louis and Spergen intervals to the north and the Stc. Genevieve to the south (Wheeler et al. ,1990). Channel development may have been locally influenced by subtle topographic variation related to basement fault zones (Sonnenberg,1985).

DISPOSITIONAL MODEL: MORROWAN CHANNELS

Detailed depositional models for Morrowan channels in eastern Colorado and southwestern Kansas have been presented by several authors (see, for example, Sonnenberg,1985; Clark,1987; Krystinik and Blakeney,1990; Wheeler et al. ,1990). These interpretations emphasize the following sequence of events:

- Maximum regression, resulting in initial channel incision into underlying platform shelf carbonates;
- Early transgressive phase, causing deposition of **basal** lag or coarse sand above a scoured surface;
- Middle **transgressive** phase, during which further aggradation of fluvial material takes place, including deposition of mainly fine – to medium – grained channel sands in stacked sequences, at times interbedded with finer grained floodplain silts and muds;

• Late transgressive phase, producing deposition of fine – grained, tidally influenced (**estuarine**) sands grading upward into tidal flat and estuarine/bay muds (this phase is also marked by a general widening of valley walls **due to** marine erosion);

• Maximum transgression, during which deposition of marine muds occurs, capping the channel – fill sequence.

In the Stewart field area, which lies on the southwestern flank of the Central Kansas uplift, three valley – fill sequences are apparent (Clark and Steinhauser, 1996). This area existed at a somewhat higher elevation than did easternmost Colorado, where seven such sequences have been identified and mapped along the paleo – axis of the Hugoton embayment (Blakeney et al. ,1990). Evidence from seismic and well – log data indicates that the channel system at Stewart field is highly linear and was structurally controlled by faulting or by local **topographic** features related to horst – graben development (C. Clark, 1996, personal communication).

The relative percentage of lag, channel, and estuarine material in any specific valley – fill sequence appears related to three possible factors: (1) location of the channel within the Hugoton embayment, (2) channel geometry, apt (3) relative rate of sea level rise. Channels along the state line between Colorado and Kansas display linear geometries and contain a significant proportion of coarse – grained lower channel and basal lag facies. Locations more marginal to the emlayment, such as those in Finney County, southwestern Kansas, were typified by stream systems of lower energy. In these areas, coarse valley fill is less abundant, whereas fine – grained fluvial and estuarine facies form a higher percentage of the total section. Channels with linear geometries ill these areas seem to have enhanced tidal action through "funneling", **thereby** resulting in a larger amount of reworked and **winnowed** fluvial material.

Krystinik and Blakeney (1990), however, from their studies in the state line area, have proposed that larger amounts of coarse channel debris reflect gradual transgression at a relatively constant rate. More rapid drowning of valley, in contrast, is interpreted by these authors to have produced fill sequences characterized by increased upper channel and tidally influenced (estuarine) deposits relative to coarse material.

Both interpretive schemes can be applied to Stewart field. The field comprises a linear channel system along the northeastern margin of the Hugoton embayment. Paleo – elevation probably permitted gradual flooding of the area only during the more extensive Morrowan **transgressive** events. Such flooding resulted in the creation of estuaries and in the deposition of **tidally** influenced sandstones, including reworked channel facies. Such sandstones are particularly abundant in the Stewart field area and **serve as** the more high – quality reservoirs.

Total thickness of the Horrowan interval in southwestern Kansas, along the eastern flank of the Hugoton embayment, ranges from 0 – 300ft (0 – 90m). In the Stewart field area, the Morrow corresponds entirely to channel fill and is up to 53. 5ft (24m) thick, being more commonly **in the range of** 10 – 35 ft (3 – 11m). Coarse – grained, basal lag deposits are rare to absent; fluvial material consists mainly of very fine to fine – grained sandstone, silt – stone, and shale. Above the valley – fill section, Morrowan or lowermost Atokan deposits comprise marine shales. This general setting makes an excellent petroleum system, including source, reservoir, and seal.

STEWART FIELD: MORROWAN RESERVOIRS

On the basis of abundant well data, three stacked valley – fill sandstones have been identified within the productive Morrow channel complex at Stewart field. Productive intervals are in very fine to fine – grained and moderate to well – sorted material that has been reworked and winnowed of fines by tidal action. **Porosities** and permeabilities range from 8% to 20% and 5 to 250 mD, respectively. A lower porosity cutoff of 12% is used to **designate** effective pay. Reservoir quality is highest in the oldest valley – fill sandstone (VF – 3) and lowest in the more radioactive middle sandstone interval (VF – 2).

The geometry, dimensions, and orientation of the total channel complex are indicated by the net pay **isopach** map. The channel is more than 5 mi (8 km) in length and ranges from 0. 25 to 0. 40 mi (0. 40 – 0. 61 km) in width. Net sandstone thickness **attains** a maximum of 45 – 55 ft (14 – 17m) at several places along the length of the channel, where abrupt changes in valley direction take place from an east – west to a northwest – southeast orientation. Increases in channel depth at these locations, marked by **isopach maxima**, are possibly related to more intense **scouring** caused by faulting in the underlying Mississippian carbonates.

The **diagenesis** of Morrowan channel sandstones has been discussed by Rader (1990). Early diagenetic products include **chlorite**, quartz overgrowths, and carbonate cement. Carbonate cement was largely removed by subsequent dissolution prior to the emplacement of hydrocarbons, at which point diagenetic alteration ceased. Burial history data suggest hydrocarbon emplacement occurred in the Late Cretaceous (Rader, 1990; Sonnenberg et al., 1990).

PRODUCTION

Reserve estimates for Stewart field are in the range of 5 to 7 million bbl of oil.

Individual Morrow wells are predicted to be capable of producing 150,000 – 200,000 bbl, including an average primary recovery of 100,000 bbl and additional recovery of 50,000 – 100,000 bbl from **waterflood** operations.

Production rates have ranged from 75 – 120 bbl per day on completion, declining to 30 – 50 bbl per day within the first year and thereafter showing little or no decline. Wells produce from depths of 4750 – 4850 ft (1440 – 1470 m) and can be drilled and completed without significant problems. This has made the field highly economical to develop.

3 – D SEISMIC SURVEY: ADVANTAGES AND LIMITATIONS

A 3 – D seismic survey was **conducted** in 1994 to help define the eastern limits of the field. This survey was intended to improve reservoir characterization for the purposes of continued field development and future waterflood operations. The total area covered by the survey was 1.5 mi^2 (3.2 km^2), centered on Sec. 7, T23S, R30W. Three dry holes drilled in 1987 appeared to define the limit of Morrowan productivity in this area. These three wells, the 7 – 6 Bulger, 7 – 7 Bulger, and 7 – 9 Bulger, all in Sec. 7, had been sited on the basis of 2 – D seismic data, which indicated **amplitude anomalies** commonly associated with Morrow channels. As displayed in the seismic model, such anomalies **consist of** a **couplet** (trough and peak) corresponding to channel fill and its lower contact with Mississippian carbonates. The Morrowan trough, in particular, becomes **prominent** at thicknesses above 25 ft (7.6 m). In the case of the 7 – 6 and 7 – 7 Bulger wells, the anomalies were associated with tight siltstone and shale channel fill.

Interpretation of 3 – D data revealed that these wells were in fact drilled on either side of sandstone – bearing fill. The inline sections suggest that the 7 – 6 and 7 – 7 wells would have been productive if drilled a few hundred feet (about 100m) to the northeast and southwest, respectively.

On the basis of this success and of anomalies evident from 2 – D data, a second 3 – D survey was performed in 1995 to the east, covering a 1.5 mi^2 (3.2km^2) area in Sec. 8, 9, 16, and; 17 (T23S, R3W). In this area, two Morrow wells had been completed at low rates, yet with sufficient reservoir pressures to suggest the presence of higher quality sandstone nearby.

Information from the 3 – D survey suggested the Morrowan valley broadened in this area, with thinning of the total fill sequence. A well drilled on an identified 3 – D anomaly, the 8 – 6 Haflich, was located 300ft (91m) southeast from one of the marginal producers, which had logged 18ft (5.5m) of Morrowan sandstone. The 8 – 6 Haflich encountered no sandstone, but instead 8ft (2.4m) of fine – grained clastics and an underlying section of highly **porous** Ste. Genevieve limestone with a transit time of 67 s/ft (221 s/m). It was **discerned** that the location lay close to the subcrop edge of the Ste. Genevieve and that the mapped 3 – D anomaly reflected increased porosity related to erosion in this interval.

Subsequent **seismic** modeling confirmed this in part. Equal thicknesses of Morrowan sandstone and porous Ste. Genevieve are capable of generating very similar responses, with the single difference of slightly stronger amplitudes in the case of Morrowan sandstone. This allowed for fine tuning of the Morrow seismic model and established the limitations of 3 – D interpretation in this area. It should provide an essential guide for exploration and development of Morrow reservoirs **elsewhere** in southwestern Kansas.

CONCLUSION

Morrowan channels with reservoir – quality sandstones exist across a broad area in the Hugoton embayment of Colorado and Kansas. Many such channels have been explored and developed, particularly in eastern Colorado. Others, as yet unexploited, undoubtedly exist in parts of western and southwestern Kansas. The data presented in this report offer a guide for prospecting the Morrowan in these underexplored areas.

More generally, Stewart field provides an example of the benefits and limitations that can result from the use of 3 – D seismic data to **delineate** thin channel sandstone reservoirs. Such reservoirs exist in many parts of North America, including the Gulf Coast region, being typical of fluvial, **deltaic**, tidal, **barrier island**, submarine channel, and other **lithofacies**. Development of these reservoirs, including enhanced recovery operations, has often been constrained by the **inability** to accurately **map** and **characterize** their occurrence. As a result, thin sandstone reservoirs constitute an important **interwell** frontier for future drilling. As the case of Stewart field makes clear, 3 – D data are an important new tool for opening this frontier, but are unlikely to resolve all difficulties resulting from geologic complexity.

Words and Expressions

embayment	湾形物,形成港湾
fluvial	河的,河流的;河流作用的;栖于河中的
aggradation	沉积
regression	复归,回归;退步,退化,消退
basal	基础的,基本的,基部的,构成基部的
transgressive	越过(范围、限度等);违反,违背(规则、法律、条约等)
estuarine	(江河口、港湾等)沉积的;江河口的; 港湾的
excavation	挖掘,发掘,挖掘成的洞,出土文物
topographic	地志的,地形学上的
partial	部分的,局部的,偏袒的,偏爱的
thereby	因此,从而,在那方面,在那附近
regressive	回归的
winnowed	扬净的, 风选的
transgression	违反,犯罪,【地】海侵,海进
tidally	潮汐地,潮水般地
porosity	多孔性,有孔性
designate	指明,指出,任命,指派
isopach	等厚线
attain	达到,获得
scouring	擦[洗]净,冲刷,洗涤
diagenesis	【地质】成岩作用,岩化作用
chlorite	【矿】绿泥石;【化】亚氯酸盐
waterflood	注水入(油井)

estimate	估计,估价,评估
conducted	引导,管理,为人,传导,进行
amplitude	广阔,丰富,振幅,物理学名词
anomaly	不规则,异常的人或物
couplet	对句; 双韵; [pl.]对联;【生】偶联体
prominent	卓越的,显著的,突出的
porous	多孔渗水的
discerned	目睹,认识,洞悉,辨别,看清楚
seismic	【地】地震的
elsewhere	在别处,往别的地方;在另外一地方
delineate	描绘
deltaic	三角洲的; 三角形的
lithofacies	岩相(术)
inability	无能力,无才能
map	绘制地图
characterize	表现……的特色,刻画的……性格
interwell	井间的

Phrases and Expression

result in	导致
on the basis of	以……为基础
be associated with	与……有关,与……有关系
due to	由于,应归于
serve as	被用作……,充当……,起……的作用
in the range of	在……范围内;在射程内
consist of	由……组成,构成

Proper Name

isopach maxima	最大等厚线
barrier island	障壁岛

Language Focus

1. Thus, predicting reservoir occurrence can be difficult using traditional subsurface methods.

(参考译文:因此,运用传统的地下方法预测储层就很困难。)

本句中 predicting reservoir occurrence 为动名词加逻辑宾语做主语,后接系动词 be + difficult 表语表示“做某件事是困难的”。句中 using 为现在分词接逻辑宾语做方式状语,意为以“运用传统的地下方法”这种方式。

2. Originally drilled and developed as a shallow Mississippian pool in 1956, the field was later expanded by unanticipated discovery in the overlying Morrowan at 4700 – 4800ft (1430 – 1460m) depth.

(参考译文:1956 年时,将该油田作为浅层密西西比油藏进行勘探和开发。后来由于在 4700 ~ 4800ft (1430 ~ 1460m) 深的上覆莫罗地层中有了意外的发现使油田得到扩展。)

本句中 Originally drilled and developed as a shallow Mississippian pool in 1956 为动词过去分词做定语,表示动作 drilled 和 developed 与逻辑主语 field 的被动关系。

3. More rapid drowning of valley, in contrast, is interpreted by these authors to have produced fill sequences characterized by increased upper channel and tidally influenced (estuarine) deposits relative to coarse material.

(参考译文:相反的是,这些作者将峡谷更快速的水淹解释为产生了充填层序,这些层序的特征为递增的上河道和受潮汐影响(河口湾)的沉积物(这些沉积物为较粗粒物质)。)

本句主干为 drowning of valley is interpreted by these authors, to have sth. characterized by sth. 为目的状语,意为“使……具有某种特征”。increased 和 influenced 为过去分词做定语表示被动关系意为“被增长的”和“受……影响的”。“in contrast” 为插入状语,表示“相反”。

4. In the Stewart field area, the Morrow corresponds entirely to channel fill and is up to 53.5 ft (24 m) thick, being more commonly in the range of 10 – 35ft (3 – 11m).

(参考译文:在斯图尔特油田,莫罗层相当于整个的河道充填层序,厚达 53.5ft (24.0m),一般为 10 ~ 35ft(3 ~ 11m)。)

本句中 the Morrow 为句子主语,corresponds 和 is 为并列谓语。句中 being more commonly in the range of 10 – 35ft (3 – 11m) 为伴随状语,进一步解释说明莫罗层的平均厚度。

5. Carbonate cement was largely removed by subsequent dissolution prior to the emplacement of hydrocarbons, at which point diagenetic alteration ceased.

(参考译文:碳酸盐胶结物在烃类进入前已溶解运移掉,成岩作用于烃类进入时停止。)

本句中 prior to 表示“在……之前”,作时间状语。句中 at which point diagenetic alteration ceased 为介词 at + 关系代词 which 引导非限定性定语从句,修饰 the emplacement of hydrocarbons。介词 at 来源于词组 cease at... point,此词组意为“停止于某一点”。

Reinforced Learning

Ⅰ. Answer the following questions for a comprehension of the text.

1. Where are the Lower Pennsylvanian Morrowan channels are productive of oil and gas within the greater Hugoton embayment of Texas, Oklahoma, Kansas, and Colorado?

2. What can you infer from the evidence from seismic and well – log data in the Stewart field area?

3. What are the factors did the relative percentage of lag, channel, and estuarine material in any specific valley – fill sequence appears relate to?

4. What did result in a larger amount of reworked and winnowed fluvial material?

5. Is it possible for operators to locate the thicker part of the relevant sandstone, when several wells encountered a thin, oil – productive sandstone?

Ⅱ. Multiple choice: choose the correct one from the alternative answers to give the exact meaning of the words.

1. I could give it only <u>partial</u> support.
A. unfair　B. incomplete　C. fond　D. Inclined

2. I have never been to that city; <u>thereby</u> I don't know much about it.
A. thereafter　B. therewith　C. therefore　D. thereto

3. He was <u>designated</u> by the President as the next Secretary of State.
A. designed　B. assigned　C. intended　D. doomed

4. She <u>attained</u> her ambition of becoming a pilot.
A. achieved　B. found　C. arrived at　D. caught up

5. His <u>conduct</u> of the business was very successful.
A. behavior　B. manners　C. deal　D. management

6. Our house is the <u>most prominent</u> one in the street; it's painted red.
A. most outstanding　B. largest

C. greatest D. most beautiful

7. The scientists mapped the surface of the moon.

A. drew B. located C. planed D. explored

8. I soon discerned that the man was lying.

A. resolved B. interpreted C. picked out D. interfered

9. Due to the extreme cold, we were unable to plant the trees.

A. Enough to B. Because of C. Proper fo D. Thanks to

10. We found that birch bark could serve as paper.

A. serve for B. serve on C. serve out D. serve with

Ⅲ. Multiple choice: read the four suggested translations and choose the best answer.

1. It is historical regression.

A. 遗憾 B. 倒退 C. 回归 D. 恢复

2. This is viewed as a consequence of our inability to understand and treat a complex problem .

A. 无力气 B. 不可能 C. 不能够 D. 有能力

3. I told you I was sorry for my little transgression, and you forgave me.

A. 冒犯 B. 海进 C. 海侵 D. 超度

4. The treasure survived until its excavation in 1978.

A. 处理 B. 挖掘 C. 维修 D. 破损

5. The two most common forms of skin cancer are basal cell and squamous cell cancers.

A. 基底 B. 表皮 C. 真皮 D. 鳞状

Ⅳ. Put the following sentences into Chinese.

1. Channel development may have been locally influenced by subtle topographic variation related to basement fault zones

2. This phase is also marked by a general widening of valley walls due to marine erosion

3. Evidence from seismic and well – log data indicates that the channel system at Stewart field is highly linear and was structurally controlled by faulting or by local topographic features related to horst – graben development.

4. Porosities and permeabilities range from 8% to 20% and 5 to 250mD,

respectively.

5. It should provide an essential guide for exploration and development of Morrow reservoirs elsewhere in southwestern Kansas.

V. Put the following paragraphs into Chinese.

1. The complete sequence is commonly not preserved, due to partial excavation by later streams that developed during subsequent regressive events. Parts of many channels appear to have remained topographic lows throughout Morrowan deposition, thereby in effect attracting reoccupation by succeeding fluvial systems. Most major channels display the effects of multiple episodes of valley – fill deposition.

2. Information presented by Montgomery (1992) for Morrowan reservoirs along the Colorado – Kansas state line suggests that the rate at which a well is produced may influence its ultimate recovery. Modeling indicates that for a given well spacing, ultimate recoveries may increase slightly (up to a maximum of 10%) if rates of daily production are reduced by 50% of their flow or pump capacity. This may be related to the fact that channel reservoirs are somewhat underpressured. No relationship was observed or implied between well spacing and ultimate recovery.

1.3 Prestack Processing of Land Data with Complex Topography

Guidance to Reading

A new wave – equation – based prestack seismic processing system is proposed. This system has only two essential elements; velocity analysis and depth migration. This approach applies truly surface – consistent statics corrections, regardless of the amount of elevation, change or of near – surface velocity variation. It uses tomography for estimating the details of shallow velocities and a finite – difference solution of the two – way wave – equation both for computation of image times and for data extrapolation in migration. A field data set that violates most of the assumptions in conventional common midpoint (CMP) processing, because of severe elevation changes and near – surface velocity variations, is successfully processed. The final depth section reveals a complicated fold – thrust geometry that was not visible after CMP processing.

Text

INTRODUCTION

Most seismic survey lines over tectonically **deformed** areas have complicated topography. Rajasekaran and McMechan (1992) proposed a new approach to prestack processing that handles both marine and land data with equal ease. This is a **wave – equation** based processing system that uses reverse – time migration. What is unique about the approach is that static corrections for extreme topographic variations are applied implicitly during migration rather than as an explicit, separate step. The goal of this paper is to briefly review the main elements in this prestack processing system and to illustrate its viability by applying it to field data with severe elevation and near – surface velocity statics.

FIELD DATA ACQUISITION AND CHARACTERISTICS

The field data used in the example below are from the Andean Orogenic Belt of western South America. The **tectonics** are dominantly compressional with a northwest trending **fold – belt** with fold **axis** parallel to the modern trench; older, mature rocks overthrust younger, immature rocks. **A wide range of** rock units ranging from salt to sandstones and **limestones, along with** carbonates and volcanics are present. The elevations vary by more than 1 km over the portion of the line from which the data were processed. This severe topography producesstatics for vertically propagating waves (reducing to a flat datum at the maximum elevation) of as much as 1700 ms. Five hundred shots were processed; these were acquired with 25 m shot spacing, 25 m geophone group spacing, and 240 receiver groups in split spreads. The near offset was 37.5 m, and the far offset was 3012.5 m. The time **sampling** interval was 2 ms with a total recording time of 8 s. The data have poor signal – to – noise **ratio** and strong ground roll with changes in character along the line. In general, shots at the higher elevations have better signal quality and coherent reflections than those at the lower elevations. Only 4 s of data were processed because no coherent events were seen below 3s in any of the shots. For both conventional and prestack processing, we assume that the structure is 2 – D and invariant **perpendicular** to the **survey** line. This is approximately true as the line is nearly perpendicular to the strike of the structure, but as described below, some 3 – D effects are still present. Noise reduction was crucial in both conventional and prestack processing of this data set.

CONVENTIONAL PROCESSING

The data were processed as a blind test because neither auxiliary geologic information, interpretations, nor well logs were made available with the data. Thus the project proceeded in the spirit of Marmousi, but without the constraints available in that exercise, and on field data rather than on synthetics. To provide initial estimates of structural geometry and velocity, conventional processing was performed.

Considerable time and effort were spent in evaluating **preprocessing** techniques to enhance the signal. Every shot was examined for noisy traces and high **amplitude** bursts, and many of these noises were manually removed. Processing was to a floating datum. The final processing flow included spreading corrections for amplitude balancing, **deconvolution**, and **filtering**. Stacking velocity analysis and **residual** static corrections were applied iteratively. Residual static corrections were estimated by maximizing the stack power in a window that included the main reflections (500 – 2000 ms).

THE PRESTACK WAVE – EQUATION SYSTEM

Overview

There are two related objectives of prestack processing; to produce the best migrated image and to accurately estimate the migration velocities. Reverse – time migration of each individual common – source gather produces images that can be compared, as a function of migration velocity, to maximize image coherence when they are stacked. Thus, imaging and velocity estimation are done iteratively.

The input data unit is the Common – source gather. Only one velocity distribution is estimated and this is the interval velocity. Transmission tomography using first – arrival traveltimes gives an estimate of the near – surface velocity distribution; deeper velocities may be estimated by iterative reflection tomography or by coherence/focussing analysis. Using the tomographic velocity distribution for the near surface and actual source and receiver positions for **wavefield** extrapolation elegantly solves the statics problems and simplifies ground – roll suppression. The number of processing steps is greatly reduced; NMO, DMO, and statics are completely eliminated, or are applied implicitly during migration, rather than as separate steps.

A typical prestack wavefield processing sequence is suggested as follows: (1) addition of survey geometry to trace **headers**, and editing and filtering noisy traces; (2) estimation of near – surface velocities by tomography; (3) data conditioning **prior to migration**, which includes tapering of the edges and reversal of time axis of each common – shot gather; (4) depth migration of each shot gather in turn, with an option to remigrate after focusing depth analysis or reflection tomography; and (5) stacking over the individual migrated source gathers to produce a depth section.

Preprocessing

For the current data set, where the information was **obscured** by noise, some preprocessing to enhance the signal was necessary. Amplitude balancing was applied to **compensate for** variations in shot size and **coupling**, noisy traces and shots were eliminated, and a band – pass filter (8 – 12 – 40 – 50Hz) and **spectral** balancing were applied within the filter band pass to each common – shot gather before prestack depth migration. Spectral balancing enhances the high – frequency signal (Pritchett, personal communication) and improves resolution in migration by increasing the usable bandwidth. For the first round of processing, no **attempt was made to** remove direct arrivals or ground roll. Each common – shot gather was tapered in time and in space to minimize edge effects in extrapolation and was time – reversed prior to migration. The data were also resampled in time to 1 ms and interpolated in space to 12. 5 m to accommodate finite – difference stability and grid dispersion requirements. Fortunately, the data did not contain large gaps in receiver locations, so interpolation was straightforward.

Tomography for near surface velocities

Migration **is sensitive to** the velocities used. This realization has opened the possibility of using migration, not only as an imaging tool, but also for estimation velocities for prestack migration. Migration may **be combined with** tomographic methods for velocity analysis.

A key step in this **implementation** of prestack processing is tomographic imaging of the near – surface part of the velocity model for use in migration (which implicitly includes velocity statics). This is done using time picks from the first arrivals as data.

Migration velocity analysis

The sensitivity of migration to velocities is exploited for estimating velocities for deeper structures. Higher velocities migrate events to greater depths; lower velocities migrate them to shallower depths. Migration velocity analysis for structure below the near surface was performed by migrating several shot records with various constant velocities and observing the depth and spatial alignment of the resulting images. The focusing was observed not only as reflection alignment in migrated common – surface location gathers, but also in the coherency of events in the stack of individual depth migrated sections.

Prestack migration

Prestack reverse – time migration is performed individually on each common – source gather. This has been implemented in both **acoustic** and **elastic** forms. We used a scalar version based on a fourth – order, finite – difference solution of the two – way wave – equation for this data set. Reverse – time migration is based on the complete reversibility of wave – equation. Reverse – time migration is ideal for handling both vertical and lateral velocity variations efficiently and accurately. Traveltimes for image conditions are computed for each shot, from the actual shot location, using the same wave – equation. The direct arrival time from the source to each depth point in the 2 – D subsurface is the image condition for migration. For complicated velocity models, this wave – equation approach to image – time computation is more accurate than ray – based methods, because arrivals with minimum traveltimes and/or maximum amplitudes can be selected for the image conditions. A very wide (10 km) aperture was used during extrapolation to facilitate the migration of steep events.

Postmigration processing and interpretation

Postmigration processing was applied to reduce some of the effects of noise in the input. Trace mixing enhances the coherence even where signals are not visible in individual shot gathers; we used five – trace, dip – guided mixing over 62.5 m. A high – pass wavenumber filter was applied to reduce the near – surface **artifacts** and to improve the **coherence** of the section. The structure seen in the final prestack result is relatively complete compared to those seen in the stack or the poststack migration. The events seen in the prestack migrated section are more coherent and continuous. The image has the characteristics of an over – thrust. Several faulted **stratigraphic** features are interpreted under the mountain. A **synclinal** feature can be inferred beneath the valley, but this structure is not as continuous as the units beneath the mountain and may be cut by faults. Two strong events, cutting the section diagonally, are interpreted as **thrust** faults.

DISCUSSION

Conventional versus prestack processing

The goal of the project was to test prestack reverse – time processing on field data with irregular topography. Conventional processing was performed initially to provide an approximate solution and to provide a basis for comparative evaluation.

Conventional processing produced a fairly good stack section, considering the quality of the data. It may be possible to improve the stack section with additional efforts but our stack appears **similar to** that obtained by professional processors prior to our analysis. Standard processing steps like static corrections, NMO, and DMO compute static and dynamic traveltime corrections assuming a reference datum that is usually flat or slowly varying. This works for most cases when the variations in elevation are small or where the floating datum follows the subsurface structural geometry. For data with large topographic changes, like those processed here, this is not sufficiently accurate.

When the moveout is nonhyberbolic and velocities vary laterally, both NMO and DMO are handicapped and may yield erroneous results. The standard static corrections are strictly valid only for vertical propagation. If the stacking velocity estimates are in error, the stack section, while it may be coherent, is no longer an accurate approximation to a zero – offset section, and the poststack migration, even with migration velocities derived independently of stacking velocities, may not give an accurate subsurface image. The best stacking velocity function is that which produces the most coherent stack and has no explicit relation to the interval velocities used in migration. Thus, the increase in signal – to – noise level produced by stacking is a subjective (albeit positive) effect that is not based on physical velocities, and the subsequent poststack migration necessarily involves corresponding approximations in migration velocity.

In the prestack processing system, the data are viewed as a wavefield that has been altered by the physical properties of the medium. There are no limiting assumptions regarding the subsurface structures, velocity of the medium, source and receiver elevations, or propagation angles. Only minimal preprocessing is required for amplitude balancing and signal enhancement. Steep **dips** (even past 90°) may be imaged without distortion as the two-way wave equation is used for extrapolation. Application of static corrections is implicit. The advantages of fold (in increasing signal-to-noise level) are still present. Migration velocities are now physical (interval) velocities, and the coherence of postmigration stacked images **is very sensitive to** them. This is because both stacking coherence and migration focusing are now the result of a single, rather than two, velocity distributions. It is this sensitivity that is the physical basis of all the depth focusing algorithms for velocity analysis. The tradeoff is that the velocity estimation and migration become iterative. Quality control is more difficult in prestack processing because a considerable amount of data needs to be processed to get an interpretable image.

Statics

The final stack of the migrated common-source gathers exhibits good coherence, showing that the statics have been applied implicitly during migration. This is achieved by estimating the near-surface velocity distribution by tomography, extrapolating the wavefield for each shot from the actual observed position on the surface, and applying the image time conditions computed from the actual source locations. By using the actual source and receiver locations on the surface, the elevation statics are applied in a truly surface consistent manner. The velocity statics (traveltime anomalies caused by the near-surface velocities variations) are handled by migrating through the velocities estimated, by tomographic imaging of first arrivals, from the data itself. Both short and long wavelength statics corrections for all angles of propagation are automatically applied during migration. Thus the static corrections are applied without any non-physical or expensive approximations to treat complex topography. Tomographic methods in general are better than conventional static correction methods for estimating long wavelength statics. In addition, there are no layering assumptions involved. The depth to which statics information can be obtained by tomography with first-break traveltimes is about 10% of the farthest offset (here about 300 m). Tomography can be used for estimating deeper velocities by including reflection as well as refraction data.

Limitations and future directions

The successful elimination of static variations requires accurate estimation of the near – surface velocity distribution. In noisy data, reliable time picks are difficult to obtain. Consistency of traveltime picks should be carefully evaluated prior to tomography. When the near surface is less complicated, reverse – time migration with accurate near – surface velocities will separate the horizontally propagating surface waves from the vertically propagating reflections and image them as high amplitude artifacts near the source locations. A high – pass, wave – number filter after migration may remove these artifacts. In the present case, a depth filter was not able to eliminate the artifacts completely in the near surface. Reprocessing after first – arrival muting was more successful.

Getting an acceptable velocity model for migration in the presence of structural complication from a data with less – than – desirable signal – to – noise ratio is very difficult. Prestack migration can only estimate a macro velocity model for the subsurface. For detailed structure and velocities, additional geologic constraints are needed.

In prestack processing, when the structure is complicated and the velocity is unknown, the only way to quality control the process is to iteratively migrate and stack selected shots in the region of interest, with a change in preprocessing or with new parameters (i. e. , velocities) at each iteration. In short, in the absence of an interpreted section or without the assistance of an area geologist, quality control becomes very tedious. Multiple depth migration runs are required.

More can be learned about the subsurface by processing data from complicated areas with different techniques and comparing the results. This is a useful approach to evaluate structural images of data from previously unexplored areas. Estimating statics via tomographic imaging is viable for data with complex topography. This may be the most efficient way of computing 3 – D statics.

A single shot migration consumed 400 cpu seconds on one CRAY – YMP processor. Although this is expensive, it must be kept in mind that this is the total cost as many of the intermediate steps are no longer required, and that this approach can handle difficult data sets that do not yield satisfactory results with less accurate treatments. This makes the system viable not just for 2 – D but also for 3 – D. The 3 – D data management is simplified by single shot migration.

True wavefield processing is possible only when complete 3 – D, three – component seismic data are acquired with adequate sampling in space. Until then a hybrid processing scheme that has good signal enhancement techniques and accurate wavefield imaging tools should be used under the guidance of additional geological and geophysical constraints.

CONCLUSION

The Marmousi experience revealed current capabilities for imaging and estimating velocities from tectonically complex areas. It identified the key problem not as imaging but as estimating velocities for imaging. This problem will be compounded when complex topography is included. Traveltime anomalies need to be corrected in a surface – consistent manner. When and how these corrections are made will determine the success or failure of the whole processing stream. Many solutions have been proposed for treatment of complex topography, but there are no previously published reports on prestack application of these to land data.

We propose a simple approach to true wavefield processing where the static corrections are applied implicitly during migration in a truly surface consistent manner. We do not know of a simpler, or a more elegant, solution to this formidable problem. We have also gone a step further and successfully applied prestack migration to a complicated land data set, and demonstrated that it does indeed work and offers significant improvements over conventional processing.

Words and Expressions

deformed	变形的
wave – equation	波动方程
tectonics	构造地质学,大地构造
fold – belt	造山(地)带,褶皱带
axis	轴线
limestone	石灰岩
sample	从……中抽样
ratio	比率
perpendicular	成直角的
survey	测量
preprocess	预处理
amplitude	波幅,振幅

deconvolution	反褶积
filtering	滤波出
residual	剩余的,残留的
wavefeild	波场
header	上部炮眼
migration	迁移
obscure	模糊的
coupling	耦接头
spectral	光谱的
implementation	地压
acoustic	声学的
elastic	弹性的
reversibility	可逆性
artifact	假象
coherence	相干
stratigraphic	倾斜
synclinal	向斜层
thrust	冲断层,逆断层
dip	倾角

Phrases and Expression

a wide range of	广泛的,一系列的
along with	连同
prior to	在……之前
compensate for	补偿
make an attempt to	试图
be sensitive to	对……敏感
be combined with	与……相结合
similar to	与……类似

Language Focus

1. The goal of this paper is to briefly review the main elements in this prestack processing system and to illustrate its viability by applying it to field data with severe elevation and near - surface velocity statics.

(参考译文:本文的目的是简要介绍该叠前处理方法的要点。并把它应用到地表高程及表层速度变化剧烈的野外数据中,以证实该方法的可行性。)

本句为主系表结构,表语由两个并列的不定式结构充当,句中 by applying it to field data 为方式状语,with severe elevation and near – surface velocity statics 做 field data 的后置定语。

2. Reverse – time migration of each individual common – source gather produces images that can be compared, as a function of migration velocity, to maximize image coherence when they are stacked.

(参考译文:各共炮点道集的逆时偏移产生的图像,作为偏移速度的函数,由叠加时产生最大图像的相干性进行对比。)

本句的主干是 Reverse – time migration produces images,句中 of each individual common – source gather 做定语修饰 Reverse – time migration。句中 that 引导定语从句修饰 images,as a function of migration velocity 这部分为插入语。

3. Using the tomographic velocity distribution for the near surface and actual source and receiver positions for wavefield extrapolation elegantly solves the statics problems and simplifies ground – roll suppression.

(参考译文:用近地表层析速度分布及波场外推时的实际炮点和接收点位置巧妙地解决了静校正问题,简化了地滚波的压制。)

本句为主谓宾结构,主语由动词现在分词结构充当,有两个并列的谓语 solves 和 simplifies。

4. It may be possible to improve the stack section with additional efforts but our stack appears similar to that obtained by professional processors prior to our analysis.

(参考译文:进一步做工作也许可能改进叠加剖面的质量,但我们叠加的成果似乎与分析前专业处理员的处理结果类似。)

本句是由 but 连接的并列句。It 为形式主语,to improve the stack section 是真正的主语,with additional efforts 做状语。句中 but 引导的并列句为主系表结构,appear 做系动词用,that 为代词,obtained 是动词过去分词做后置定语,prior to our analysis 为时间状语。

5. If the stacking velocity estimates are in error, the stack section, while it may be coherent, is no longer an accurate approximation to a zero – offset section, and the poststack migration, even with migration velocities derived independently of stacking velocities, may not give an accurate subsurface image.

(参考译文:如果叠加速度估算不正确,虽然它可能是相干的,但却不再是零炮检距剖面的准确的近似，即使偏移速度不是由叠加速度推导出来的，也得不到一个准确的地下界面图象。）

本句为复杂句，总体来说是由 If 引导的条件句 If the stacking velocity estimates are in error 加主句 the stack section is no longer an accurate approximation to a zero – offset section, and the poststack migration may not give an accurate subsurface image 构成。主句由 and 连接的两个并列句构成，其中 while it may be coherent 和 even with migration velocities derived independently of stacking velocities 为插入语，用来进一步说明主语 the stack section 和 the poststack migration。

Reinforced Learning

Ⅰ. Answer the following questions for a comprehension of the text.

1. What is a typical prestack wavefield processing sequence?

2. What is the key step in the implementation of prestack processing?

3. What is reverse – time migration based on? What can be handled by reverse – time migtation?

4. For complicated velocity models, is wave – equation approach to image – time computation more accurate than ray – based methods? Why?

5. What's the goal of the project mentioned in the text?

Ⅱ. Multiple choice: choose the correct one from the alternative answers to give the exact meaning of the words.

1. In that province a conventional political system was absent.

A. accepted　B. conservative　C. traditional　D. formal

2. She's proud of her ring because of its unique design.

A. strange　B. distinctive　C. certain　D. odd

3. We think such information should be made explicit and not left vague.

A. implicit　B. special　C. clear　D. uncertain

4. We quickly accommodated ourselves to our new surroundings.

A. contained　B. adapted　C. adopted　D. changed

5. The government failed to implement the plan.

A. fulfill　B. improve　C. imply　D. arrange

6. He decided to take the easy option and give them what they wanted.

A. choice　B. chance　C. opportunity　D. optimum

7. Nothing can compensate for losing my husband.

A. take for B. live for C. search for D. make up for

8. This procedure does not completely eliminate the possibility of an accident.

A. remove B. elevate C. reduce D. level

9. The ratio of pupils to teachers was 30 to 1.

A. velocity B. rate C. rite D. interval

10. I was chosen, along with twelve other artists.

A. go with B. except for C. together with D. regardless of

Ⅲ. Multiple choice: read the four suggested translations and choose the best answer.

1. The tectonics are dominantly compressional.

A. 大地构造 B. 建筑构造 C. 建筑学 D.（物理）状态

2. Migration is sensitive to the velocities used

A. 移民 B. 移居 C. 迁徙 D. 偏移

3. For both conventional and prestack processing, we assume that the structure is 2 – D and invariant perpendicular to the survey line.

A. 平行 B. 垂直 C. 倾斜 D. 重合

4. Every shot was examined for noisy traces and high amplitude bursts, and many of these noises were manually removed.

A. 振幅 B. 海拔 C. 纬度 D. 速度

5. For the current data set, where the information was obscured by noise, some preprocessing to enhance the signal was necessary.

A. 程序 B. 加工 C. 处理 D. 预处理

Ⅳ. Put the following sentences into Chinese.

1. In general, shots at the higher elevations have better signal quality and coherent reflections than those at the lower elevations.

2. This realization has opened the possibility of using migration, not only as an imaging tool, but also for estimation velocities for prestack migration.

3. The structure seen in the final prestack result is relatively complete compared to those seen in the stack or the poststack migration.

4. The best stacking velocity function is that which produces the most coherent stack and has no explicit relation to the interval velocities used in migration.

5. Tomographic methods in general are better than conventional static correction methods for estimating long wavelength statics

V. Put the following paragraphs into Chinese.

1. The goal of conventional processing is to produce an image that will be an approximate zero – offset section (at least in a kinematic sense). This is achieved as long as most of the assumptions about earth layers (flat), moveout (hyperbolic), reflections (precritical), and lateral velocity variations (none) are met. Some deviations are accommodated, but only if they are sufficiently small. A more satisfactory solution is to treat the data as a complete wavefield.

2. The strong variations in elevation suggest massive structures that are 3 – D and produce additional out – of – plane noise that is difficult to identify and eliminate in a 2 – D line. Vertical geophones record only the vertical component of the wave – field; when large structures with high angles are involved, the reflected compressional wave will not be only vertical. Structure – induced noise can be correctly incorporated only with 3 – D acquisition and processing.

Chapter 2 Reservoir Characterization

2.1 Dynamic Reservoir Characterization of Vacuum Field

Guidance to Reading

Time – lapse multicomponent ***seismic*** *surveying enables* ***dynamic*** *reservoir characterization and the production of a dynamic reservoir model. This, in turn, assists in producing structured economic and technical decisions that will extend reservoir life and improve recovery while reducing risk and environmental impact.*

This article briefly describes the 4 – D, 3 – C technique and a research application of it at Vacuum Field, New Mexico, by the Reservoir Characterization Project (RCP) at the Colorado School of Mines. This technique has the potential to provide the most complete information needed for efficient reservoir characterization. This article will discuss the technique' s possibilites for determining anisotropy and permeability, and conclude with a brief case history of research at Vacuum Field in New Mexico.

Text

4 – D, 3 – C SEISMIC

The simplest definition of **time – lapse** (or 4 – D) seismic is merely **comparing** one 3 – D survey with a repeat survey or surveys taken in the same geographic location at a later time. Determination of the optimal timing of these surveys is linked to the reservoir model and to economics.

Multicomponent (or 3 – C) seismology involves recording two horizontal components and one vertical component. This method of recording seismic data provides significantly more information about the rock and fluid properties of reservoirs and their changes than can be achieved from conventional P – wave seismic surveys alone. Comparative traveltime or **velocity** measurements, **amplitudes**, and frequencies of P – and S – waves enable the discrimination of rock and fluid properties, their characteristics, and their changes over time.

When combined into time – lapse multicomponent (4 – D, 3 – C) seismology, the resulting method is a tool for volume resolution: i. e., it provides the ability to sense changes in the bulk rock/fluid properties of the reservoir with time. Velocity and **attenuation** measurements contain information on the fluid state and distribution within reservoir rocks, particularly in low – aspect ratio (cracklike porosity or fractured) rock.

ANISOTROPY

Shear – wave **anisotropy** can provide information on a finer scale than ordinary seismic resolution. Anisotropy is a measure of fine – scale structure within rock and reservoir **fabric**. It is a **link to** volume resolution of seismic data and to seismic determination of important reservoir characteristics including porosity, permeability, fluids, and flow pathways. By linking seismic shear – wave anisotropy to reservoir parameters, better reservoir management can be done. For instance, attenuation of split shear waves in anisotropic media and anisotropic behavior of seismic waves in general give us a potential measure of permeability within a reservoir. The directional permeability **aligns parallel to** the fast shear – wave orientation. The slower split shear – wave is affected by pore structure **compliance** and is a prime indicator of permeability, whereas the faster split shear wave is affected by fluid state within the pores or fractures.

By linking anisotropy structure to permeability structure of the reservoir, we can seismically **calibrate** permeability for reservoir modeling and flow **simulation**. This technology can help reservoir management at virtually all stages in the life cycle of a reservoir. The prediction of reservoir performance is determined largely by permeability and permeability structure. Reservoir production will be enhanced if the areal sweep efficiency can be increased and zones of the reservoir can be processed efficiently so as not to **bypass** zones of low permeability. With 4 – D, 3 – C seismic surveying and dynamic reservoir characterization, we can predict and monitor reservoir **conformance**.

PERMEABILITY

The ability to sense bulk rock/fluid properties with 4 – D, 3 – C seismology enables characterization of the most important transport property of a reservoir, namely permeability. Permeability in the interwell region must be defined and **gridded** into reservoir modeling for accurate flow simulation. Because of the high volume resolution of 4 – D,3 – C seismic we can more accurately **delineate** reservoir fluid **compartments** and their changes with time.

As a result, we can monitor the sweep efficiency of a production process to see if reserves are bypassed by channeling around lower permeability parts of the reservoir and the rate at which the channeling occurs. In doing so, we can change injection patterns to sweep the reservoir more efficiently. Not only can we monitor reservoir performance but we can predict it ahead of time. The greatest economic benefit of this technology will come in linking volumetric bulk rock/fluid property variation from seismic to **geocellular** reservoir modeling and simulation for predicting reservoir performance and guiding reservoir management.

CASE STUDY

A time – lapse (4 – D), multicomponent (3 – C) **pilot** study was conducted in Vacuum Field, Lea County, New Mexico, where the San Andres carbonates produce from an average depth of 4300 ft. This is a mature field which has been maintained above bubble point pressure by water flood since 1978 and is now in the early stages of CO_2 flooding.

Two 3 – D, 3 – C surveys were acquired eight weeks apart. Between the surveys, 50 000 000 ft^3 of CO_2 was injected into Central Vacuum Unit (CVU) well 97 and allowed to soak. Subsequent to seismic **acquisition**, the CO_2 was **extracted** out of the same borehole.

Research conducted by RCP demonstrates that reservoir heterogeneity is more **pervasive** than previously thought, making prediction of reservoir fluid flow more difficult and the need for monitoring the CO_2 flood vital. During this study, research was underway while new data **trickled in. Beginning with well logs**, cores, and a previously acquired regional 3 – D data set, a model of a complex **compartmentalized** reservoir began to emerge. The first **iteration** of multicomponent data, **available** for interpretation in 1996, yielded higher resolution images of **spatially variant** rock properties. The second iteration of 3 – D, 3 – C data led to a time – lapse image of the CO_2 bank flowing away from the well bore along a highly permeable fracture zone.

3 – D INTERPRETATION

Various P – wave **attributes** extracted from the 3 – D data sets indicate reservoir heterogeneities at the San Andres level; the most powerful and convincing attribute is **coherence**. Evidence of the existence of **faulting** in the reservoir was **met with** much **adversity due to** the fact that tectonic activity in the area had greatly **diminished** by the time the Guadalupian – age San Andres carbonates were deposited. The coherency attribute from 3 – D P – wave data was used to determine if faults were indeed influencing the path CO_2 would follow once injected.

The main distinguishing feature **separating** seismic discontinuities caused by faults **from** other discontinuities **related to** noise and dipping reflectors is **dip**. In order to emphasize fault delineation, the coherency attribute computed from the seismic data was f – k fan – filtered to mute events with dips less than 4 ms per trace (approximately 0 – 20°).

The same coherency flow was **applied to** the 3 – D compressional wave surveys. South and west of the CVU – 97 CO_2 injection well is a third fault that exhibits a **curvilinear** shape as it bends northward into a larger northeast – trending fault.

4 – D,3 – C INTERPRETATION

The goal of interpretation in this project was to characterize the reservoir and attempt to image any changes in the San Andres **resulting from** dynamic reservoir processes **associated with** the injection of CO_2. Numerous attributes from all data sets were extracted and examined toward this end. Shear – wave velocity anisotropy provided by far the highest degree of volume resolution, and was also the attribute which sensed the dynamic properties of the reservoir associated with CO_2 injection.

These measurements were made by differencing the slow and fast shear – wave **isochrons** from a horizon just above the San Andres top to the base of the San Andres zone. This difference was normalized by the fast shear – wave (S1) isochron to remove anisotropy effects from the shallower subsurface above the San Andres reservoir. Clearly there are differences between the initial and repeat anisotropy maps. This is expected with the additional pressuring of the reservoir that **took place** between the surveys. Note that most of the differences appear in the north – west portion of the survey where the wells exhibit better production/injection characteristics.

A difference map of the initial anisotropy values minus the repeat values over the San Andres interval shows a large **anomaly** centered 600 ft south and updip of the CVU – 97 CO_2 injection well. This difference map was multiplied by 100 to approximate a percent difference. The anomaly represents approximately a 12% difference (above a plus or minus 6% difference background) between surveys.

The initial anisotropy map shows an area of near zero anisotropy in the region of the 4 – D anomaly indicating either: (1) the rocks have no open fractures, or (2) open fractures exist in two **conjugate** directions.

The difference in the anomalous area represents a base – survey to repeat – survey S1 velocity increase of 17%. Kuster – Toksoz modeling was used to simulate this effect by changing the **geometry** of low – aspect ratio cracks. The shear – waves **responded to** a change in pore aspect ratio or preferential opening of microfractures resulting from the injection of CO_2. The faster shear – wave (S1) velocity was attenuated less with the resulting change in low – aspect ratio crack porosity. Both S1 and the slow shear – wave were affected by the injection of CO_2, but the characteristics of the anisotropy anomaly favor the S1 as having the greatest amount of change. The change in **viscosity** and/or **saturation** of the fluid in the fractures may have affected the rigidity of the fracture system, **resulting in** an increase in S1 velocity, but **quantification** of this change has not been modeled. This analysis favors the preferential closings of microcracks **perpendicular** to the maximum stress direction in the **vicinity** of CO_2 injection **in response to** the unification of the stress field by pressuring of the reservoir and the presence of CO_2.

The Kuster – Toksoz model predicts a change in P – wave velocity **as well**. A P – wave velocity increase of 7% (significantly less than the 17% S1 velocity change) would result if the model were correct. A P – wave time difference of the 4 – D interpretation on an horizon in the injection interval was calculated and reveals a 7% velocity increase as predicted.

The RCP and its industry partners are continuing to expand this research to monitor a full – scale WAG CO_2 flood in the same location. **At least** three additional 3 – D, 3 – C surveys will be acquired in the multiwell injection program which will deliver approximately 40 times the volume of CO_2 of this study over a one – year period.

CONCLUSIONS

Time – lapse multicomponent (4 – D, 3 – C) technology provides the most complete information currently available for economically efficient **hydrocarbon exploitation**. Using this technology, comparative analyses and computer – simulated models reveal changes in a reservoir's dynamic properties. Differences between surveys can indicate changes in the producing reservoir and these changes, after calibration through the reservoir model, can predict reservoir performance.

Dynamic reservoir characterization can maximize **incremental recovery** of a reservoir without a large increase in operating costs. An economic **incentive** exists to use this technology early in the life cycle of a project **so that** it can guide development. For example, the determination of permeability and monitoring **nonsymmetric** fluid flow will help prevent leaving bypassed hydrocarbons behind.

Dynamic reservoir characterization will be transferable to other enhanced recovery operations, including **waterflooding**. Substantial cost savings can occur by using it to guide infill or horizontal drilling **rather than** blanket development drilling. It is our opinion that further research will reveal that this methodology has widespread application in all phases of development (from discovery through **depletion**) and could aid in the exploration phase via direct detection of hydrocarbons.

Words and Expressions

seismic	地震,地震的
dynamic	动态的
time – lapse	延时的
velocity	速度
amplitude	振幅(声音,无线电波等的)
attenuation	衰减
anisotropy	各向异性
fabric	结构,组织,构造
align	校准
compliance	可塑性
calibrate	校准,使标准化
simulation	模拟
bypass	绕过

conformance	波及
grid	网格(化)
delineate	描述,勾画
compartment	分隔间,室
geocellular	地质细胞
pilot	(小规模)试验性的
acquisition	获得
extract	萃取
pervasive	遍布的,普遍的
well log	测井
compartmentalized	划分的
iteration	迭代
available	可得到的,可利用的
spatially	空间地
variant	不同的
attribute	属性,特性
coherence	相干性
faulting	断层(作用)
adversity	逆境
tectonic	构造的
diminish	消失,减弱
dip	倾斜,偏角
curvilinear	曲线的
isochron	等时线
anomaly	异常,反常
conjugate	共轭
geometry	几何结构
viscosity	黏性
saturation	饱和度
quantification	量化
perpendicular	垂直的
vicinity	附近
hydrocarbon	烃类
incremental	增加的

recovery	采收率
incentive	刺激,鼓励
nonsymmetric	非对称的
waterflooding	注水
depletion	枯竭

Phrases and Expression

compare with	与……相比
link to	与……相连接
parallel to	与……平行
trickle in	缓缓流入
begin with	以……开始
lead to	导致
meet with	遭受
due to	由于
separate from	分开,区别
relate to	与……相关
apply to	应用
result from	由……引起
associate with	与……相关
take place	发生
respond to	对……做出反应
result in	导致
in response to	对……做出反应
as well	也
at least	至少
so that	因此
rather than	并非,而不

Language Focus

1. The simplest definition of time – lapse (or 4 – D) seismic is merely comparing one 3 – D survey with a repeat survey or surveys taken in the same geographic location at a later time.

(参考译文:延时(或四维)地震最简单的定义不过是用一个重复的测量

或以后在同一地理位置进行的测量与原来的测量进行对比。)

本句的主语是 definition, taken in the same geographic location at a later time 是过去分词短语,做 survey or surveys 的后置定语。

2. Not only can we monitor reservoir performance but we can predict it ahead of time.

(参考译文:我们不但能够监测油藏特性,而且还能对其进行超前预测。)

本句为倒装句,如果 not only 位于句首,并且 not only... but (also) 连接两个句子时,not only 后面的句子要用倒装结构。

3. This is a mature field which has been maintained above bubble point pressure by water flood since 1978 and is now in the early stages of CO_2 flooding.

(参考译文:这是一个壮年期油田,自从 1978 年就通过注水把压力维持在饱和压力以上,并且现在已经处于 CO_2 驱替的早期阶段。)

本句是由 and 连接的两个并列句,其中 which has been maintained above bubble point pressure by water flood since 1978 是定语从句,用来修饰先行词 field。

4. The main distinguishing feature separating seismic discontinuities caused by faults from other discontinuities related to noise and dipping reflectors is dip.

(参考译文:区分由断层引起的地震不连续面和其他与噪声和倾斜反射层有关的不连续面的主要辨别特征是倾角。)

本句主干为主+系+表结构,即 feature is dip。separating seismic discontinuities caused by faults from other discontinuities related to noise and dipping reflectors 是现在分词作后置定语,修饰主语 feature。其中 caused by faults 是过去分词作后置定语,修饰 discontinuities, related to noise and dipping reflectors 也是过去分词作后置定语,修饰 other discontinuities。

Reinforced Learning

Ⅰ. Answer the following questions for a comprehension of the text.

1. What does multicomponent (or 3-C) seismology involve?

2. What is anisotropy?

3. How can we seismically calibrate permeability for reservoir modeling and flow simulation?

4. Can the Kuster-Toksoz model predict a change in P-wave velocity?

5. What does the time – lapse multicomponent （4 – D,3 – C） technology provide the most complete information currently available for?

Ⅱ. Multiple choice：choose the correct one from the alternative answers to give the exact meaning of the words.

1. Pretending to faint was merely an artifice.

A. similarly B. only C. barely D. scarcely

2. Giving advice at the right time has to involve a great deal of intelligence.

A. include B. exclude C. solve D. resolve

3. We are looking for dynamic persons to be salesmen.

A. faithful B. clever C. diligent D. energetic

4. Do you take seriously his prediction of a government defeat?

A. decision B. action C. forecast D. behavior

5. The government has taken a measure to maintain the stability of prices.

A. gain B. increase C. keep D. enhance

6. Several cars are available within this price range.

A. obtainable B. impossible C. responsible D. popular

7. Having one or more distinguishing marks.

A. big B. important C. noticeable D. effective

8. His illness diminished his health.

A. polished B. changed C. promoted D. weakened

9. We cannot emphasize too much the importance of learning English.

A. say B. stress C. express D. ignore

10. It's a complex question and your answer was too pat.

A. difficult B. complicated C. tough D. perfect

Ⅲ. Multiple choice：read the four suggested translations and choose the best answer.

1. Comparative traveltime or velocity measurements, amplitudes, and frequencies of P – and S – waves enable the discrimination of rock and fluid properties, their characteristics, and their changes over time.

A. 速度 B. 高度 C. 长度 D. 宽度

2. Shear – wave anisotropy can provide information on a finer scale than ordinary seismic resolution.

A. 革命 B. 解决 C. 分解 D. 分辨率

3. Research conducted by Reservoir Characterization Project (RCP) demonstrates that reservoir heterogeneity is more pervasive than previously thought, making prediction of reservoir fluid flow more difficult and the need for monitoring the CO_2 flood vital.

A. 容量 B. 质量 C. 均质性 D. 非均质性

4. The same coherency flow was applied to the 3 – D compressional wave surveys.

A. 横波 B. 纵波 C. 微波 D. 声波

5. A difference map of the initial anisotropy values minus the repeat values over the San Andres interval shows a large anomaly centered 600 ft south and updip of the CVU –97 CO_2 injection well.

A. 价值 B. 标准 C. 数值 D. 重视

Ⅳ. Put the following sentences into Chinese.

1. This method of recording seismic data provides significantly more information about the rock and fluid properties of reservoirs and their changes than can be achieved from conventional P – wave seismic surveys alone.

2. For instance, attenuation of split shear waves in anisotropic media and anisotropic behavior of seismic waves in general give us a potential measure of permeability within a reservoir.

3. As a result, we can monitor the sweep efficiency of a production process to see if reserves are bypassed by channeling around lower permeability parts of the reservoir and the rate at which the channeling occurs.

4. The coherency attribute from 3 – D P – wave data was used to determine if faults were indeed influencing the path CO_2 would follow once injected.

5. Note that most of the differences appear in the northwest portion of the survey where the wells exhibit better production/injection characteristics.

Ⅴ. Put the following paragraphs into Chinese.

1. Permeability is the ability of the formation to conduct fluids. From usage the name for fluid conductance capacity of a formation is permeability. It is a property of the porous medium and is measure of capacity of the medium transmitting fluids. The measurement of permeablility, then, is a measure of the fluid conductivity of the particular material.

2. Although oil reservoirs are characterized as porous media with certain

porosities and permeabilities, they are almost never homogeneous beds with constant properites. Generally, there are numerous strata with wide – ranging properties. In terms of enhanced oil recovery, the divergence of reservoir permeability is a significant factor.

2.2 Challenges in Reservoir Characterization (Ⅰ)

Guidance to Reading

Despite today's high activity level and the many recent apparent advances within reservoir characterization practice and technology, the province – average recovery factors have not increased significantly, production forecasts are still notoriously in error, and the mainstream day – to – day geoscience/reservoir engineering approach to modeling, mapping, gridding, visualizing, and forecasting the behavior of reservoirs in a typical oil company has not changed noticeably during the last five years. From a summary of the state – of – the – art and current trends within reservoir characterization practice and research, this paper suggests and discusses new avenues and focal points for the future.

Text

INTRODUCTION

Despite today's high activity level and the many recent apparent advances within reservoir **characterization** practice and technology, the province – average recovery factors have not increased significantly, production forecasts are still notoriously **in error**, and the mainstream day – to – day geoscience/reservoir engineering approach to modeling, mapping, **gridding**, visualizing, and forecasting the behavior of reservoirs in a typical oil company has not changed noticeably during the last five years.

The number of technical papers published and the number of reservoir description conferences, seminars, forums, and courses arranged annually, however, have increased dramatically. These have, **in effect**, made all new advances, approaches, ideas and results instantly available to every oil company and field – development team in the world. The lack of notable effect is therefore somewhat difficult to understand. Perhaps it is too early to tell. Perhaps oil and gas fields that came onstream between 1987 and 1992 and that **benefited from** the use of three – dimensional (3 – D) seismic data even for development planning, an integrated team – approach to the studies, excellent **outcrop** analogs for geological model control, an ultra – fine simulation grid system, "numerical rocks" that are outcrop controlled and conditional to seismic data, well observations, and other information, horizontal wells that were cored to provide lateral **variograms**, etc. , will demonstrate that reservoir description R&D actually pays off with forecasts becoming correct and oil recovery increasing. Or, could we possibly be facing a classical implementation problem? Perhaps we do not practice in our field studies what we **preach** at conferences. Also could it be that if everyone writing papers and going to conferences (including us) started applying the new tools, technology, and insight available today on specific reservoirs **rather than** working on new and general R&D theories and/or universal reservoir characterization problems, recoveries actually would start increasing? After all, each field really is a new "research" project!

Even if the large and easy reservoirs have been found and developed in many basins, we are not outsmarting Nature to give up more of its oil now than she did before. Even recently predicted production profiles turn out to be surprisingly **erroneous**. So what can be done? What are the major challenges in reservoir characterization research? How should we focus? Who should do the research? Which are the areas with the greatest potential payoff?

Suggestions for future R&D activities are scattered throughout this paper, but we believe that in order to really **outsmart** Nature, you have to know her. Hence, detailed reservoir **tomography** by some known (e. g. , seismic) or as – yet undiscovered technology, which yields images of all faults, the correct structure map, and geological architectural flow – unit and **barrier** details down to 1 – m resolution is on top of the reservoir characterization R&D wish list.

THE GOALS

The main goals of reservoir characterization research are to aid field – development and reservoir – management teams in (1) describing the reservoir in sufficient detail (the detail required depends on the **recovery mechanism**), (2) outsmarting Nature to obtain higher recoveries with fewer wells in better positions at minimum cost through **optimization**, for a given reservoir description, and (3) reducing to a minimum uncertainty in production forecasts.

The degree to which geoscientists and engineers have delivered in the past is a good indicator of the need for future R&D in this area.

THE PAST, OR IS HINDSIGHT AN EXACT SCIENCE?

A recent review of many water – flooded oil fields discovered, appraised, and evaluated in the United Kingdom North Sea in the 1970s and then produced through the 1970s and 1980s showed large percentage overruns on capital costs of developments. The average overrun was 95%, with a maximum of 97.4%! O&M costs were on average 140% higher than planned. The first oil came 1 – 3 yr **behind schedule**. On average, only 65% of the planned oil **plateau** rate was achieved, and the timing of oil recovery was delayed because water break-through times were much shorter than predicted. Water as well as total liquid handling capacities were underestimated, **so that** most platforms were facility – constrained after only a surprisingly short time. Water **injection** rates also were nearly always overestimated. What went wrong in the planning phase? Why were there such bad predictions? After all, even then, all fields were evaluated and optimized by means of numerical simulation! Not enough data? Poor data? Poor use of data?

When the history books on the United Kingdom continental shelf (UKCS) are finally written, the reasons for bad predictions will probably be the following (L. P. Dake and E. T. DeBoer, 1988, personal communication): (1) Only 2 – D seismic data were available, **resulting in** too few detected faults and incorrect structure maps. (2) Simulation models were much too **homogeneous**, so that "everything" was averaged away. There was insufficient degree of property variability and too little **focus on** facies variation (i. e., lack of a detailed geological model). (3) Simulation grids were much too coarse. Driving forces cannot be modeled accurately without spatial resolution. (4) Vertical communication in the simulation models was exaggerated, not allowing for thief zones. (5) Lateral communication in simulation models was exaggerated, with all pay continuous and too few faults.

On the basis of these observations, one would expect that the least homogeneous fields would exhibit the worst agreement between actual behavior and pre – production predictions. According to a recent paper by Corrigan, this **rule of thumb** holds in most cases. Recipes for prediction success (i. e., field behavior that is according to, or better than, forecast) and for prediction disaster can be formulated.

This above analysis **applies only to** the specific fields on the UKCS. We believe, however, that a similar analysis of the development history of other areas would yield comparable results.

Past performance is not very flattering for the underground sciences! Poor reservoir characterization practices and inadequate representation of reservoirs with large grid blocks receive most of the blame. To be fair, the possibilities were also limited, since only 2 – D seismic data usually were available.

In order to focus future R&D in the right direction, it could be worthwhile at this time to make the following: (1) A complete portfolio analysis for various areas of interest, where the fields are classified according to **depositional** environment, recovery mechanism, etc. (2) A comprehensive **post – mortem** review of the pre – production estimates and forecasts against actual behavior, leading to perhaps very interesting conclusions and recommendations for the industry. (3) A list of the most typical problems and pitfalls as well as the smart solutions historically encountered and devised by innovative field – development teams. (4) An "I wish I had and I wish I could" list from the "underground scientists" to provide research directions. (5) Recommendations for reducing uncertainties, including **contingency** planning and flexibility arrangements.

This analysis would expose the major general and province – specific R&D challenges ahead. Also, a good balance between market pull (i. e. , short – term problem solving research) and technology push (i. e. , high risk and long – term research) would result.

THE PRESENT: CURRENT PRACTICE IN A TYPICAL COMPANY

Significant technological advancements have occurred within the last 5 – 10 yr in reservoir geology, **geophysics**, and **petrophysics** as well as in reservoir engineering. However, we claim that these advancements, so far, have had only limited **impact on** the routine day – to – day operations of a typical oil company, although there are significant exceptions. Most of the new developments are still in the research labs of universities and research institutes, or at the R&D departments of the oil companies, struggling to become accepted and be taken into routine use. We now give a brief presentation of the contributions of the various disciplines to the development of an important field.

Geophysics: The Structural Model and a Lot More

Seismic data usually find fields, reveal their lateral/vertical extent, provide the reservoir surface **topography** (i. e. , depth map for top reservoir and sometimes for different horizons within it), supply some of the most important **parameters** (A, h) for the HCPV calculation, and reveal where the more significant faults are located. Rather useful things to know when one is constructing a reservoir model!

Today, there is no substitute for a high – quality 3 – D seismic interpretation. Maps derived from 2 – D seismic data are poor substitutes since fields actually appear different when mapped from 2 – D and 3 – D data. The change in HCPV with time is commonly not **due to** dramatic changes in N/G (net – to – gross ratio), Φ, or S_w, but rather due to changes in seismic interpretation, such as when a 3 – D survey finally becomes available, or a new GOC/OWC position is detected, or perhaps a new geological model is reinforced by production data.

Seismic acquisition, processing, and interpretation techniques have been refined steadily over the years. Of all the "underground sciences," geophysics has probably undergone the most significant technological change in the last decade. We believe that continued advancement and technological gains in this area are a **prerequisite** for any significant improvements in reservoir characterization. Seismic resolution and detectability have improved steadily. If this will continue at the same rate is an open question. Using attribute techniques, VSP data, time – lapse seismic monitoring techniques, etc. , seismic interpretations already aid in (1) reservoir architecture mapping, because sometimes it is possible to follow a channel sand, to distinguish sand from shale, etc. , (2) mapping reservoir properties like N/G, Φ, and S_w across the field, (3) locating fluid contacts, and (4) monitoring fluid fronts. The integration of logs, cores, VSP, and 3 – D seismic data is now taking place quickly and conveniently on powerful workstations. Database improvements and digital seismic data storage have resulted in dramatic improvements in efficiency.

Interwell – seismic interpretations may soon routinely yield pre – production information about lateral between – well pay/nonpay continuity. Time – lapse seismic monitoring using permanently installed geophones on the floor of the North Sea might enable frequent mapping of fluid – front positions during production. This would constitute a significant technological breakthrough and greatly aid in reservoir management.

Many companies do not use their 3 – D seismic data to their full extent. By using inversion and other techniques, the 3 – D data might reveal essential geological features and important **heterogeneities**. Also, we recommend that alternative interpretations, not just sensitivities, be prepared by having several skilled geophysicists, even from different companies, analyze the same data. When several interpretations are considered, appraisal wells can be put in the least robust [i. e., insensitive to variations in the (uncertain) interpretations] and production wells in the most robust positions.

Petrophysics: The Log Analysis

When the first well has been **drilled** and logged, the petrophysicist starts to work. Based on data from a suite of well logs and various theoretical and empirical equations, the analyst finds values for the significant petrophysical properties. **Porosity**, **permeability**, water and/or oil saturation, and the net – to – gross ratio are usually the most important.

Logging tools have changed significantly in the last 5 – 10 yr. New tools and MWD have been developed, and the older tools have been improved, providing more data, better precision, and improved resolution. Changes in analysis have been much less pronounced. Databases, fast computers, and high – quality **plotters** have reduced the manual side of the work and improved the quality and reproducibility of the results, but the basic techniques are still more or less the same. **Visualization** of the **facies**, natural **fractures**, and the **dip** of layers encountered in the wells is now commonplace.

Production Geology: Describing the Reservoir

In a field – development team, it is usually the production or reservoir geologist who coordinates the pulling together of all relevant data in order to construct a map version, a grid – block version, and a 3 – D visualization of the geological domain.

The job is to build a quantitative and sufficiently detailed geological description of the reservoir that agrees with all the available data (hard as well as soft). The input data are the structural model and whatever else the geophysicist provides, static well data such as cores and log – derived properties from the petrophysicist, dynamic test data from the reservoir engineer, and in addition, the geoscientist's general knowledge of the processes that created and modified the reservoir at hand. Using data from well logs and cores (if available), one will identify the various **sedimentological** building blocks, flow units, or **lithofacies** along the well path, trying to correlate these between wells. Today, this work is mostly done by hand, although some software can facilitate the process. Well – to – well correlation is performed on 2 – D cross sections or fence diagrams through several wells. These tasks require both skill and imagination from geologists, and they are wide open to subjective judgment. 2 – D and 3 – D software are now available to assist in these tasks.

When the basic geological structures have been established, the reservoir is usually divided into a number of layers, typically 5 – 20. The boundaries between the layers may have a structural interpretation derived from seismic data, or they may be simple surfaces based on various interpolation techniques between a limited number of wells. In each layer, the average petrophysical properties, estimated by the petrophysicist, are either given a constant value or more commonly distributed laterally according to different contour maps. The maps may be drawn by hand by the geologist, using knowledge of the depositional environment, or generated by computer using various interpolation schemes between the observed well values.

When the gross volume of the reservoir has been established and the basic petrophysical properties have been mapped throughout the reservoir, HCPV can be calculated. This volume, or actually a range of volumes obtained by an uncertainty analysis and the base – case geological model, including major uncertainty ranges for geological features which will affect production (Hal – dorsen and Damsleth, 1990) (e. g. , aquifer size, barrier sizes, fault – sealing capacity, and a possible number of missed faults; Heffer and Bevan, 1990) are then handed over to the reservoir engineers so that sensitivity studies may be performed.

Reservoir Engineering: The Dynamics

Although more advanced representations of geological models in a numerical simulation grid are coming into use, most reservoir simulations are still performed with coarsely gridded simple layer – cake models with constant or computer – interpolated properties in each layer.

Everyone is aware that input data to a simulation model are uncertain. Thus, it is common practice to perform a **sensitivity** analysis for those parameters that are believed to be most significant. The simulation model is the major tool for finding the effects of everybody's uncertainty. The usual procedure is to keep all parameters but one at their base – case value and then vary a single parameter to evaluate the effect on the output. After cycling through the parameters in this manner, the plausible range of the output will be known when the parameters are varied within a plausible range, one at the time. When several parameters are varied simultaneously, however, the effect cannot be established in this way.

Recently, ideas from statistical experimental design have been used in the planning and analysis of sensitivity runs. This approach may lead to a significant reduction in the number of simulation runs, or more information may be obtained. Interactions between different input parameters can be evaluated by this technique.

Optimizing the production strategy is also usually the responsibility of the reservoir engineers. Finding the ideal number of **wells** in the right positions, deciding the best **perforation** intervals, choosing the optimal plateau rate and capacities, and planning a suitable **offtake** strategy, **taking** the various static and dynamic uncertainties **into account**, is a **formidable** task.

The final step is history matching. After a period of production or after a long – term production test, the initial part of the true production profile becomes available. Generally, this will **differ from** the profile generated during pre – production simulations. The engineer will then make some adjustments in the simulation model (e. g., introduce a new sealing fault, extend the shale length, and/or adjust the relative permeability) in order to obtain a match between the real and simulated profiles. This process is repeated several times during the lifetime of a field. Despite some 20 published papers on automatic and adaptive history matching, a practical tool for reducing the number of runs is still missing.

Also, geoscientists must be in the "driver's seat" when geological input data are changed. This process can never be fully automated, and nonuniqueness is always a worry.

The Team

There is an increasing trend in the industry to incorporate all the above disciplines into one team, which also includes facility engineers and economists. Such a team sits together, perhaps with the "geotable" in the middle, and works very closely. Members of a team should necessarily understand each other, respect each other, act as a devil's advocate to each other, and keep each other informed. The focus should be on innovation and creation of value through the team approach, leading to a customer orientation with focus on "my output is your input." In many ways, you do not work for your boss; you work for your colleague.

Words and Expressions

characterization	描述方法,界定方法
grid	网格
outcrop	露头,露出地表
variogram	变量图
preach	竭力鼓吹,宣传
erroneous	错误的,不正确的
outsmart	智胜,比……更机灵
tomography	X线断层摄影术
barrier	障碍
recovery	采收率
mechanism	机制,机理
optimization	最佳化,最优化
hindsight	后见之明,事后聪明
plateau	高原
injection	注射,注入
homogeneous	同性质的,同类的
depositional	沉淀的,沉积的
post-mortem	事后的
contingency	应急措施
petrophysics	岩石物理学
geophysics	地球物理学
topography	地形学,地形测量学
parameter	参(变)数,参(变)量
prerequisite	先决条件
heterogeneity	异质性,不均匀性断层
porosity	孔隙度

drill	钻井勘探
permeability	渗透性
plotter	描绘器,图形显示器
visualization	可视化
facies	(地质)相,相图
fracture	断层
dip	(地层的与水平方向形成的)倾角
sedimentological	沉积学的
lithofacies	岩相
sensitivity	敏感,敏感度
well	油井,天然气井
perforation	穿孔,打孔
offtake	(从油槽中)将油排尽
formidable	非常艰难的

Phrases and Expression

in error	错误地
in effect	实际上,事实上
benefit from	通过……获益
rather than	与其……倒不如……
behind schedule	落后于预定计划
so that	以便
result in	引起,导致
focus on	对……予以关注
on the basis of	以……为基础
rule of thumb	经验法则
apply to	适用于
impact on	影响
due to	由于
take... into account	考虑
differ from	与……不同

Language Focus

1. Hence, detailed reservoir tomography by some known (e. g. , seismic)

or as – yet undiscovered technology, which yields images of all faults, the correct structure map, and geological architectural flow – unit and barrier details down to 1 – m resolution is on top of the reservoir characterization R&D wish list.

（参考译文：因此，由已知技术（如地震）或尚未发现的技术得到详细的储层的层析成像，这种层析成像能够以 1m 的分辨率产生所有断层的图像、正确的构造图、地质结构中的流通单元和屏障的细节，因而应摆在油藏描述研究与开发进程表的首位。）

本句是主系表结构，句子主干为 reservoir tomography is on top of the reservoir characterization R&D wish list。句中 which 引导非限定从句修饰 reservoir tomography。

2. However, we claim that these advancements, so far, have had only limited impact on the routine day – to – day operations of a typical oil company, although there are significant exceptions.

（参考译文：可是，我们要声明，迄今为止，这些进展对典型油气公司的日常工作并没有产生多大影响，尽管某些公司例外。）

本句是主谓宾结构，句子的宾语由 that 引导的宾语从句充当，而宾语从句又包含了 although 引导的让步状语从句。

3. Maps derived from 2 – D seismic data are poor substitutes since fields actually appear different when mapped from 2 – D and 3 – D data.

（参考译文：根据二维资料做出的构造图质量是很差的，因为二维资料和三维资料解释的构造实际上是完全不同的。）

本句是由 since 连接的表示因果关系的复合句。主句中 derived from 2 – D seismic data 是过去分词短语充当 Maps 的后置定语。而从句中 when mapped from 2 – D and 3 – D data 充当时间状语。

4. Also, we recommend that alternative interpretations, not just sensitivities, be prepared by having several skilled geophysicists, even from different companies, analyze the same data.

（参考译文：此外，我们建议，让一些有经验的、甚至是不同公司的地球物理专家分析相同的资料，做一些不同的解释。）

本句主句是主谓宾结构，宾语由 that 引导的宾语从句充当。recommend 后接宾语从句时需要用虚拟语气，即 should be prepared，should 可以省略。

5. The focus should be on innovation and creation of value through the team approach, leading to a customer orientation with focus on "my output is

your input".

（参考译文：重点是通过团队作业方法进行革新和创造，形成一个面向用户的工作方法。）

本句为主系表结构，leading to a customer orientation with focus on "my output is your input"为分词结构做状语。

Reinforced Learning

Ⅰ. Answer the following questions for a comprehension of the text.

1. What are the main goals of reservoir characterization research?

2. Various disciplines have made contributions to the development of an important field. What are they?

3. What is a prerequisite for any significant improvements in reservoir characterization?

4. What are the most important values for the significant petrophysical properties?

5. How do you understand "in the driver's seat" in the last paragraph but one?

Ⅱ. Multiple choice: choose the correct one from the alternative answers to give the exact meaning of the words.

1. We must not underestimate the challenges which lie ahead.

A. minimize　B. exaggerate　C. maximize　D. overlook

2. The flood resulted in a considerable reduction in production.

A. led to　B. resulted from　C. due to　D. owe to

3. We have gained sufficient experience to tackle this problem.

A. few　B. adequate　C. moderate　D. minimum

4. This old tree still yields apples every year.

A. submits　B. bears　C. gives in　D. surrenders

5. Many firms are focusing on increasing their markets overseas.

A. depending on　B. concentrating on

C. relying on　D. working on

6. Our regional measures have had a significant impact on unemployment

A. affect　B. impress　C. influence　D. expect

7. No other country at that time had an organized public opinion remotely

comparable to Britain's.

A. compared B. contrast C. parallel D. familiar

8. This information is freely available to anyone wishing to see it.

A. reliable B. flexible C. accessible D. possible

9. The television is a poor substitute for human companionship.

A. instrument B. device C. appliance D. replacement

10. A political unit consisting of an autonomous state inhabited especially by a predominantly homogeneous people.

A. diverse B. different C. various D. identical

Ⅲ. Multiple choice: read the four suggested translations and choose the best answer.

1. When the first well has been drilled and logged, the petrophysicist starts to work.

A. 钻井 B. 训练 C. 排水 D. 打孔

2. The fields are classified according to depositional environment, recovery mechanism, etc.

A. 恢复 B. 采收率 C. 重获 D. 复原

3. Of all the "underground sciences," geophysics has probably undergone the most significant technological change in the last decade.

A. 地球物理学 B. 岩石学 C. 物理学 D. 地质学

4. Porosity, permeability, water and/or oil saturation, and the net – to – gross ratio are usually the most important.

A. 饱和 B. 渗透性 C. 孔隙度 D. 繁荣

5. One will identify the various sedimentological building blocks, flow units, or lithofacies along the well path.

A. 外观 B. 岩相 C. 页岩 D. 表面

Ⅳ. Put the following sentences into Chinese.

1. Suggestions for future R&D activities are scattered throughout this paper, but we believe that in order to really outsmart Nature, you have to know her.

2. The degree to which geoscientists and engineers have delivered in the past is a good indicator of the need for future R&D in this area.

3. Today, there is no substitute for a high – quality 3 – D seismic interpretation.

4. Visualization of the facies, natural fractures, and the dip of layers encountered in the wells is now commonplace.

5. Recently, ideas from statistical experimental design have been used in the planning and analysis of sensitivity runs.

V. Put the following paragraphs into Chinese.

1. Past performance is not very flattering for the underground sciences! Poor reservoir characterization practices and inadequate representation of reservoirs with large grid blocks receive most of the blame. To be fair, the possibilities were also limited, since only 2 - D seismic data usually were available.

2. Seismic data usually find fields, reveal their lateral/vertical extent, provide the reservoir surface topography (i. e., depth map for top reservoir and sometimes for different horizons within it), supply some of the most important parameters (A, h) for the HCPV calculation, and reveal where the more significant faults are located. Rather useful things to know when one is constructing a reservoir model!

2.3 Challenges in Reservoir Characterization (Ⅱ)

Guidance to Reading

Despite today's high activity level and the many recent apparent advances within reservoir characterization practice and technology, the province - average recovery factors have not increased significantly, production forecasts are still notoriously in error, and the mainstream day - to - day geoscience/reservoir engineering approach to modeling, mapping, gridding, visualizing, and forecasting the behavior of reservoirs in a typical oil company has not changed noticeably during the last five years. From a summary of the state - of - the - art and current trends within reservoir characterization practice and research, this paper suggests and discusses new avenues and focal points for the future.

Text

NUMERICAL MODELING OF GEOLOGICAL RESERVOIR HETEROGENEITY

Most predictive tools employed in reservoir engineering practice can only handle physical quantities that vary in a **deterministic** manner in space. The rate of deterministic spatial variability is further limited by constraints on the number of grid blocks in the study. If we want to investigate the effects of input uncertainties on production forecasts, we **are faced with** simulating a great number of realizations, sensitivities, and "what ifs," since the description must be deterministic each time.

One of the single most important developments in reservoir characterization in recent years is the possibility of modeling detailed geological heterogeneity (both in a deterministic and **stochastic** manner) due to new tools, techniques, data, and more available grid blocks, particularly near injection and production wells. A few years ago, we gave a broad overview of the stochastic modeling topic with a then fairly comprehensive list of references. The excerpts below are largely taken from that overview.

Deterministic Reservoir Models

The traditional deterministic approach to reservoir characterization was described in the previous section. The main **geometric** architecture of the reservoir is modeled based on a detailed **zonation** of wells and possible correlations between wells. The petrophysical properties are assumed **either** constant within each zone **or** distributed laterally according to an interpolated contour map. These maps may capture large – scale lateral variation, but they will always be smooth, and they will not give a realistic description of the variability of the phenomenon.

Stochastic Reservoir Models

There are several reasons why stochastic techniques are used to describe deterministic reservoirs: (1) incomplete information, (2) complex spatial disposition of reservoir building blocks, (3) rock property variability, (4) unknown relationships between property value and the volume used for averaging (the problem of scale), (5) relative abundance of static over dynamic reservoir data, and finally (6) convenience and speed.

Stochastic modeling in the current geoscience, reservoir engineering, and hydrological literature usually **refers to** the generation of synthetic geological architecture and/or property fields in one, two, or three dimensions that are conditioned to observations and that possess a number of desirable geofeatures. The underlying goal of this geological quantification is to expose the effects of uncertainties in the geological description on the virgin, present, and future states of the reservoir.

To approach reality, heterogeneity must be introduced at a fine scale in the study since it is one of the most important factors governing fluid flow. The various recovery processes, however, have different needs **in terms of** detailed description. There are several different approaches to the stochastic modeling of heterogeneities. The choice of technique **depends on** the objective and scale of the study, the theoretical skills of the people involved, software availability, and most important, the available input data and geological understanding of the reservoir under study.

It is convenient to **distinguish between** two main classes of stochastic models: **discrete** and continuous.

Discrete Models

Discrete models have been developed to describe geological features of a discrete nature. These include locations and dimensions of sand bodies in **fluvial** rocks; **distribution** and sizes of shales suspended in sands; distribution, **orientations**, and lengths of fractures and faults; and lithofacies modeling.

In all these cases, a point in space will **belong to** one and only one of a limited number of classes, and the stochastic model controls how the class values at each point interact. For example, the model can control how one sand body may erode into another, how and if fractures may cross, and how different lithofacies **tend to** attract or repulse each other. Important measures, such as the accessible sand fraction and the floodable sand fraction, may be computed without doing actual flow simulations. Geological guidance is of vital importance in the model – building phase.

Continuous Models

Continuous models, on the other hand, have been developed to describe phenomena that vary continuously. Examples include rock **properties**, seismic **velocities** and dimension parameters (such as top of reservoir, OWC, etc.).

Each point in the reservoir space or in the reservoir area has one **distinct** value for the variable(s) of interest. The stochastic model describes **mean** level, or possible lateral or vertical trends, for the variable(s); variability around the mean; the strength of the correlation between neighboring points; and the covariation of the variables under study, if there is more than one.

Except for trends in the mean, most continuous models assume some kind of stationarity within the reservoir. That is, the **statistical** properties of the reservoir do not vary in space. This assumption is not always **valid**. Geological guidance and experience with the reservoir under study are important in building continuous models as well, but the approach is somewhat more mechanical.

Hybrid (two – stage) Models

Discrete models are closer to the geologist's interpretation of the reservoir, and they **are** usually better **suited for** the modeling of large – scale heterogeneities and reservoir **discontinuities**. Continuous models are well suited for modeling the spatial distribution of rock properties, but assume (more or less) stationarity. The natural idea, which has gained significant interest lately, is to combine the best of the two into a hybrid model. Most discrete and continuous models may be combined in a hybrid approach. At stage one, a discrete model is used to describe the large – scale heterogeneities in the model. At stage two, different continuous models are used to describe the spatial variation of the petrophysical parameters within each class in the discrete model.

Almost any stochastic technique can be used for conditional stochastic simulation. In conditional stochastic simulation, the goal is to introduce small – scale and/or large – scale heterogeneities in the reservoir model in a realistic and time – efficient way while still honoring the observations. "Noise" is added to an interpolated surface in a systematic way. At the location of the observations, the noise is zero, so that the observed values are honored. The resulting realization will give a much more realistic visual impression **compared to** the **interpolation**. Hopefully, the **dynamic** flow behavior of the resulting simulated realization will also be much closer to reality. Provided that the stochastic model chosen agrees with general geological expertise and honors all the observed data, we believe that the actual choice of stochastic model often is of minor importance.

COMPUTING TRENDS IN RESERVOIR CHARACTERIZATION

Today, computers are essential in every part of the petroleum business. In reservoir characterization and reservoir management, computers have hundreds of applications within the various technical and commercial disciplines. Broadly speaking, oil companies acquire, edit, integrate, process, interpret, and visualize data, and then generate results and forecasts which form the basis for economic and operational decisions. The main drive in all companies and disciplines is now toward (1) increased computational and input – output speed and memory in order to handle more data, to produce more precise forecasts and results, and to investigate and optimize the field – development plan and/or future production strategy for several subsurface "parallel realities," (2) rapid **access** and cross – discipline communication (storage, sharing, and integration), (3) visualization of results, and (4) convenient, effective, and user – friendly work tools and processes.

Production geology and the reservoir visualization task are now being converted into screen disciplines much like geophysics. Some companies already have come a long way toward the integrated **workbench** approach. All ingredients are **retrieved** from discipline databases, and specialized software and tools are used for mapping, interactive editing, displaying, rotating, cutting, slicing, etc. It is only a matter of a few years before most companies have reservoir visualization stations, which are the focal point for all disciplines in the team. The goal, however, must be that reservoir visualization software and hardware be so easy to operate that the new tools and techniques quickly move from research labs to field – development teams. When these integrated platforms **come into common use**, we should see sizable improvements in efficiency, discipline integration, data consistency, and total quality. If the production geologist is to sit in the "driver's seat" for this development and/or the subsequent application, universities should perhaps include a little more computer science, graphics, mathematics, and statistics in their geology curriculums.

In the context of computing, reservoir characterization challenges for the future translate directly to future hardware, software, and improved application challenges. We have briefly discussed the current computing trends within the various petroleum engineering disciplines. Possible "geoscience fiction" and other trends and developments that may lead to better reservoir characterization and management include the following: (1) Improved databases and retrieval systems; digital storage of seismic data. (2) Every discipline is in the team and on the "highway of information." (3) Customer orientation: My output is his input. Is the receiving format okay? How can I improve my product? (4) A "geotable" (a large, say 2m × 1m, tilted, color LCD screen on which maps and cross – sections may be displayed and interactively edited) and "geopen" (a penlike editing device for the "geotable"). (5) Stochastic models of property variability conditioned to all available information. (6) Virtual georeality, where the reservoir can be "visited" and inspected. (7) Massively parallel supercomputers. Software rather than hardware will soon be the key to improvements. Computers alone will not solve all our problems. They are only very convenient means to an end.

THE FUTURE CHALLENGES

Although some elements of the reservoir characterization future are here today (at least in research laboratories), many challenges remain! Until seismic resolution (detectability) is down to a few meters or some other technique yields a clear deterministic picture of reservoir **anatomy**, we believe that developments in applied field – scale reservoir characterization R&D will continue along the hybrid line described in the previous section. Also, static data sources such as seismic can give only indirect information about dynamic fluid – flow properties (e. g. , permeability via Φ, N/G, facies type, trends which correlate with permeability, or time – lapse front position information). The challenges are to (1) have enough control data in dimensionless form (e. g. , from outcrops) and classic geological knowledge to ensure that what is being generated is realistic. (2) Quickly be able to generate architecture and point – value realizations, conditional to all data including core, log, VSP, seismic, etc. (3) Conveniently grid the new realizations. It will soon be common to have 10^6 grid blocks. A pressure solver combined with CAD may proved to be a viable approach. (4) Screen realizations cheaply in terms of their production potential, connectivity, volumetric **sweep**, **floodability**, and ultimate recovery, and then carry the worst, average, and best (with respect to, e. g. , recovery or NPV) realization forward. (5) Optimize well positions and offtake strategy with streamline and front – tracking models, which are cheap, fast, and almost correct. (6) Perform detailed 3 – D, three – phase modeling with 10^6 – 10^9 grid blocks, to be able to optimize facility needs and estimate the size of the error bars on the predicted production profiles. (7) Display in 3 – D geological realizations and "movies" of the subsequent flow calculations. (8) History matches the models very fast, possibly in real time, if permanent monitoring of pressure, contacts, fluid fronts, etc., are available.

It might be useful to divide the future into two periods: pre – tomography and post – tomography. During the first period, stochastic modeling at all scales, gridding with CAD, and numerical modeling of many realizations will develop into an art. During the second period, the large – scale geological architecture will be known, and the main stochastic focus will be toward generating conditional fine – scale property fields in 3 – D. However, this will not mean that since we will then know the geological architecture down to 1m that error bars on forecasts will be zero, the **optimum** positions of injection and production wells will be so obvious that we do not even have to **search for** optimum positions with a trial and error procedure, etc.

Detailed knowledge about the geological architecture will be a vast improvement, but some very important issues remain uncertain. For example, assuming that all the faults have been captured and mapped, are the faults open or closed? Should we use the steady – state or the unsteady – state relative permeability (both are available and very different)? Hence, in addition to a deterministic detailed model of the reservoir, other R&D results must be available, such as in – situ measured relative permeability and residual saturations, fault sealing capacities calculated from appraisal programs with permanent pressure recorders, etc.

Imagine that everything is known about the reservoir, both architecture and properties. What is now the major challenge? A fine enough grid to allow the important interaction between driving forces, recovery process, and heterogeneities, and an endless amount of optimization runs to select the optimal number of wells in their optimal positions, offtake strategy, etc. Thus, a fully known and gridded reservoir description down to the meter – scale means that the focus will be **shifted from** geological "what ifs" **to** operational and optimization "what ifs." Hence, the capacity to cheaply run a large number of repeated simulations using objective functions both for steering offtake through time ("putting brains on simulators") and for ranking "what ifs" in terms of their outcome attractiveness must be provided for.

In summary, the major future reservoir characterization research challenges are to: (1) Practice in field – development teams what is preached at conferences! (2) Learn from past field developments. Why were actual and predicted performance different? (3) Focus on both the most relevant and pressing specific problems and opportunities in your field portfolio as well as on the longer term technologies with higher risk and higher potential. (4) Develop a 100% reliable **direct hydrocarbon indicator** (DHI). Stop looking for oil fields with expensive exploration and appraisal wells, which are dry most of the time! (5) Achieve a dramatic seismic resolution improvement. The industry wanted 1 – m resolution at typical North Sea reservoir depths before the turn of the century! (6) Develop sources, receivers, acquisition, processing, and interpretation technology such that all maps of faults, large – scale geological architectures, field extents, fluid contacts, fluid fronts, facies types, and other properties are arrived at directly from seismic or equivalent tomography – science data. (7) Develop and routinely use permanent pressure recorders to assess sealing capacities of faults prior to and during the production phase. (8) Increase use of pressure coring to obtain the correct unaltered relative permeabilities and residual saturations, which constitute that starting point for many EOR processes. (9) Determine fluvial architecture from long – term production tests. (10) Collect dimensionless outcrop data from analogs of the most important field types in the province portfolio. (11) Convert production geology into an effective screen discipline. Provide tool kits for generating 3 – D point values of interdependent properties in and around the deterministic large – scale geologic architecture, all conditional to core, log, VSP, and seismic data in the various databases. (12) Develop methodology and procedures for optimization via repeated experimentation with a simulation model. For each field optimize the interplay between heterogeneities, wells, production strategy, and a predetermined success factor (e. g., plateau rate and duration, NPV, RF) by optimizing the offtake strategy, number of wells, position of wells, handling capacities, gas lift (Edwards et al., 1990), etc., through well – planned experiments ("brains on simulators").

Thus, in a futuristic dream, we can imagine that oil, gas, and water can be distinguished directly from some DHI with no need to look for oil with expensive wells, that horizontal (or "snake" or whatever) wells traverse the whole reservoir and are 1000 – 5000 m long and with large – diameter pipe, that the seismic signal yields a resolution (detectability) of 1 m with every important geological detail captured, that Gullfaks field, for example, is gridded into 4 billion grid cells and simulated in 1 hr computer time (3 – D, three phase) with all topside facilities and constraints included, that it is possible to have real time animation of a simulation process on a computer screen, that a "brain on a simulator" arrives at the optimal offtake strategy through time, and that fluid fronts are monitored continuously by repeated seismic and that all wells, even plugged and abandoned exploration and appraisal wells, have permanent monitoring of rates and pressure.

An important question arises: Who should do the research to make all this come true? Within reservoir characterization research, there is an enormous duplication of effort, even if nothing is really secret. The leader – follower discussion in this area is really not about who invents something first, but who uses it in a practical application first. Whereas a few years ago, all companies sent their geologists to the same outcrops to measure sand and shale lengths as well as permeability patterns with **minipermeameter** tools, multicompany **consortiums** now operate together in a cost – effective manner.

Universities, public or private research institutions, and company research laboratories should cooperate and specialize. Universities and research institutions have the tools and methods, the industry has the problems and challenges. Each year, the industry should provide to universities a list of problems/challenges/opportunities/"I wish I could—I wish I had." If that were done, theses and dissertations could be **aimed at** these problems and challenges.

All this research will lead to improved reservoir description tools, techniques, and practices, which in turn should help us get better predictions. But will all this also lead to higher overall recovery factors? We firmly believe the answer is yes, but perhaps not before seismic or some other technology provides an x – ray, ultrasound, or NMR picture of true internal reservoir anatomy and the positions of fluid fronts through time.

Words and Expressions

deterministic	确定性的
stochastic	随机的
geometric	几何的
zonation	成带，分带
discrete	离散的
fluvial	河的

distribution	分布,分布状态
orientation	方向,方位
property	特性,性质
velocity	速度,速率
distinct	清楚无误的,明确的
mean	平均值
statistical	统计学的
valid	确凿的,令人信服的
discontinuity	不连续性
interpolation	插值,插值法,内插法
dynamic	动态的,不断变化的
outstrip	比……速度更快,把……抛在后面
simulator	模拟器,模拟装置
access	(对计算机存储器的)访问,存取
workbench	工作台,作业台
retrieve	(计算机系统)检索
anatomy	对内部结构(或运作)的研究
sweep	驱扫
floodability	可注水性
optimum	有最佳效果的
minipermeameter	便携渗透(性试验)仪
consortium	财团,联合企业

Phrases and Expression

be faced with	面临
either. . . or. . .	要么……要么……
refer to	有关
in terms of	就……而言,从……方面说来
depend on	随……而定
distinguish between	辨别,识别(两者)之间的不同
belong to	属于
tend to	趋向
except for	除……之外

be suited for 相称，合适
compared to 与……相比
come into use 开始被使用
search for 搜索，搜寻
shift from... to... 从……转为……
aim at 以……为目标

Proper Name

hydrocarbon indicator 烃类检测

Language Focus

1. One of the single most important developments in reservoir characterization in recent years is the possibility of modeling detailed geological heterogeneity (both in a deterministic and stochastic manner) due to new tools, techniques, data, and more available grid blocks, particularly near injection and production wells.

(参考译文：由于新的工具、技术、资料和更多的网格的获得(特别是在接近注水井和生产井的地方)，近年来在油藏描述方面最重要的一个发展是详细描述地质模型的非均质性(以确定的和随机的方法)。)

本句为主系表结构。due to 部分做原因状语，表明详细描述地质模型的非均质性这种可能性产生的原因。

2. Geological guidance and experience with the reservoir under study are important in building continuous models as well, but the approach is somewhat more mechanical.

(参考译文：在制作连续模型时地质指导和对油藏的经验也是很重要的，但这种方法更机械一些。)

本句的主干是由 but 连接的并列句结构。Geological guidance and experience 是并列主语，with the reservoir under study 为 with 结构做后置定语修饰 experience。

3. In conditional stochastic simulation, the goal is to introduce small-scale and/or large-scale heterogeneities in the reservoir model in a realistic and time-efficient way while still honoring the observations.

(参考译文：条件随机模拟中的目的是在油藏模型中以现实和实时的方

法从地层观察结果引进小规模的和(或)大规模的不均一性。)

本句为主系表结构。表语由不定式结构 to introduce small - scale and/or large - scale heterogeneities in the reservoir model in a realistic and time - efficient way 充当。while still honoring the observations 做时间状语。

4. Provided that the stochastic model chosen agrees with general geological expertise and honors all the observed data, we believe that the actual choice of stochastic model often is of minor importance.

(参考译文:假定所选择的随机模拟模型与总的地质经验一致且尊重所有观测到的资料,我们相信随机模型的实际选择通常是不太重要的。)

本句是由 provided that 引导的表示假设关系的复杂句。主句为 we believe that the actual choice of stochastic model often is of minor importance,是主谓宾结构,宾语由 that 引导的宾语从句充当。

5. The goal, however, must be that reservoir visualization software and hardware be so easy to operate that the new tools and techniques quickly move from research labs to field - development teams.

(参考译文:尽管如此,其目标必须是:油藏可视化软件和硬件应易于操作,以便使新工具和新技术从实验室迅速普及到开发队伍中去。)

本句主干为主系表结构。第一个 that 引导表语从句,第二个 that 为 so... that 结构中的 that。

Reinforced Learning

Ⅰ. Answer the following questions for a comprehension of the text.

1. Why are stochastic techniques used to describe deterministic reservoirs?

2. What is the underlying goal of the geological quantification?

3. What are the two main classes of stochastic models?

4. What are geological features of a discrete natures?

5. What are the reservoir characterization challenges for the future in the context of computing?

Ⅱ. Multiple choice: choose the correct one from the alternative answers to give the exact meaning of the words.

1. He refused to allow his secretary to handle confidential letters.

A. sell B. operate C. manage D. cope with

2. The government has placed tight constraints on spending this year.

A. stress B. strain C. depression D. restriction

3. The lion approached its prey.

A. contacted B. begun C. came near D. discovered

4. He got the distinct impression that Melissa wasn't best pleased.

A. different B. clear C. definite D. distinguished

5. All living things depend on the sun for their growth.

A. rely on B. come on C. aim at D. refer to

6. These plants have medicinal properties.

A. possession B. qualities C. ownership D. shares

7. This new boiler generates more heat than the old one.

A. produces B. causes C. gathers D. collects

8. The old assumptions are no longer valid.

A. lawful B. leagal C. convincing D. official

9. It is important to ensure that delegates have been properly briefed.

A. guarantee B. assure C. assume D. insure

10. Do you know the optimum temperature for the growth of plants?

A. best B. worst C. minimum D. medium

Ⅲ. Multiple choice: read the four suggested translations and choose the best answer.

1. One of the single most important developments in reservoir characterization in recent years is the possibility of modeling detailed geological heterogeneity.

A. 同一性 B. 变化 C. 恒定 D. 异质性

2. There are several different approaches to the stochastic modeling of heterogeneities.

A. 随机的 B. 连续的 C. 离散的 D. 混合的

3. Discrete models have been developed to describe geological features of a discrete nature.

A. 随机的 B. 连续的 C. 离散的 D. 混合的

4. The main geometric architecture of the reservoir is modeled based on a detailed zonation of wells and possible correlations between wells.

A. 方向 B. 分布 C. 成带 D. 地区

5. Examples include rock properties, seismic velocities and dimension parameters.

A. 速率　　B. 形状　　C. 强度　　D. 方位

Ⅳ. Put the following sentences into Chinese.

1. To approach reality, heterogeneity must be introduced at a fine scale in the study since it is one of the most important factors governing fluid flow.

2. Important measures, such as the accessible sand fraction and the floodable sand fraction, may be computed without doing actual flow simulations.

3. Continuous models, on the other hand, have been developed to describe phenomena that vary continuously.

4. Except for trends in the mean, most continuous models assume some kind of stationarity within the reservoir.

5. Production geology and the reservoir visualization task are now being converted into screen disciplines much like geophysics.

Ⅴ. Put the following paragraphs into Chinese.

1. Most discrete and continuous models may be combined in a hybrid approach. At stage one, a discrete model is used to describe the large – scale heterogeneities in the model. At stage two, different continuous models are used to describe the spatial variation of the petrophysical parameters within each class in the discrete model.

2. Today, computers are essential in every part of the petroleum business. In reservoir characterization and reservoir management, computers have hundreds of applications within the various technical and commercial disciplines. Broadly speaking, oil companies acquire, edit, integrate, process, interpret, and visualize data, and then generate results and forecasts which form the basis for economic and operational decisions.

Chapter 3 Geologic Structure Analysis of Reservoirs

3.1 Geologic Aspects of Naturally Fractured Reservoirs

Guidance to Reading

Most of today' s producing naturally fractured reservoirs were discovered accidentally. We should revisit the subject of how to explore for these reservoirs. Another is because significant volumes of hydrocarbons reside in these reservoirs — particularly in fields abandoned because of improper testing and evaluation or because the wells did not intersect the natural fractures.

Unfortunately rules of thumb and, naturally fractured reservoirs do not mix well. What appears to work in one might fail miserably in the next. Consequently, each naturally fractured reservoir exploration play must be an individual research project.

This text discusses selected geologic aspects that describe, mostly qualitatively key characteristics of the fractures and the places which are important in hydrocarbon production.

Text

BACKGROUND

Stearns **defines** a natural fracture **as** a macroscopic **planar** discontinuity that **results from** stresses that exceed the **rupture** strength of the rock. Nelson defines it as a naturally occurring macroscopic planar discontinuity in rock **due to** deformation or physical **diagenesis**.

It follows that a naturally fractured reservoir is a reservoir that contains fractures that result from natural, man – made, stress differences that existed in the rock at the time it fractured. These natural fractures can **have** a positive, **neutral**, or negative **effect on** fluid flow.

Open fractures that are **uncemented** might have, for example, a positive effect on oil flow but a negative effect on water or gas flow due to **coning**.

These fractures **tend to** close as reservoirs are depleted due to increases in net normal stresses across the fractures. Not **taking** this closure or partial closure **into account** can lead to overly optimistic forecasts of reservoir performance.

It is, therefore, of **paramount** importance to have knowledge of **magnitude** and direction of **in situ** principal stresses; **azimuth**, dip, spacing, and **aperture** of fractures; and a good idea **with respect to** fracture **porosity** and permeability. Partially mineralized fractures might provide better ultimate hydrocarbon recovery because the partial mineralization can **act as** a natural **proppant**, thus keeping the fracture open during depletion.

Totally mineralized natural fractures, on the other hand, could create permeability barriers to all types of flow. This could generate small compartments within the reservoir and, **in turn**, uneconomic or marginal recovery.

In my opinion, virtually all reservoirs contain at least some natural fractures. However, if the effect of these fractures on fluid flow is **negligible**, the reservoir can be treated (from a geologic and a reservoir engineering point of view) as a "conventional" reservoir. In this I agree with Nelson and **regard** only those reservoirs in which the fractures have an effect (either positive or negative) on fluid flow **as** naturally fractured.

Reservoir rock, by definition, must be porous and permeable. However, contributions to total porosity and permeability by the **matrix** and by the fractures must be separated. Therefore, precise determination of both matrix and fracture porosity, and matrix and fracture hydrocarbon **saturation** is important to accurately calculate the distribution between matrix and fractures of in – place hydrocarbons. Matrix and fracture permeabilities are equally important **parameters** for calculating true flow capacities.

Igneous, **sedimentary**, or **metamorphic** rocks can, under the right conditions, be the origin of acceptable reservoir rock. Although, most hydrocarbon accumulations occur in sandstones or **carbonate** rocks, I have evaluated commercial fractured reservoirs in shales, **anhydrites**, coal seams, sandstones, limestones, dolomites, volcanics, and igneous metamorphic reservoirs. Naturally fractured reservoirs can be found in all types of traps, all over the world, and throughout the **stratigraphic** column.

FRACTURE GENERATION AND FORM

Fractures result from various causes. Landes and Nelson list them as:

(1) Structural deformation associated with folding and faulting. Faulting tends to generate cracks along the fault line which, in turn, produces a zone of **dilatancy**. Dilatancy is probably responsible for a large part of the migration and accumulation of petroleum in fracture reservoirs.

(2) Rapid and deep erosion of overburden that permits expansion, **uplift**, and fracturing along planes of weakness.

(3) Volume shrinkage due to such events as: dewatering in shales, cooling of igneous rocks, or **desiccation** in sedimentary rocks.

(4) **Paleokarstification** and solution collapse.

(5) Fracturing through release of high pore – fluid pressure (those that approach the **lithostatic** pressure) in geopressured sedimentary **strata**.

(6) The rare **meteorite** impact that causes complex, extensively **brecciated**, fractured reservoirs.

Fracture **morphology** relates to the characteristics and / or filling along natural fracture surfaces. Nelson says fracture morphology can be considered as open, deformed, mineral – filled, or **vuggy**.

Open fractures are uncemented and do not contain any secondary mineralization; i. e. , there has been no alteration of the original fracture surface. Fracture width is usually very small, probably no larger than one pore diameter, but such fractures increase the matrix permeability significantly in a direction parallel to fracture strike (s). On the other hand, open fractures have negligible effect on permeability **perpendicular** to fracture strike(s).

Although there are exceptions, porosity of open fractures is usually a fraction of a percent.

Deformed fractures include **gouge** – filled fractures and slicken – sided fractures. The gouge **is composed of** the finely **abraded** material resulting from grinding or sliding motion that occurred along shear fractures in friable rocks. Gouge drastically reduces fracture permeability. A slickenside is the result of frictional sliding along a fracture (small fault) plane that polished the fracture surface. A polished, **striated** surface along fractures may increase permeability parallel to the fracture, but it also drastically reduces permeability perpendicular to the fracture. Slickensides, **as well as** gouge filling, can cause strong permeability anisotropy to develop in an otherwise **isotropic** reservoir.

Mineral – filled fractures are filled, or partially filled, with postfracture formation mineralization (most commonly quartz or calcite). Completely filled fractures can be formidable permeability barriers. On the other hand, partial fracture filling (mineralization) could have positive effects on hydrocarbon recovery because the secondary minerals could act as natural proppants. The strong **calcite** or quartz prevents fracture closure as the reservoir is depleted. I have seen apertures of partially mineralized fractures in cores of up to 1 inch.

Fractures along which vugs have developed can provide significant reservoir porosity and permeability. Because of their irregular and somewhat round shape, vuggy fractures probably do not close as the reservoir is depleted. Vuggy fractures usually result from acid waters **percolating** through fractures. In the extreme, such processes can lead to the development of karst and, therefore, very **prolific** reservoirs.

MECHANICAL BEHAVIOR OF ROCK

It has long been recognized that the mechanical properties of rocks are controlled by the combined influence of intrinsic and environmental parameters.

Intrinsic rock parameters include such things as composition, grain size, matrix porosity and permeability, bed thickness, and pre – existing mechanical discontinuities. Environmental properties include effective confining pressure (the difference between lithostatic and pore fluid pressure), temperature, time (strain rate), differential stress, and perhaps even pore fluid composition.

If environmental parameters are constant, rock composition basically determines the strength and **ductility** of various rock types. This obviously influences how difficult or easy it is to fracture the rock. Everything being equal, **based on** composition alone, the **lithology** most susceptible to fracture is quartzite followed in descending order by dolomite, quartz – cemented sandstone, calcite – cemented sandstone, and limestone.

Studies on the effect of grain size on fracture abundance have found, in general, that the finer the grain size the greater the strength, the lower the ductility and, therefore, the greater the fracture intensity.

In like manner laboratory studies of the effect of matrix porosity have shown that the lower the porosity, the greater the fracture intensity in a given rock type.

Bed thickness also influences fracture spacing. Both outcrop and production data show that thinner beds contain more closely spaced fractures.

Environmental properties include effective pressure, temperature, strain rate, differential stress, and pore fluid composition.

Effective or confining pressure **plays** an important **role in** rock behavior and, therefore, in the generation of fractures. It has been demonstrated experimentally that rock strength and ductility increase with increasing effective pressure. Consequently, rocks deformed at shallower depths might be more fractured than the same rocks deformed under large overburden pressure.

Strain rate at which deformation occurred can be an important environmental parameter. In general, as the strain rate gets higher, rocks become increasingly **brittle**. However, to be an important parameter, strain rates must change several orders of magnitude. For example, rocks deformed by meteorite impact would be significantly more fractured than if deformed by slow tectonic deformation. However, rocks that were influenced by unexceptional strain rate variations within a long – term geologic process probably do not vary a great deal in fracture development.

CLASSIFICATION

Stearns and Nelson, from a geologic point of view, have classified natural fractures as tectonic, regional, and diagenetic.

Tectonic fractures. These were described by Stearns and Nelson as: "Those whose origin can, on the basis of orientation, distribution, and morphology, be attributed to or be associated with, a local tectonic event." The vast majority of all tectonic fractures **fall into** one of two categories: fractures caused by folding processes and fractures caused by faulting processes.

Fractures associated with faults can result from the same far – field stress differences that caused the faulting. Consequently, shear fractures can be considered **miniatures** of the fault, and their two orientations can be determined from the attitude of the controlling fault.

Tectonic fractures are the most important fracture type with respect to hydrocarbon production. Numerous reservoirs produce from tectonic fractures, including the Palm Valley gas field of Central Australia, Aguarague gas field of Argentina, and offshore oil reservoirs of Mexico.

Regional fractures. They have been defined by Nelson and Stearns as "those (fractures) which are developed over large areas of the earth's crust with relatively little change in orientation, show no evidence of offset across the fracture plane, and are always perpendicular to major bedding surfaces." These fractures seem unrelated to local structures, are probably due to surface forces, tend to develop in an **orthogonal** pattern, and seem almost **omnipresent**.

Orientation of regional fractures remains constant within 10° ~ 15° over 100 miles. Because there is no offset across the fracture plane, there is no host rock damage which makes regional fractures very conducive to fluid flow.

Diagenetic fractures. These form due to diagenetic changes in the rock. Most commonly they are (1) desiccation, (2) **syneresis**, (3) thermal gradients, and (4) mineral phase changes. Each of these processes or conditions can produce stress differences large enough to cause **tensile**, or extension, fractures associated with a reduction in bulk volume during diagenesis.

They are initiated by body rather than surface forces; i. e., they are started by forces in the body rather than external to it as is the case for tectonic fractures. An example of contractional fractures is the Permian Council Grove Formation of the Panoma Field (Kansas).

UNDISCOVERED NATURALLY FRACTURED RESERVOIRS, WHY AND HOW?

Many naturally fractured reservoirs should have been economic but were abandoned because of (1) incorrect pressure **extrapolations**, (2) poor completions, and / or (3) failure of the borehole to **intersect** the natural fractures.

Incorrect pressure extrapolations in fractured reservoirs might occur if the infinite acting **radial** flow period is not reached during a pressure **transient** test. This can lead to the **erroneous** conclusion that the reservoir is depleting.

Conventional completions are typically performed in intervals that meet certain porosity, permeability, and water saturation **cutoff** criteria. This is risky in naturally fractured reservoirs where the largest degree of natural fracturing could be associated with the lowest porosities and matrix permeabilities. Furthermore, there are instances where the largest fracture intensity is found in the thinner beds.

Commercial production of hydrocarbons is not possible from an unfractured, tight matrix. However, hydrocarbons can flow very efficiently from the tight matrix into the natural fractures. One key to success is to ensure fractures with high dips are intersected by directional or horizontal wells.

DSTs and RFTs are powerful techniques, but care must be exercised in their interpretation because they are not fully diagnostic in naturally **fractured** reservoirs. For example, if only the tight matrix is tested, these tools will correctly indicate very low permeability and no flow capabilities. Even when a fracture is tested, recovery may be only mud lost into the fractures during drilling operations.

Most natural fractures of commercial importance are vertical or near vertical. Therefore vertical wells do not stand the same probability of success as directional or horizontal wells in naturally fractured reservoirs.

SUMMARY AND CONCLUSIONS

There is no doubt that natural fractures are a contributing factor in most reservoirs and virtually all structural traps. However, in too many cases they are ignored or, at best, only given **token** consideration. There is today a substantial database for predicting both fracture intensity and fracture orientation.

Furthermore, specific detection of fractures from modern log **suites** and / or well test data is now possible. Combine our ability to predict fracture orientation and spacing with our ability to measure fractured reservoir in situ properties with our ability to control directional drilling, and it becomes obvious that greater attention must be paid to the natural fractures in our reservoir rocks.

Only if we do begin to utilize all fracture data will we then begin to **optimize** our profit margin from fractured reservoirs, and most reservoirs are fractured.

Words and Expressions

planar	平面的
rupture	破裂
diagenesis	成岩作用
neutral	中立的
uncemented	未胶结的
coning	锥进
paramount	最高的,主要的
magnitude	大小
in situ	原位
azimuth	方位角
aperture	缝隙

porosity	孔隙度
proppant	支撑剂
negligible	可忽略的
matrix	基质,基岩
saturation	饱和度
parameter	参数
igneous	火成的
sedimentary	沉积的
metamorphic	变质的
carbonate	碳酸盐
anhydrite	硬石膏
stratigraphic	地层学的
dilatancy	膨胀,扩张
uplift	隆起
desiccation	干燥
paleokarstification	古岩溶作用
lithostatic	地压的
strata	地层
meteorite	陨星
brecciated	角砾岩的
morphology	形态学
vuggy	多孔的
perpendicular	垂直的
gouge	裂缝泥
abraded	研磨的
striated	有条纹的
isotropic	各向同性的
calcite	方解石
percolate	渗入
karst	岩溶
prolific	多产的
ductility	可塑性
lithology	岩性
brittle	易碎的

miniature	微型
orthogonal	正交的
omnipresent	无所不在的
syneresis	脱水
tensile	伸张
extrapolation	推断
intersect	相交,相贯
radial	径向的
transient	瞬间的
erroneous	错误的
cutoff	中止
fractured	断裂的
token	象征性的
suite	程序组合
optimize	使最优化

Phrases and Expression

define . . . as	把……定义为
result from	源于
due to	由于
have . . . effect on	对……有影响
tend to	往往
take . . . into account	把……考虑在内
with respect to	关于
act as	担任,充当
in turn	相应,转而
regard . . . as	把……视为
be composed of	由……组成
as well as	和……一样
base on	基于
play . . . role in	在……中起作用
fall into	分成

Language Focus

1. Stearns defines a natural fracture as a macroscopic planar discontinuity that results from stresses that exceed the rupture strength of the rock.

（参考译文：Stearns 把天然裂缝定义为一个宏观的不连续面，这个面是由超过岩石破裂强度的应力造成的。）

本句中两个 that 从句都是定语从句，其中前一个 that 引导的定语从句用来修饰先行词 discontinuity，后一个 that 引导的定语从句用来修饰先行词 stresses。

2. It follows that a naturally fractured reservoir is a reservoir that contains fractures that result from natural, man – made, stress differences that existed in the rock at the time it fractured.

（参考译文：由此可见，天然裂缝性储集层是具有裂缝的储集层，岩石中的这些裂缝是由天然的应力差造成的，而不是人工形成的。）

本句 It follows that ... 中的 it 为形式主语，而 that 引导的从句为句子的真正主语。后三个 that 引导的都是定语从句，分别修饰先行词 reservoir、fractures 和 differences。

3. Studies on the effect of grain size on fracture abundance have found, in general, that the finer the grain size the greater the strength, the lower the ductility and, therefore, the greater the fracture intensity.

（参考译文：岩石颗粒大小与裂缝发育程度关系的研究表明，通常岩石颗粒越细，岩石强度越大，可塑性越低，于是产生的裂缝强度较大。）

本句的主干是 Studies have found that...，其中 that 引导的从句是做 found 的宾语。the finer... the greater... 是经典的 the more... the more... 句式，译为“越……越……”，后边的 the lower... the greater... 也是此句式。

4. Combine our ability to predict fracture orientation and spacing with our ability to measure fractured reservoir in situ properties with our ability to control directional drilling, and it becomes obvious that greater attention must be paid to the natural fractures in our reservoir rocks.

（参考译文：如果我们能把预测裂缝的方向和间距、测量裂缝性储集层特性以及控制定向钻探三者结合在一起，那么显而易见，我们必须对储集岩的天然裂缝给予更多的关注。）

本句为祈使句（表条件）+ and + 主句（表结果）的句式。祈使句动词 combine 后接两个并列的 with，把三个 our ability 结合在一起。每个 ability 后面的不定式短语充当后置定语。主句部分 it 做形式主语，that 引导主语从句是主句真正的主语。

5. Only if we do begin to utilize all fracture data will we then begin to optimize our profit margin from fractured reservoirs, and most reservoirs are frac-

tured.

（参考译文：只有在我们开始利用所有的裂缝资料时，我们才可以从裂缝性储集层中优化利润率，且大多数储集层都是有裂缝的。）

本句为强调句的一种，当 only if 从句位于句首，主句需要部分倒装。

Reinforced Learning

Ⅰ. Answer the following questions for a comprehension of the text.

1. It has long been recognized that the mechanical properties of rocks are controlled only by the influence of intrinsic parameter. Is it right? Why?

2. If environmental parameters are constant, for the various rock types what does rock composition basically determine?

3. What do the environmental properties include?

4. From a geologic point of view, what have Stearns and Nelson classified natural fractures as?

5. Many naturally fractured reservoirs should have been economic but were abandoned. Why?

Ⅱ. Multiple choice: choose the correct one from the alternative answers to give the exact meaning of the words.

1. If your liabilities exceed your assets, you may go bankrupt.

A. occupy B. expel C. deliver D. surpass

2. She was always optimistic, even when things were at their worst.

A. healthy B. brave C. cheerful D. indifferent

3. My wages are the principal source of my income.

A. main B. stable C. lasting D. permanent

4. Our ultimate objective is the removal of all nuclear weapons.

A. great B. eventual C. strong D. recent

5. Can you explore the market possibility for us?

A. ask B. investigate C. explode D. determine

6. The next – best solution is to abandon the project altogether.

A. desert B. conduct C. finish D. hold

7. Preventing abnormal or excessive accumulation of fat in the liver.

A. prevention B. formation C. collection D. consumption

8. Scientists have studied the migration of fish over long distances.

A. life　　B. existence　　C. style　　D. movement

9. That country remained neutral in the war.

A. negative　　B. positive　　C. subjective　　D. impartial

10. The damage to my car is negligible.

A. severe　　B. insignificant　　C. acute　　D. obvious

Ⅲ. **Multiple choice: read the four suggested translations and choose the best answer.**

1. Reservoir rock, by definition, must be porous and permeable.

A. 柔软的　　B. 无孔的　　C. 多孔的　　D. 坚硬的

2. Open fractures that are uncemented might have, for example, a positive effect on oil flow but a negative effect on water or gas flow due to coning.

A. 未脱水的　　B. 未结晶的　　C. 未风化的　　D. 未胶结的

3. Matrix and fracture permeabilities are equally important parameters for calculating true flow capacities.

A. 参数　　B. 标准　　C. 单位　　D. 特征

4. Stearns and Nelson, from a geologic point of view, have classified natural fractures as tectonic, regional, and diagenetic.

A. 结晶的　　B. 成岩的　　C. 诊断的　　D. 沉积的

5. Consequently, rocks deformed at shallower depths might be more fractured than the same rocks deformed under large overburden pressure.

A. 破裂　　B. 变形　　C. 分割　　D. 溶蚀

Ⅳ. **Put the following sentences into Chinese.**

1. In like manner laboratory studies of the effect of matrix porosity have shown that the lower the porosity, the greater the fracture intensity in a given rock type.

2. However, rocks that were influenced by unexceptional strain rate variations within a long – term geologic process probably do not vary a great deal in fracture development.

3. Most natural fractures of commercial importance are vertical or near vertical.

4. There is no doubt that natural fractures are a contributing factor in most reservoirs and virtually all structural traps.

5. Only if we do begin to utilize all fracture data will we then begin to opti-

mize our profit margin from fractured reservoirs, and most reservoirs are fractured.

Ⅴ. **Put the following paragraphs into Chinese.**

1. Secondary porosity (also known as induced porosity) is the product of geologic processes occurring after deposition and has no direct relation to the form of the sedimentary particles. Secondary porosity can be due to solution, recrystallization (重结晶), dolomitization (白云石化), or fractures.

2. Most fracture porosities reported in the literature range between about 0.01 and 10%. However, it is important to emphasize that fracture porosity is strongly scale – dependent. For example, if a 20 ft drilling break is encountered, the fracture porosity within those 20 ft is 100%.

3.2 Analysis of Fault Traps

Guidance to Reading

More risks are associated with fault traps than with simple four – way – dip closures. Additional analysis is required to properly assess trap risk. Good appraisal of fault traps begins with accurate fault mapping. This text focuses on the following topics: mapping faults including discussions on the aliasing problem, fault shape, 3 – D data, en echelon faults and the coherence cube; a general discussion of fault traps; juxtaposition traps and the use of "Allan sections"; fault – sealing traps and the three mechanisms that cause fault – zone capillary properties to differ from unfaulted rock—Clay smear, grain crushing and diagenesis.

Text

INTRODUCTION

Good **appraisal** of fault traps begins with **accurate** fault mapping. Even on 3 – D data sets, accurate fault mapping requires **construction** of fault surface maps. Mapping of either fault throw or vertical separation **contours** on fault surface maps is highly recommended to help avoid **aliasing** (incorrectly connecting) faults. **Coherency** processing appears to offer potential for helping to correctly link fault **segments**.

Juxtaposition traps: Faults may trap **hydrocarbons** if they **juxtapose**

rocks with significantly different **capillary properties** or if the capillary properties of the fault zone itself have **sealing** capability. Juxtaposition **traps** need to be **evaluated** by carefully mapping the **stratigraphy** of **the hanging wall and the footwall** along the fault surface.

Fault – seal traps: Fault – seal **traps** depend on the fault zone itself to seal. The sealing potential of fault zones can be **estimated qualitatively** from knowledge of the net/gross ratio of the affected **section** and the amount and timing of **displacement**. The sealing potential of fault zones can be estimated **semi – quantitatively** by the use of computer programs **calibrated** with local examples.

Fault trap risks: Fault traps have two major types of risks which **unfaulted four – way – dip closures** do not share. The first risk involves how the faults are mapped. The second risk involves the **sealing** behavior **associated with** trapping fault. These two risks are independent and either can cause an apparently attractive prospect to **result in** a dry hole.

MAPPING FAULTS

When faults are mapped from well control or 2 – D **seismic** data, the possibility of aliasing faults is very high. If fault segments are incorrectly connected, fault traps on the resulting maps may be totally different than the true subsurface structure.

Aliasing problem

When **addressing** the aliasing problem, it is imperative that all significant fault surfaces be mapped. Faults in different tectonic provinces **tend to** have characteristic shapes. Faults which have **atypical** shapes for the **tectonic province** in which they occur should be **scrutinized** carefully for possible aliasing.

A shape which may be reasonable in one tectonic setting may be highly unlikely in another tectonic environment.

Fault shape

The term fault shape, as used here, **refers to** the shape of the fault surface, not to the shape of the fault trace on a structure map. Except **in the case of** vertical faults or **horizontal** beds, the trace of a fault is the result of the intersection of two **dipping**, non – **planar** surfaces. Fault traces can be determined by integrating structure and fault surface maps, but the traces are not **intuitive** and cannot be easily determined if the fault surface itself is not mapped.

Although beyond the scope of this article, fault shape is important in other **respects**. Fault shape controls structure shape in the hanging wall. Fault shape may also provide valuable information about the sand – shale ratio in parts of the section.

3 – D data

Aliasing of faults on 3 – D seismic data is less of a problem than with well and 2 – D seismic data. Not only are the seismic lines much closer spaced and properly migrated in three dimensions, but fault interpretations can also be tied by interpreting carefully selected **arbitrary** lines. Tying fault interpretations with arbitrary lines **drastically** reduces fault aliasing.

Unless the data is extremely clear and every line in a 3 – D data set is interpreted, aliasing is still possible and fault surface maps are still recommended. Most interpreters initially interpret every fifth or tenth line in a 3 – D survey. During this phase of the seismic interpretation, constant reference to continually updated fault surface maps is recommended.

Kinks or unexpected bends in the fault surface suggest an interpretation problem which is much easier to correct immediately than to come back and reinterpret later. Fortunately, many of the interactive software packages make the generation of fault surface maps very easy during interpretation of 3 – D seismic data.

En echelon faults

Even if fault surface maps are made during the interpretation of 3 – D seismic data, **en echelon** (unconnected, **sub – parallel**) faults may be incorrectly linked. This incorrect interpretation can be particularly costly because an en echelon fault pattern such as that illustrated can produce a downthrown high. Unfortunately the **ramp** between the two en echelon faults will cause hydrocarbons to leak.

A good check on the interpretation of a critical fault is to contour either the **throw** or the vertical separation of the fault on the fault surface map. An incorrect interpretation of en echelon faults can produce **perturbations** in the throw or vertical separation contours which can alert an interpreter to the interpretation problem. Mapping fault throw or vertical separation from a 3 – D seismic survey **by hand** is very time consuming. Fortunately some software packages are available which make the process much easier.

If throw is contoured on a fault surface, care must be taken that the values reflect true throw, i. e. , **offset perpendicular** to the fault **strike** and not apparent throw measured at some other angle to the fault strike. Apparent throw is always less than true throw and mapping apparent throw can produce near random contours with no physical significance. True throw can only be determined after the fault surface has been mapped.

Coherence cube

A recent advance in seismic processing is the **coherence cube**. Coherency processing **consists of** assigning a **numerical** value to the continuity of each trace relative to **adjacent** traces. Areas of coherent data can be displayed as white or light gray and areas of discontinuities, such as faults, can be displayed as dark gray. Examining time slices of seismic data displaying coherency instead of **amplitude** appears to offer real potential in determining how faults are connected.

FAULT TRAPS

Even when faults are interpreted correctly, fault traps carry significant seal risks compared to unfaulted four – way – dip closures. A fault trace on a structure map is not a seal, it is a line on a map. Fault traps can be sealed in one of two ways. Juxtaposition traps result from the juxtaposition of reservoir **lithologies** on one side of a fault with sealing lithologies on the other side of the fault. Fault – seal traps are sealed by the fault zone itself.

A complete discussion of seals is beyond the scope of this article, but a brief discussion is appropriate. Seals are rocks which have capillary properties which make it difficult for a non – wetting liquid such as oil or gas to enter the pores. Reservoir rocks have capillary properties which allow hydrocarbons to enter the **pores**, and which allow hydrocarbons to be produced at economic rates.

Some rocks are neither seals nor reservoirs and some rocks can be seals under some conditions and reservoirs under other conditions. More complete discussions of seals are referred to in other papers.

Juxtaposition traps

Juxtaposition traps occur where reservoir lithologies on one side of a fault are juxtaposed against a sealing lithology on the other side. In the U. S. Gulf Coast, juxtaposition traps are usually thought to occur where sands are juxtaposed against shales across a fault, but they can also occur, at least **in theory**, where sands with different capillary properties are juxtaposed across a fault. The best method to evaluate the potential for a juxtaposition trap is to map the stratigraphy at the fault surface in both the hanging wall and the footwall. These maps are sometimes **referred to as** "Allan" fault plane maps or "Allan sections" after Urban Allan who popularized their use.

Allan sections

Allan sections require that both the hanging wall and footwall of a prospect be mapped. Drilling a fault closure without mapping both sides of the fault and constructing an Allan section is accepting an unnecessary risk. Construction of accurate Allan sections requires that fault surface and structure maps be properly integrated. Fault – surface and structure map in tegration ensures that intersection of the stratigraphy with the fault surface is properly located. Allan sections constructed from structure maps which have not been integrated with fault surfaces can be inaccurate and result in a mistaken assessment of prospect risk. Allan sections can be constructed routinely by hand or can be generated by some computer software programs.

Allan section use

The use of Allan sections has become fairly well established within the industry. Traditional Allan sections depict juxtaposition of **strata** at the present time. The juxtaposition of strata **at times** in the past may have been very different. In areas where **charge was limited to** a short period of time, it may be necessary to construct paleo Allan sections **as well as** present – day Allan sections. The **utility** of **paleo** Allan sections in areas which are currently receiving charge, such as the U. S. Gulf Coast, has not been established. Paleo Allan sections can be constructed by hand if paleo structure maps have been constructed. The author **is unaware of** any computer software packages which can routinely construct paleo Allan sections.

Fault – seal traps

The significance of fault – seal traps is still a matter of debate. M. W. Downey **points out** that for a fault zone to **act as** an effective seal, the entire fault zone **in contact with** the hydrocarbon – bearing reservoir must have favorable capillary properties. If only a small window in the fault surfacc has capillary properties similar to a **porous** Gulf Coast sand, enormous quantities of hydrocarbons can be lost in geologically short time periods. Downey recognizes that fault – seal traps can exist, but regards them as **rarities**. Other workers provide compelling evidence of significant fault – seal traps.

Fault zones themselves can act as seals if fault – zone capillary properties are significantly different from the unfaulted – reservoir capillary properties. Three mechanisms which can cause the capillary properties of the fault zone to differ from the unfaulted rock are clay smear, grain crushing or **cataclasis**, and **diagenesis**. These three mechanisms are discussed in more detail below.

Clay smear

Clay **smear** refers to a process by which **ductile** shale layers are smeared along a fault zone. Clay smears have been lab created, observed in **outcrop** and core, and inferred from **log** interpretation. Clay smear potential is primarily a function of the thickness of shale and the distance of the shale **from the point of interest**. The contribution of any individual shale to clay smear potential increases with increasing shale thickness and decreases with distance from point of interest. The clay smear potential at any point is the sum of contributions from all shales which have moved past that point.

In theory, the amount of clay smear can be expected to be a function of shale **ductility**, fault angle, effective stress, etc. , **in addition to** shale thickness and distance from the point of interest. These secondary controls are difficult, if not impossible to calculate. Clay smear potential needs to be calibrated **locally**, making the **tacit** assumption that the secondary **variables** controlling clay smear are similar for all local examples. A given clay smear potential may usually be sealing in one area, e. g. , the Niger Delta, while it may usually be non – sealing in a different environment, e. g. , the North Sea.

Clay smear potential can be estimated in a general way from net/ gross ratios and fault displacement, or can be calculated **on a point – by – point basis** along a fault surface using computer software. The results from either approach should be calibrated with local examples of sealing and non – sealing faults. Where calibrated, this analysis has proven successful in assessing risk in fault traps.

Grain crushing

Grain – crushing or cataclasis associated with faults can result in significant reductions in grain – size and **permeability** in fault zones. Such **cataclastic** zones can have capillary pressures of one to two orders of **magnitude** greater than unaltered rock and have the potential for trapping **up to** several hundred feet of hydrocarbon column. Cataclasis can be expected to be more important in **indurated** rock and at higher confining pressures. Increasing fault displacement should also increase cataclasis. Although cataclasis is a theoretically reasonable way of creating fault seal traps, specific examples of hydrocarbon accumulations related to this process have yet to be documented.

In the Gulf Coast, faults which offset a sandstone against itself do not appear to seal. R. G. Gibson documented a similar relationship in two fields in the Columbus Basin, Trinidad. These fault – seal failures suggest either that cataclasis is not a significant process in poorly **lithified** sands or that offset on these faults has been insufficient to create significant cataclastic zones. The former explanation appears preferable as grain size diminution can occur in very early stages of displacement in indurated rocks.

S. D. Knott refers to numerous North Sea reservoir examples where **intra – reservoir** faults seal. Some of these faults probably seal **due to** cataclastic **deformation** in the fault zone, but individually documented examples are lacking. Most of the faults analyzed by Knott are **post – depositional** faults and as such might be expected to **be more prone to** cataclasis.

Diagenesis

Diagenesis is widely recognized as a process which can affect petrophysical properties near a fault zone. **Cementation** along a fault can lower **porosities** and **permeabilities** by an order of magnitude relative to rocks farther away from the fault zone.

Diagenesis and **cataclasis** can be combined to increase the sealing potential of a fault. Cementation of cataclasites can drastically reduce their porosity and permeability. Grain size reduction caused by cataclasis increases the surface areas of grains, increasing diffusive mass transfer processes (such as pressure solution). Even if no fluid flow occurs within the fault zone, the fault zone may be **preferentially** cemented due to these **diffusion** controlled processes.

Although diagenesis has the potential to create impermeable rock, diagenetic processes tend to be **patchy** and often result in tight rock **alternating with** permeable rock. As the effectiveness of a seal depends more on continuity than on average capillary properties, fault traps sealed by diagenetic properties are probably rare.

This article has **focused on** the sealing potential of faults. Faults can also act as **fluid conduits**, and **fracturing** associated with faults can result in excellent reservoirs in otherwise tight rocks. A detailed discussion of the controls on fluid flow within a fault zone is beyond the scope of this article, but flow **is more likely to** occur during fault movement. Fluid flow possibility during fault movement could cause buried or inactive faults to be more likely to form traps than faults which show evidence of recent activity.

Words and Expressions

appraisal	评价,鉴定
accurate	精确的,准确的
construction	建造,作图
contour	轮廓,等高线,以等高线标示
aliasing	混淆
coherency	相干性
segment	部分,断片
trap	圈闭(一是种能阻止油气继续运移并能在其中聚集的场所)
hydrocarbon	碳氢化合物
juxtapose	并列,并置
capillary	毛细管作用的
property	性质
evaluate	评价,评估
stratigraphy	地层学,此层成层情况
seal	封闭,密封
estimate	估计,判断
qualitatively	从质的方面,定性地
section	刨面
displacement	位移
semi – quantitatively	半定量地
calibrate	校准,测定
unfaulted	无断层的
seismic	地震的,因地震引起的

address	谈论,演说
tectonic	地壳构造上的
province	地区
atypical	非典型的,不合规则的
scrutinize	仔细检查,细看
horizontal	水平的
trace	痕迹
dipping	倾头现象
planar	平面的
intuitive	直观的,直觉的
respect	方面
arbitrary	任意的,随心所欲的
drastically	大大地,彻底地
kink	扭结
en echelon	雁列式的,雁行的
sub – parallel	近平行的
ramp	断口,斜面
throw	纵距,距离
perturbation	扰乱,混乱
offset	衬托出
perpendicular	垂直,垂线
strike	走向
coherence	相干性
cube	数据体
numerical	数字的,以数字表示的
adjacent	临近的,相邻的
amplitude	振幅
lithology	岩石学
pore	孔隙,毛孔
strata	地层
charge	充电,充填
utility	效用
paleo	古,旧

porous	多孔的
rarity	稀有,罕见
cataclasis	压碎,岩石的碎裂
diagenesis	成岩作用
smear	涂抹
ductile	易延展的,塑性的
outcrop	(脉矿的) 露出,(岩石)露头
log	录井
ductility	延展性
locally	局部地
tacit	默许的,不言而喻的
variable	变量
point – by – point	逐点详述的
permeability	渗透性
cataclastic	碎裂的
magnitude	量,数量
indurate	使硬化
lithify	使石化
intra	内,在内
deformation	变形
post – depositional	沉积期后的
cementation	胶结作用
porosity	孔隙度,多孔性
permeability	渗透率,渗透性
cataclasis	断裂作用
diffusion	散布性的,扩散性的
preferentially	优先地
impermeable	不渗透性的
patchy	分布不均的,不规则的
fluid	流体
conduit	管道,通道
fracturing	断裂

Phrases and Expression

depend on	取决于
be associated with	与……有联系
result in	导致
tend to	往往,倾向于
refer to	指代,指的是,提及
in the case of	在……情况下,就……而说
by hand	用手工的
consist of	由……组成
in theory	理论上
refer to... as	把……称作,把……当做
at times	有时
be limited to	限制在,局限于
as well as	和……一样,除……之外(还)
be unaware of	不知道,不清楚
point out	指出
act as	充当,起……作用
in contact with	与……有联系
from the point of interest	距研究点
in addition to	除了……之外(还有)
due to	由于,因为
on... basis	在……基础上
up to	达到
due to	由于,因为
be prone to	有……倾向,易于
focus on	集中于,集中研究
be likely to	有可能
alternate with	交替,轮流

Proper Name

the hanging wall and the footwall	上盘和下盘
four – way – dip closures	四向倾没圈闭

Language Focus

1. When addressing the aliasing problem, it is imperative that all significant fault surfaces be mapped.

（参考译文：谈论断层混淆问题时，绘制所有的重要断面图是必不可少的。）

本句中 When 之后省略了主语 people 这时用分词短语 addressing the aliasing problem 作状语，主句 it is imperative that... 结构中，that 之后的从句是主语从句，it 是形式主语，that 之后的从句要用虚拟语气，谓语动词要用 should do，其中 should 可以省略。本句中 be mapped 前省略了助动词 should。

2. Faults which have atypical shapes for the tectonic province in which they occur should be scrutinized carefully for possible aliasing.

（参考译文：对构造区内具有独特形状的断层应当仔细核查，以免造成混淆。）

本句中 Faults 是主语，should be scrutinized 是谓语，which have atypical shapes for the tectonic province in which they occur 是定语从句，其中，定语从句中含有定语从句 in which they occur。句中 they 指代 faults，for possible aliasing 是目的状语。

3. Not only are the seismic lines much closer spaced and properly migrated in three dimensions, but fault interpretations can also be tied by interpreting carefully selected arbitrary lines.

（参考译文：断层的三维解释，不仅有密度大的地震测线，可在三维空间中进行准确的偏移，而且还可以通过解释精心选择的任意测线进行连接对比。）

本句是由 not only... but also 引导的并列句，其中 not only 放在句首，句子要部分倒装。Be 动词放在主语之前。but also 引导的句子不倒装。故 be 动词 are 放在了主语 the seismic lines 之前。句中 carefully selected 作定语修饰 arbitrary lines。

4. Allan sections require that both the hanging wall and footwall of a prospect be mapped.

（参考译文：Allan 剖面图要求绘制远景圈闭上盘和下盘的图件。）

本句中 require 表示要求。表示要求、建议、命令的动词引导的宾语从句要用虚拟语气，谓语动词要用 should do，其中 should 可以省略。句中 be mapped之前省略了助动词should。

5. Allan sections constructed from structure maps which have not been integrated with fault surfaces can be inaccurate and result in a mistaken assessment of prospect risk.

(参考译文:未综合断面图,仅根据构造图绘制的Allan剖面可能不精确,可能导致对远景区风险性作出错误评估。)

本句中Allan sections是主语,谓语有两个(can be inaccurate和result in)。句中constructed from structure maps which have not been integrated with fault surfaces是定语。句中constructed from structure maps是分词短语作定语,which have not been integrated with fault surfaces是定语从句修饰先行词structure maps。

Reinforced Learning

Ⅰ. Answer the following questions for a comprehension of the text.

1. What is highly recommended to help avoid aliasing faults?

2. Which has greater risks, fault traps or unfaulted four – way – dip closures?

3. What are the three mechanisms which can cause the capillary properties of the fault zone to differ from the unfaulted rock?

4. What is the function of the combination of diagenesis and cataclasis?

5. What does this article mainly focus on?

Ⅱ. Multiple choice: choose the correct one from the alternative answers to give the exact meaning of the words.

1. He is always <u>accurate</u> in what he says and does.

A. close B. correct C. faithful D. inexact

2. The application of the methods can guarantee the <u>coherency</u> of associated data in DB system.

A. inherent B. cohesiveness

C. coherence D. understandability

3. The company dominates this <u>segment</u> of the market.

A. section B. separate C. bend D. whole

4. The choice of players for the team seems completely <u>arbitrary</u>.

A. accused B. subjective C. costed D. committed

5. The gardener estimated that it would take him four hours to weed the garden.

A. reckoned B. evaluated C. appreciated D. allowed

6. A fur coat has more utility in winter than in autumn.

A. facility B. quality C. service D. usefulness

7. These young students lives in adjacent rooms.

A. advised B. adjusted C. adjective D. adjoining

8. He seemed to have an intuitive knowledge of how I was feeling.

A. unlogical B. interact C. spontaneous D. illogical

9. A bullet goes from this gun with a velocity of 3000 feet per second.

A. ratio B. speed C. vehicle D. price

10. The earth is for the most part covered with water and mountains.

A. in most cases B. mostly C. gradually D. obviously

Ⅲ. Multiple choice: read the four suggested translations and choose the best answer.

1. When addressing the aliasing problem, it is imperative that all significant fault surfaces be mapped.

A. 住址 B. 称呼 C. 谈论 D. 对付

2. Although beyond the scope of this article, fault shape is important in other respects.

A. 尊敬 B. 问候 C. 重视 D. 方面

3. A good check on the interpretation of a critical fault is to contour either the throw or the vertical separation of the fault on the fault surface map.

A. 投掷 B. 距离 C. 射程 D. 冒险

4. In areas where charge was limited to a short period of time, it may be necessary to construct paleo Allan sections as well as present – day Allan sections.

A. 填充 B. 收费 C. 指控 D. 掌管

5. A single sealing lithology can provide both top and lateral seals.

A. 后来 B. 侧向的 C. 最新的 D. 侧音的

Ⅳ. Put the following sentences into Chinese.

1. Mapping of either fault throw or vertical separation contours on fault surface maps is highly recommended to help avoid aliasing (incorrectly connect-

ing) faults.

2. Fault traps have two major types of risks which unfaulted four – way – dip closures do not share.

3. Kinks or unexpected bends in the fault surface suggest an interpretation problem which is much easier to correct immediately than to come back and reinterpret later.

4. If throw is contoured on a fault surface, care must be taken that the values reflect true throw, i. e., offset perpendicular to the fault strike and not apparent throw measured at some other angle to the fault strike.

5. Juxtaposition traps occur where reservoir lithologies on one side of a fault are juxtaposed against a sealing lithology on the other side.

V. Put the following paragraphs into Chinese.

1. A fault trap occurs when the formations on either side of the fault have been moved into a position that prevents further migration of petroleum. For example, an impermeable formation on one side of the fault may have moved opposite the petroleum bearing formation on the other side of the fault. Further migration of petroleum is prevented by the impermeable layer. In a fault trap, a permeable bed, overlain by an impermeable bed, is faulted against impermeable beds.

2. Fault traps are also common. Again, there must be a porous and permeable reservoir rock that is sealed above by a fine – grained, relatively impermeable bed. But the real trap is provided by the fault, which prevents further updip migration either by the fine – grained material in the fault itself (the so – called "fault gouge" that results from the movement on the fault plane) or by the bringing of a fine – grained relatively impermeable bed on the other side of the fault to the position that truncates(切断) the reservoir.

3.3 Geometry and Evolution of the Frontal Part of the Magallanes Foreland Thrust and Fold Belt (Vicuna Area), Tierra del Fuego, Southern Chile

Guidance to Reading

The Magallanes foreland thrust and fold belt is a thin – skinned foreland thrust and fold belt of Paleocene to Oligocene age that deforms Upper Jurassic through Neogene volcanic, volcaniclastic, and siliciclastic strata of the Magallanes basin, southern Andean Cordillera, Chile. This paper is a detailed description and analysis of the geology and structural evolution of the thrust front (Vicuna area of southern Tierra del Fuego). Reflection seismic and well data, together with 1:50,000 *scale geological mapping, have been used in the analysis.*

Text

INTRODUCTION

The **Cordillera Darwin** and the **Magallanes thrust** and fold belt of **Tierra del Fuego** form the southernmost part of the **Andean Cordillera** at the tip of South America. This part of the Andean Cordillera started to form as a result of the closure of the Rocas Verdes marginal basin in the middle of the Cretaceous. The thrust belt is bounded to the south by the **crystalline** rocks of the Cordillera Darwin and to the north by the **undeformed foreland** of the Magallanes **basin**. The Magallanes basin is an important **hydrocarbon province** in both Argentina and Chile. This paper is a detailed description and analysis of the Magallanes thrust and fold belt and **focuses on** the Vicuna area located at the front of the thrust belt on Tierra del Fuego, southern Chile. Here, northward – directed contractional **deformation** during the **Oligocene – Miocene** has thrust Jurassic and Cretaceous volcaniclastic and clastics over the **Paleogene – Neogene** siliciclastic sediments of the Magallanes basin. The structures found in the Vicuna area are classic examples of thrust – front structures. The structures include fault – propagation folds, duplexes, and triangle zones, which are potential traps for hydrocarbons in the area. An understanding of the geometries, **kinematic** and dynamic evolution of these structures, analyzed for the first time in this paper, is fundamental for future successful exploration and exploitation. Although hydrocarbon shows have been detected in shallow wells in the Vicuna area, productive wells are located farther north of this area.

Thrust – front structures are formed where thin – skinned foreland fold and thrust belt deformation terminates against the undeformed foreland to the **orogen**. These thrust – front structures commonly produce antiformal structures that form major traps in hydrocarbon provinces such as the Canadian Rocky Mountains, the Wyoming thrust belt, and the Neuquen basin in the Andean **foothills** belt.

This paper describes the geology and structure of the Vicuna area and develops a **tectonic** model for the evolution of this part of the Magallanes thrust and fold belt. The relationships of the frontal structures to those in the foreland and the detailed structural geometry and kinematic evolution of the mountain front have been determined. There, on the mountain front, reflection seismic lines show an abrupt change in structural style from the thrust belt to the foreland basin. Three – line and area – balanced structural cross sections have been constructed from depth – converted interpretations of seismic lines and 1:50. 000 scale surface geological mapping. The cross sections have been palinspastically restored to check for balance, and to calculate the shortening. Progressive forward kinematic models were constructed from balanced cross sections in order to constrain the structural interpretation.

REGIONAL GEOLOGY

The first geological descriptions of Tierra del Fuego were made by Darwin (1846) in the area that is known today as Cordillera Darwin. Harambour et al. defined three major structural domains in the southern branch of the Andean Cordillera.

(1) A southern crystalline domain is formed by **Paleozoic** to Early Mesozoic polydeformed and metamorphosed basement rocks. The main phase of deformation affecting these rocks is Albian to Coniacian Andean deformation represented by folds in the inner part of the belt. The Paleozoic – rocks form a major stack of thrust sheets that were uplifted during the Paleogene. These basement rocks are bound to the south by the remains of the Rocas Verdes marginal basin . To the north the basement rocks are thrust over **Jurassic** and **Cretaceous** rocks of the Magallanes basin.

(2) A central domain is formed by dominantly Cretaceous clastic rocks in the east – northeast – trending Magallanes thrust and fold belt. The sole thrust of this belt appears to be located within Jurassic strata, **close to** the boundary with the underlying Paleozoic basement.

(3) A third domain is formed in the foreland area to the north, which is the vast, roughly flat, relatively undeformed region of the Magallanes basin. Strata in the foreland **consist of** Middle to Upper Jurassic volcanics and **volcaniclastics**, and Cretaceous to upper Tertian siliciclastic sediments.

EVOLUTION OF THE MAGALIANES BASIN

The pre – Jurassic geological history of the Magallanes basin is poorly understood. Herve et al. suggested that the upper Paleozoic basement rocks evolved as an **accretionary prism** related to a subduetion zone at the Pacific margin of Gondwanaland.

The Magallanes basin began to evolve as an exten – sional basin in the Middle – Late Jurassic to Early Cretaceous. Jurassic rocks of the Tobifera Formation directly overlie the basement and consist of an heterogeneous suite of siliceous volcaniclastic and volcanic rocks together with marine and nonmarine siliciclastic rocks deposited in **grabens** and half grabens. These rocks show large changes in thickness **ranging from** being absent on some basement highs **to** more than 2000 m thick in the graben areas. The Jurassic volcanic and volcaniclastic rocks are overlain unconformably, to the north of the Vicuna area, by the Lower Cretaceous fluvio – deltaic and marine sandstones and shales of the Springhill Formation. The Springhill sandstones are interpreted as transgressive, shallow – marine to fluvial shoreline sandstones and form the major hydrocarbon reservoir in the Magallanes basin. The existence of the Springhill sandstone in the Vicuna area is uncertain. The oldest rocks that **crop out** at the surface **correspond to** the Vicuna formation and subsurface data available for this study were not definitive on this subject.

The Cretaceous section forms a northward transgressive **clastic** sedimentary sequence that thickens toward the south. Through time, deeper water facies retrogressed toward the north. These rocks were deposited on the passive northern margin of the Magallanes basin. Basin subsidence in the Early Cretaceous is thought to be a result of the decay of the thermal anomaly **associated with** the Jurassic extension. **In contrast**, the Late Cretaceous and Paleogene – Neogene subsidence was driven by tectonic – loading of the encroaching thrust belt from the south.

Albian through Paleogene contraction of the Jurassic rift system gave rise to the Magallanes foreland thrust and fold belt and formation of the Magallanes foreland basin. Paleogene – Neogene infill of the foreland basin consists of up to 5000m of wedge – shaped **siliciclastic** rocks that onlap onto the Cretaceous **sediments** toward the north. A Maastrichtian – lower Eocene unconformity of regional extent may correspond to a change in direction of sediment supply as a result of uplift of the Magallanes thrust and fold belt to the south and west.

THRUST SYSTEMS

The geological map of the Vicuna area shows east – northeast – trending structures, with a difference in structural style between the thrust and fold belt to the south and the foreland to the north. In the south, three major north – northeast – verging thrust sheets make up the thrust and fold belt; the Colo – Colo, Bahia Bell, and Vicuna thrust sheets from south to north, respectively. Rocks within these thrust sheets young toward the south, and thrusts place older rocks on top of younger rocks. Map – scale folds within the allochthonous rocks have axial traces trending parallel to thrusts. Only in areas where fold **axes** plunge laterally can thrusts be seen to cut folds. North of the Vicuna thrust sheet, in the foreland basin, the outcropping Paleogene – Neogene section shows anticlinal culminations 3 – 5 km in width. These thrust – cored anticlines commonly are tighter than their adjacent **synclines** and the fold axial traces are slightly **oblique** to the major structures in the thrust and fold belt.

Magallanes Thrust and Fold Belt

The Magallanes thrust and fold belt in the Vicuna area is characterized in all seismic sections by two differing packages of reflections above 3 s, an upper and a lower package. The upper package is characterized by steeply south – dipping reflections that merge at depth into one gently south – dipping reflection. These reflections can be correlated with south – dipping thrusts mapped at the surface. This package of reflections is interpreted to be an imbricate fan. The lower package is characterized by gently south – dipping reflections that are interpreted to be a **duplex**. Both thrust systems involve Upper Jurassic and Cretaceous rocks.

The bounding thrust faults in the imbricate fan system outcrop at the surface and show a listric geometry. The listric nature of the thrust faults is expressed in the seismic lines by an upward loss in amplitude of the reflectors toward the land surface. This loss in amplitude is interpreted to be the result of the increase in dip angle of the fault. In some cases, it is possible to define folds within individual thrust panels from the seismic lines but, **in general**, little clear detail can be observed. The sole thrust of the imbricate system **merges into** a strong, gently south – dipping reflection, located near 3s in two – way travel-time. This reflection has been interpreted as the basement – cover contact in all three sections because it marks the limit between different reflective responses above and below. The basement – cover contact appears to be **offset** by extensional faults that dip steeply both to the south and to the north. In some cases, location of thrust – fault ramps appears to be directly associated with the position of extensional faults.

Folds in the **imbricate fan** are of kilometric size and generally show a northward vergence with short and steep anticlinal forelimbs. At cross section, scale thrusts always cut through the forelimbs of anticlines and, in some cases, the forelimbs are overturned. Folds become tighter near thrust faults. Within the multilayered Cretaceous sequence, folds typically have a chevron morphology. Locally, however, outcrop – scale cylindrical folds occur in the more competent carbonates of the Vicuna Formation. Fold morphologies and the relationships with thrust faults indicate that folding in the imbricate thrust sheets was generated by fault propagation.

The internal structure of the duplex is poorly imaged on seismic lines and does not crop out at the surface. Thus, it is difficult to determine the dimensions and geometries of individual horses. The floor thrust of the duplex may be located near the basement – cover contact and forms the basal detachment of the Magallanes foreland thrust and fold belt in the Vicuna area.

The leading edge of the imbricate system is an inter – cutaneous wedge with characteristics similar to the structure at the southern Canadian Rocky Mountain thrust front. In the Vicuna area, a triangle zone is developed at the leading edge of the imbricate fan system, where the fore – land – vergent sole thrust is buried and terminates at depth against a foreland – dipping, hinterland – verging thrust. The detailed structure inside this triangular block is difficult to determine because it is poorly imaged in the seismic sections. A fore – land – dipping monoclinal structure is developed in the autochthonous package in front of the thrust wedge. Minor thrusting in the footwall to the triangle zone has deformed the overlying Paleogene – Neogene sections.

Foreland of the Magallanes Thrust Belt

The foreland area **is composed of** lithologically distinct foreland – basin rocks and displays a structural style that is different from the Magallanes thrust and fold belt discussed previously. The characteristics of the northern part of the seismic lines are broad areas of mainly flat reflections and narrow zones with dipping reflections that can be correlated with anticlinal structures outcropping on the surface. To the north of the Vicuna area, where well data are available, the base of the Cretaceous has been correlated with the first strong reflector above the basement – cover contact. The second strong reflector is correlated with the Cretaceous – Paleogene – Neogene boundary. In the Vicuna area this boundary is marked by downlapping reflections related to Paleogene – Neogene sediments. These downlapping reflections suggest a progradational sequence, possibly formed as the sediments were fed into the basin from the active and growing mountain belt to the south. The foreland basin sediments have been divided into three distinct seismostratigraphic packages.

A syncline – anticline pair can be seen at the surface in the foreland area in all three sections. The seismic lines reveal that, at depth, the anticlinal cores show different thrust structures whose geometries vary both laterally and vertically. Variation in these structures is interpreted to be a function of distribution of detachment levels and relative competencies of different formations. Other minor detachments related to mechanically weak horizons, but not imaged on the seismic sections, are located throughout the foreland.

Pop – up structures and triangle zones are developed as a result of minor listric thrust faults branching upward from the various detachment levels . These structures commonly are stacked in a vertical sense such that they give rise to complex structures in the cores of the major anticlines. The Miraflores anticline is a typical example of the structural style in the foreland area.

CONCLUSIONS

The Vicuna area of the Magallanes thrust and fold belt displays two distinct structural styles as shown by both surface exposures and in seismic sections—that of the thrust belt itself and that of the foreland basin. Contractional deformation occurred in the Oligocene – Miocene and the fold and thrust structures trend west – northwest – east southeast. Two distinct tectonostratigraphic assemblages can be identified. the pretectonic wedge and the syntectonic wedge; both thicken toward the south. The pretectonic wedge consists of Upper Jurassic and Cretaceous strata and forms the thrust and fold belt. The syntectonic wedge is composed of Upper Cretaceous and Paleogene – Neogene siliciclastic units and forms the fill of the Magallanes foreland basin.

Two vertically stacked thrust systems are found in the Magallanes thrust and fold belt: an upper imbricate fan system above and a lower duplex. The sole thrust of the imbricate fan forms the roof thrust to the duplex in the southern part of the area. At the front of the imbricate fan an intercutaneous wedge with a buried leading edge is formed. The imbricate fan system has an important footwall **ramp** that cuts through 3 km of the Paleogene – Neogene sequence. Tertian sediments of the foreland basin have been uplifted along a passive roof "back thrust" at the triangle zone at the front of the imbricate fan system. The underlying duplex is formed by a number of horses of varying size, resulting in a corrugated roof thrust along part of its length. The floor thrust of the duplex detaches close to the basement – cover contact.

To the north, in the foreland area, the structural style is controlled by the existence of three principal detachment levels within the sedimentary package. Structures in the foreland verge toward the hinterland as well as toward the foreland. Thrust – tip anticlines are tight and separated by broad synclines.

The sequence of thrusting is forward, from hinterland to foreland in the Magallanes thrust and fold belt, and from the upper detachment to the lower detachment in the foreland area. The amount of shortening calculated for the Vicuna area from the cross sections is approximately 60% and is in accordance with the facies changes recorded across the Vicuna area and with shortening estimates in the region south of Vicuna.

Words and Expressions

crystalline	结晶质的
undeformed	无形变的
foreland	前陆
basin	盆地
hydrocarbon	碳氢化合物,烃
province	范围,领域
deformation	(尤指受压)变形
Paleogene – Neogene	古近纪—新近纪(或系)的
Oligocene	渐新世
Miocene	中新世
kinematic	运动学的
orogen	造山带

foothills	山麓丘陵
tectonic	地壳构造上的
Paleozoic	古生代
Jurassic	侏罗纪的,侏罗系的
Cretaceous	白垩纪的
volcaniclastic	火山碎屑岩的
graben	地堑
clastics	(岩石)碎屑(状)的
siliciclastic	硅质碎屑的
sediments	沉积物
axes	轴
syncline	向斜
oblique	偏斜的
duplex	复式断块
offset	抵消
ramp	斜坡

Phrases and Expression

focus on	对(某事或做某事)予以注意
close to	靠近
range from... to	在……中变化
consist of	由……组成
crop out	(岩石、矿石等)露在地面,显露出来
correspond to	相当于
be associated with	与……联系在一起
in contrast	相比之下
in general	一般而言,总的来说
merge into	合并,结合
be composed of	由……组成

Proper Name

Cordillera Darwin	达尔文山脉
Magallanes thrust	麦哲伦冲断褶皱带
Tierra del Fuego	火地岛

Andean Cordillera	安第斯山脉
accretionary prism	增生棱锥体
imbricate fan	叠瓦扇

Language Focus

1. An understanding of the geometries, kinematic and dynamic evolution of these structures, analyzed for the first time in this paper, is fundamental for future successful exploration and exploitation.

(参考译文:对本文中首次分析的这些构造的几何形态、运动学及动力学演化过程的理解,是未来成功地勘探和开发该区油气资源的基础。)

本句是主系表结构,句子主干为 An understanding is fundamental for future successful exploration and exploitation。句中 of the geometries, kinematic and dynamic evolution of these structures 为所有格形式。句中 analyzed for the first time in this paper 为过去分词结构修饰 An understanding。

2. The main phase of deformation affecting these rocks is Albian to Coniacian Andean deformation represented by folds in the inner part of the belt.

(参考译文:影响这些岩石的主要变形幕是以该构造带内部的褶皱所代表的阿尔布期至柯尼亚克期的安第斯变形幕。)

本句是主系表结构,句子主干为 The main phase of deformation is Albian to Coniacian Andean deformation。句中 affecting these rocks 为现在分词结构作后置定语修饰 deformation。句中 represented by folds in the inner part of the belt 为过去分词作后置定语修饰 Albian to Coniacian Andean deformation。

3. Jurassic rocks of the Tobifera Formation directly overlie the basement and consist of an heterogeneous suite of siliceous volcaniclastic and volcanic rocks together with marine and nonmarine siliciclastic rocks deposited in grabens and half grabens.

(参考译文:Tobifera 组的侏罗系岩层直接覆盖在基岩之上,它是由沉积于地堑和半地堑内的硅质火山碎屑和火山岩以及海相和非海相的硅质碎屑岩组成的一个非均质单元。)

本句包含了两个并列谓语 overlie 和 consisit of。句中 deposited in grabens and half grabens 为过去分词结构作后置定语修饰 siliceous volcaniclastic and volcanic rocks together with marine and nonmarine siliciclastic rocks。

4. Only in areas where fold axes plunge laterally can thrusts be seen to cut folds.

(参考译文:只有在褶皱轴横向倾没处才能见到冲断层切割褶皱。)

本句为 only 前置的倒装句,还原为正常的语序为 Thrusts can be seen to cut folds only in areas where fold axes plunge laterally。

5. The characteristics of the northern part of the seismic lines are broad areas of mainly flat reflections and narrow zones with dipping reflections that can be correlated with anticlinal structures outcropping on the surface.

(参考译文:在地震剖面的北段,以大范围的平反射和可能相当于地面背斜构造的狭窄的倾斜反射区为特征。)

本句为复杂句,主句是主系表结构,其中又包含了由 that 引导的定语从句。句中 with dipping reflections that can be correlated with anticlinal structures outcropping on the surface 是 with 结构修饰 narrow zones。That 从句修饰 reflections。

Reinforced Learning

Ⅰ. Answer the following questions for a comprehension of the text.

1. What forms the major hydrocarbon reservoir in the Magallanes basin?

2. How did the Magallanes foreland thrust and fold belt and the Magallanes foreland basin come into being?

3. What is the thrust and fold belt to the south Vicuna area made up of ?

4. What are the two vertically stacked thrust systems found in the Magallanes thrust and fold belt ?

5. What is a typical example of the structural style in the foreland area?

Ⅱ. Multiple choice: choose the correct one from the alternative answers to give the exact meaning of the words.

1. I was surprised by the abrupt change of subject.

A. rude　　B. Exaggerate　　C. sudden　　D. steep

2. It's important to draw out a child's potential capacities.

A. threatening　　B. prospective　　C. present　　D. past

3. The fundamental problem remains that of the housing shortage.

A. financial　　B. essential　　C. moderate　　D. minimum

4. The product will now be made available throughout the market.

A. reliable　　B. flexible　　C. accessible　　D. possible

5. The working of this machine corresponds to that of the human brain.

A. depends on B. communicates with

C. equals D. responds to

6. Commercial exploitation of resources threatens our survival.

A. explanation B. exposure C. using D. expectation

7. When the railway disappeared, other industries associated with it closed down.

A. compared to B. contrasted with C. paralleled with D. related to

8. The disease is characterized by weakening of the immune system.

A. described B. depicted C. featured D. approached

9. The extension of the deadline gives us a breathing space.

A. expansion B. addition C. surplus D. delay

10. Experiments reveal that walking is much more healthful than running.

A. show B. claim C. decide D. acclaim

Ⅲ. Multiple choice: read the four suggested translations and choose the best answer.

1. The Magallanes basin is an important hydrocarbon province in both Argentina and Chile.

A. 脸盆 B. 流域 C. 内港 D. 盆地

2. The structures include fault – propagation folds, duplexes, and triangle zones.

A. 成对物 B. 复式公寓 C. 复式断块 D. 双的

3. Thrust – front structures are formed where thin – skinned foreland fold and thrust belt deformation terminates against the undeformed foreland to the orogen.

A. 造山带 B. 前陆 C. 褶皱 D. 断层

4. Progressive forward kinematic models were constructed from balanced cross sections in order to constrain the structural interpretation.

A. 几何学的 B. 数学的

C. 运动学的 D. 影像学的

5. The syntectonic wedge is composed of Upper Cretaceous and Paleogene – Neogene siliciclastic units and forms the fill of the Magallanes foreland basin.

A. 火山碎屑岩 B. 岩屑

C. 页岩 D. 硅质碎屑岩

Ⅳ. Put the following sentences into Chinese.

1. The structures include fault – propagation folds, duplexes, and triangle zones, which are potential traps for hydrocarbons in the area.

2. Thrust – front structures are formed where thin – skinned foreland fold and thrust belt deformation terminates against the undeformed foreland to the orogen.

3. The Cretaceous section forms a northward transgressive clastic sedimentary sequence that thickens toward the south.

4. The foreland area is composed of lithologically distinct foreland – basin rocks and displays a structural style that is different from the Magallanes thrust and fold belt discussed previously.

5. Pop – up structures and triangle zones are developed as a result of minor listric thrust faults branching upward from the various detachment levels .

Ⅴ. Put the following paragraphs into Chinese.

1. In the southern part of the Vicuna area, two different thrust systems have been found: an upper imbricate fan that deforms Upper Jurassic and Cretaceous strata, and a younger, lower duplex composed of Cretaceous and probably Upper Jurassic rocks. The imbricate fan is characterized by fault – propagation folding in which Iistric thrust faults merge downward into a sole thrust that probably is located within the Upper Jurassic stratigraphy. I bis fan system generates an intercufancous wedge with a well – developed triangle zone at its leading edge. The sole thrust of the upper imbricates forms the roof thrust of the underlying duplex.

2. In the northern part of the Vicuna area, the syntectonic sedimentary wedge of the foredeep consists of Late Cretaceous through Paleogene – Neogene siliciclastics that have been deformed and uplifted by passive back thrusting at the triangle zone. The structural style in the foreland region shows three main subhorizontal detachment levels located within the sedimentary wedge as a result of the progressive transfer of slip from the thrust belt to the foreland. Minor blind thrusts produce stacked "pop up" and triangle structures that result in complex geometries in the cores of anticlines.

Chapter 4 Structural Influence on Reservoir Formation

4.1 Structural Influence on Hydrocarbon Entrapment in the Northwestern Red Sea, Egypt(Ⅰ)

Guidance to Reading

The northwestern part of the Egyptian Red Sea has attracted the attention of many geologists because it lies at the triple junction of the main rifts between the Red Sea, the Gulf of Aqaba, and Gulf of Suez. The geometry of the fault system in this area of the basin clearly indicates an extensional setting. The area has a southwestward regional dip, and it has experienced more extension than the rest of the Gulf of Suez.

Six tectonic stages, different in their stress history, sedimentary fill, and depositional setting, are recognized for the northwestern Red Sea: (1) *Cambrian to early Cretaceous stage*; (2) *late Cretaceous to Oligocene stage*; (3) *early Miocene stage*; (4) *early to middle Miocene stage*; (5) *middle to late Miocene stage*; *and* (6) *post – Miocene stage.*

Text

INTRODUCTION

The area that forms the **scope** of this study **lies in** the northwestern Red Sea, Egypt, at the **triple junction** of the main **rifts** between the Red Sea, **Gulf** of Aqaba(亚喀巴湾), and Gulf of Suez(苏伊士湾)(Figure 1). The area is **delineated** by 26°49′ and 27°32′N **latitude** and 33°29′ and 34°05′E **longitude** and **embraces** an area of almost 2508 km^2, being 57 km long and 44 km wide. The most characteristic **topographic** features of the study area are the exposures of the Precambrian basement massifs at three major localities: the Esh Mellaha range to the northwest, Shadwan Island to the northeast, and the Red Sea Hills to the southwest (Figure 4. 1. 1). The Esh Mellaha range has a **more or less** complete pre – Miocene (prerift) sequence on its western side and is

onlapped to the south by a Miocene reef complex at Gebel Abu Shaar **plateau** (Figure 4.1.2).

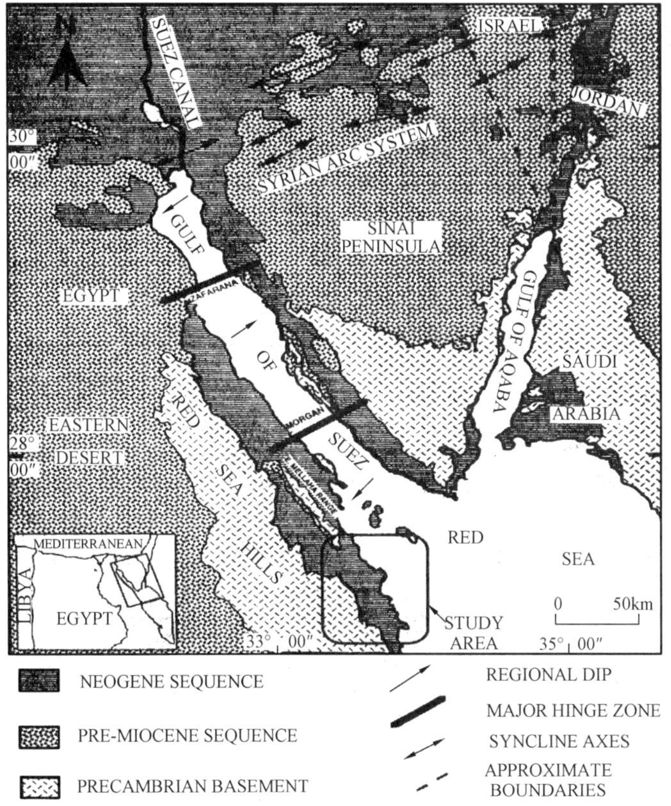

Figure 4.1.1 Regional structural elements and geometry of the Gulfbf Suez region showing the surface geology, major hinge zones, and regional dips in the subbasin (Modified from Moustafa)

The study area has an excellent potential for hydrocarbon accumulation because the rifting of the Red Sea produces favorable conditions for (1) synrift (Miocene) organic - rich, oil - and/or gas - **prone** source rock **deposition**; (2) a suitable **maturity** regime for generating hydrocarbons; (3) the development of fractures in the Precambrian basement, and the accumulation of sandstone and carbonate reservoirs, **ranging** in age **from** Precambrian **to** Miocene; (4) the presence of potential fine - grained **clastic** and evaporite seals; and (5) several types of traps for accumulation of hydrocarbons (Salah, 1994).

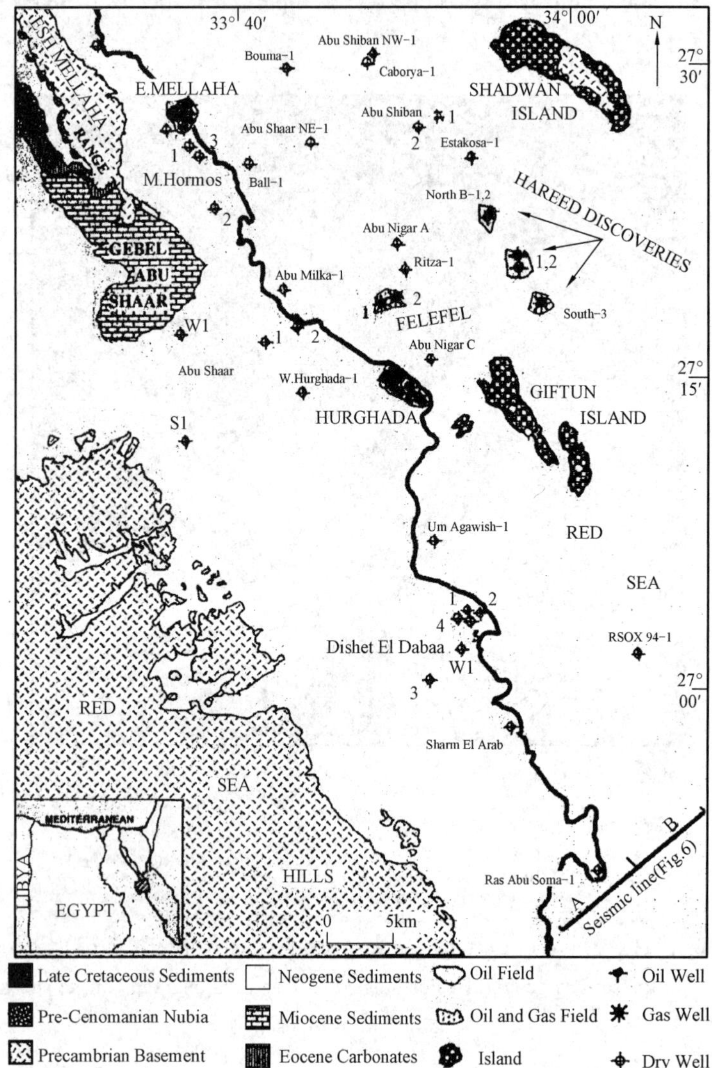

Figure 4. 1. 2 Location map of the study area showing the oil arid/or gas fields and exploratory wells(Modified from Salah,1994)

Some commercial oil and/or gas fields such as Hurghada, Esh Mellaha, Hareed, and Felefel have been discovered already. The oldest discovery, Hurghada oil field, was made in 1914 by the Anglo Egyptian Oil Company, and the recent Hareed group of oil and/or gas fields were discovered in 1988 by Conoco, Esso, and Gulf Canada oil companies (Figure 2).

For almost 90 years, the geology and the hydrocarbon potential of the Gulf of Suez and the Red Sea have been the subject of numerous investigations. The regional structural setting and the geologic history of the Gulf of Suez and the Egyptian Red Sea were the matter of interest of many researchers and continue to be the focus of many current research programs. Among past and recent papers covering different aspects of the evolution, development, sedimentation, and hydrocarbon **habitat** of the area of interest are those by El – Tarabili (1970), El – Ayouti (1980), Abdine (1981), Chenet et al. (1984), Sultan and Suchultz (1984), Angelier (1985), Richert et al. , (1986), Grafunkel (1988), Lyberis (1988), Meshref et al. (1988), Montenat et al. (1988), Beydoun (1989), Beydoun and Sikander (1992), Crossley et al. (1992), Fichera et al. (1992), Hughes and Beydoun (1992), Mitchell et al. (1992), and Salah (1994).

The purposes of this study were to (1) clarify the structural configuration of the northwestern Red Sea, and (2) highlight the distribution and trends of basinwide structural highs and lows that could act as focus for migration and accumulation of hydrocarbons.

The definitions of the **lithostratigraphic** units in the Gulf of Suez and the Red Sea have been studied by many authors, such as Hume (1911), Abdallah et al. (1963), EGPC (1964, 1974), Barakat et al. (1986), Darwish (1992), and Darwish and El – Araby (1993). The stratigraphic section of the northwestern Red Sea ranges in age from Precambrian to Holocene and can be classified into two **megasequences**: prerift (pre – Miocene) and synrift (Miocene to Holocene)

HISTORY OF EXPLORATION

Exploration for hydrocarbons in the northwestern Red Sea has included the use of geophysical prospecting and exploration drilling (EGPC, 1986).

Geophysical Prospecting

The first magnetic and gravity surveys were **flown over** the study area at the end of World War I by **a variety of** oil companies, including Anglo Egyptian Oil, Standard Oil Company, and Eastern Oil Company. In 1964, the Egyptian General Petroleum Corporation, **together with** some other oil companies (including Gulf of Suez Petroleum Company and General Petroleum Company) organized **magnetic** and **gravity** surveys over the Gulf of Suez region. Ten years later, a magnetic survey was made by the Gulf of Suez Petroleum Company (EGPC,1986). This survey led to the discovery of several oil and gas fields (e. g. ,Hareed and Felefel) in the province, especially in its southernmost part where the seismic surveys are of poor quality because of the Miocene evaporite noise.

Many seismic surveys have been conducted in the study area. The first **reconnaissance survey** was made in the middle 1950s by the Compagnie Oriental Des Petroles d' Egypt. The most recent marine survey was **conducted** by Conoco in 1987, and the most recent onshore survey was performed by the Asamera Egypt Limited Company in the northern part of the study area during 1990, and by Esso Egypt in the southern part of the study area during 1991. The interpretation of these seismic surveys has led to the identification of several potential wildcat locations, especially in the onshore part of the investigated area.

Exploration Drilling

The first well drilled in the study area was the Hurghada - 1; it was completed in 1913 by the Anglo Egyptian Oil Company. The well, located on the western side of the Gulf of Suez, tested a horst block, defined by surface mapping (Figure 2). The well led to the discovery of the first oil field in the northwestern Egyptian Red Sea. This discovery encouraged several other companies to explore for hydrocarbons in the area, among them the African Prospecting Company, the Eastern Petroleum Company (EPC), and the Sinai Petroleum Company in the middle 1920s. EPC drilled several wells on Giftun Island in the northwestern part of the Red Sea (Figure 2). Unfortunately, all these wells were dry. Drilling was **adversely** affected by World Wars I and II, but some wells were drilled between 1938 and 1950 on the western coast of the Red Sea in the Dishet El Dabaa and Abu Shaar areas (Figure 2). No discoveries were made at that time. During the last 20 yr, more intensive drilling has resulted in the discovery of the Esh El Mellaha oil field in 1982 by the Canadian Superior Oil Company, the Hareed oil and gas discoveries in 1987, and the Felefel condensate discovery in 1989 by Conoco.

STRUCTURAL ANALYSIS

The study area was the subject of intensive surface and subsurface geological and geophysical investigations for hydrocarbon prospecting and exploration. Among these studies are those by Said (1962, 1990), Robson (1971), Moustafa (1976), Bayer et al. (1988), Evans (1988), Richardson and Arthur

(1988), Salah (1989, 1994), Meshref and Khalil (1990), Hughes et al. (1991), and Hammouda (1992).

The Gulf of Suez rift represents a northern extension of the Red Sea. The rift constitutes a large depression that lies below sea level in its **axial** portion. The Suez rift trends in a north – northwest – south – southeast direction, separating the African plate from the Sinai microplate (Figure 1). The direction of the plate motion during the rift was studied by Abd El – Gawad (1970), who demonstrated that two pairs of shear zones in Arabia and Africa show a lateral displacement that **is consistent with** that observed along the Gulf of Aqaba fault zone. McKenzie et al. (1970) matched the coastline of the Arabian Peninsula with that of the African Red Sea to detect the precise direction of plate motion. Both reached the same conclusion, namely that the general movement of the Arabian plate relative to the African plate was toward the northeast. The contrasting widths of the northern portion of the Red Sea rift zone and the southern Gulf of Suez suggest that left – lateral movement along the Gulf of Aqaba strike – slip zone has allowed significantly more crustal extension within the Red Sea than has been achieved within the Gulf of Suez (Robertson Research Group, 1985).

The amount of extension was calculated at the northern, central, and southern parts of the Gulf of Suez by Meshref and Khalil (1990). They constructed three representative structural cross sections and calculated 5.1, 14, and 23 km of extension and an increase of 11%, 17%, and 33% of the initial width in the northern, central, and southern parts of the Gulf of Suez, respectively. Evidence from previous results shows that the northwestern sector of the Red Sea has experienced more extension than the other parts of the Gulf of Suez (Meshref and Khalil, 1990).

The limits of the Gulf of Suez rift are defined by laterally persistent fault zones on both sides of the rift system. These fault zones generally trend northwest – southeast, with basement rocks exposed on the upthrown side; they become less well defined to the north (Robertson Research Group, 1985).

The fault system geometry of the basin indicates an extensional setting. Generally, the Gulf of Suez is subdivided into three sub – provinces, which are **in accordance with** the dominant structural dip of the **sedimentary** cover (Moustafa, 1976). These sub – provinces are separated by two major transfer faults or **hinge** zones by most of the geologists working in the Gulf of Suez. The northern is the Zafarana hinge zone and separates the northern sector of the Gulf of Suez with its general dip to the southwest from the central sector, which dips to the northeast. The second hinge zone is the Morgan hinge zone and separates the central sector of the Gulf from the southern sector, which dips to the southwest (Figure 1).

TECTONIC INFLUENCE ON SEDIMENTATION PROCESSES

In this section of the paper, we **attempt to** establish a link between the stratigraphic units, lithofacies, and the tectonic evolution of the northwestern sector of the Red Sea. The timing of rifting is date as late **Oligocene** to early **Miocene**. Dating the basaltic igneous activity in the Suez area has placed the rift between 19 to 24 Ma (Fichera et al. ,1992). Litho – and biofacies analyses of the stratigraphic sequence have suggested an age of late Oligocene to early Miocene (Salah, 1989, 1994). Cochran and Martinez (1988) established the initiation of rifting from the time of evolving the oceanic crust of the Red Sea and indicated that this rifting started about 23 Ma. Moretti et al. (1986) concluded that the main rifting phase was in the early Miocene.

In general, the tectonic evolution occurred in six stages.

Stage 1 (Cambrian to Early Cretaceous)

During stage 1, continental to shallow marine sandstone with thin shale, dolomite, and limestone interbeds predominated and formed the Pre – Cenomanian sediments. These sandstones, previously **known as** the Nubia Sandstone, form one of the reservoirs in the northern Red Sea, e. g. , Hurghada oil field.

Stage 2 (Late Cretaceous to Oligocene)

Uplift and erosion preceded a widespread transgression from the north at the beginning of the late Cretaceous. This uplift and erosion are believed to have been produced by Tethyan rifting (Said, 1962). A southward – directed onlap resulted in overstepping of the Cenomanian and Turonian sequence, which consists of interbedded sandstones and shales (Raha and Abu Qada formations) in the lower part and carbonates (Wata Formation) in the upper part. These sandstones and limestones act as potential reservoirs in some oil fields in the Gulf of Suez.

During the Senonian there was a transition from a mainly clastic facies in the lower unit (Matulla Formation) to a dominantly carbonate facies in the upper unit (Duwi and Sudr formations). The upper unit forms the main source rock for the Gulf of Suez oil (Salah, 1989).

The Esna Formation was deposited in the Paleocene. Part of this deposition eroded simultaneously with the uplift of the Syrian arc system (Said, 1962), which caused the thinning of the Esna Formation throughout the area, with complete erosion in some places.

The Esna Formation was overlain by the Eocene carbonates of the Thebes Formation, which formed as a result of widespread transgression during the Eocene. Both units are potential source rocks in the Gulf of Suez basin (Salah, 1989).

Locally, this carbonate shelf is overlain by **conglomeratic** red beds of Oligocene age, known as Tayiba Red Beds. This unit is considered to be an indicator of initial rifting during the Oligocene.

Stage 3 (Early Miocene)

Stage 3 represents the time at which the Arabian plate started to move away from the African plate and is known as the "early clysmic event" (Robertson Research Group, 1985). Tensional stress led to faulting, which caused some parts of the basin to subside below sea level. The early Miocene Nukhul Formation, deposited as a variety of facies, reflects the heterogeneity of the environmental setting and is the product of the different tectonic settings of the separate fault blocks (Meshref and Khalil, 1990). The Nukhul Formation consists of conglomeratic and brecciated sandstone (a reservoir facies) with some thin shale interbeds in the lower member (Shoab Ali Member), making the unconformity between the Miocene and the pre-Miocene sequences. The upper member (Ghara Member) consists of **anhydrite** (indicating deposition in a supratidal/sabkha setting), shallow-marine limestones and shales (suggesting shallow shelf deposition), and continental sandstone (representing subaerial deposition).

Khalil and Meshref (1988) suggested two phases of **propagation** for the initiation of the rift. Deposition during the initial phase of the rift is represented by the sedimentation patterns of the Shoab Ali Member, which is restricted only in the most southern part of the Gulf of Suez. The initial propagation phase was followed by the widespread Nukhul basin caused by the second propagation phase, which opened the entire Gulf of Suez. The termination of the propagation was produced by two major factors: (1) the counterclockwise rotation of the Arabian and Sinai plates away from the African plate that resulted in increasing the lithospheric strength to the north, and (2) the preexisting east – northeast compressional tectonic feature of the Syrian arc system (Khalil and Meshref, 1988).

Stage 4 (Early to Middle Miocene)

Stage 4 was the most active stage, with maximum tensional stress resulting in rapid subsidence and the formation of major half – grabens and troughs. The Rudeis Formation was deposited during stage 4, while farther south in the Red Sea, sea – floor spreading began (Fichera et al., 1992). Renewed faulting and uplift occurred during the so – called "mid – clysmic event." The shoulders of the rift began to rise, and coarse sands and conglomerates (reservoir facies) were deposited near the margins of the subsiding rift during the middle Miocene (Robertson Research Group, 1985). Fine – grained sediments accumulated in deeper marine settings (source facies), forming a prolific reservoir of submarine turbidites and coarser sandstones. Stage 4 is known as the main subsidence phase by Khalil and Meshref (1988).

Stage 5 (Middle to Late Miocence)

The climate in the Gulf of Suez and the northern sector of the Red Sea changed during stage 5, and marly evaporite cycles (seal facies), highly calcareous shale (source facies) with localized areas of sandstone, and conglomeratic beds (reservoir facies) were deposited, forming the Kareem and Belayim formations. The **culmination** of the **evaporitic** sequence, South Gharib and Zeit formations, occurred during the late Miocene. The main **constituents** were salt and anhydrite, with thin interbeds of shale (seal facies) (Fawzy and Abdel – Aal, 1984).

Stage 6 (Post – Miocene to Holocene)

Stage 6 began with what are called the "late clysmic events," which were a result of further **continental movement** and reactivation of the Aqaba **wrench fault** (Robertson Research Group, 1985). This reactivation of faults produced large – scale subsidence in some parts of the area. The post – Miocene sediments were deposited in different environmental settings (Abd El – Shafy, 1990), which include deep – marine, shallow – marine, restricted, and continental settings. The **paleontological** evidence suggests that a connection to the Indian Ocean existed through the Red Sea during the Pliocene (Abd El – Shafy, 1990).

Words and Expressions

scope	(活动)范围,机会,余地
rift	裂缝,裂口,断裂,长峡谷
gulf	海湾;鸿沟
delineated	描绘的
latitude	纬度
longitude	经度
embrace	拥抱
topographic	地质的,地形学上的
onlap	上超,超复;盆地边部沉积逐渐尖灭
plateau	高地,高原
prone	倾向于;俯卧的
deposition	沉积作用,沉积物
maturity	成熟,完备,成热
clastic	【地质】碎屑
habitat	栖息地,聚集地
lithostratigraphic	岩石层位学的
megasequence	巨层序或大层序
magnetic	磁的,有磁性的
gravity	地心引力,重力
conduct	管理,行为,引导
adversely	逆地,反对地
condensate	冷凝物
constitute	组成
axial	轴的,轴向的
sedimentary	沉积的,沉淀性的
shale	页岩,泥板岩
hinge	枢纽,节点,合页
Oligocene	渐新世
Miocene	中新世
conglomeratic	聚结

anhydrite	硬石膏,无水石膏；硫酸钙矿
propagation	动植物,繁殖,(声波,电磁辐射等)传播
constituent	要素,组分
Holocene	全新世
culmination	顶点
evaporitic	蒸发的
paleontological	古生物学的

Phrases and Expression

lie in	躺在,位于,在于
more or less	差不多,几乎;大约
ranging ... from ... to	范围从……到……
fly over	飞过;飞到另一个地方去;完成
a variety of	多种的
together with	和,加之
be consistent with	与……相一致
in accordance with	根据,依照;与……一致,合乎
attempt to	试图
known as	被叫做,被认识

Proper Name

reconnaissance survey	勘测
triple junction	三联点;三重点;三重接头;三向连接构造
reconnaissance survey	勘测
continental movement	大陆板块运动
wrench fault	扭转断层;横推断层

Language Focus

1. The regional structural setting and the geologic history of the Gulf of Suez and the Egyptian Red Sea were the matter of interest of many researchers and continue to be the focus of many current research programs.

(参考译文:苏伊士湾和埃及红海的区域构造背景和地质演化史曾是许多研究人员感兴趣的课题,而且目前仍是许多研究课题的焦点所在。)

本句中 setting 与 history 是并列主语,句中 of the Gulf of Suez and the

Egyptian Red Sea 所属结构是 setting 和 history 的定语。句中 the matter of interest of many researchers 为双重所属结构，中心词为 matter，翻译成"许多研究人员感兴趣的课题"。句中 were 与 continue 是并列谓语。

2. The interpretation of these seismic surveys has led to the identification of several potential wildcat locations, especially in the onshore part of the investigated area.

（参考译文：通过对这些地震资料的解释，特别是对陆上部分探区的资料的解释，确定了几口有利的探井井位。）

本句的主干是 the interpretation has led to the identification, especially in the onshore part of the investigated area 部分为主语补足语，进一步解释说明主语。

3. The well located on the western side of the Gulf of Suez, tested a horst block, defined by surface mapping.

（参考译文：该井位于苏伊士湾的西侧，是根据地面构造图设计的井位，钻探目标是一地垒块。）

本句的主干是 the well located on the western side of the Gulf of Suez。句中 tested a horst block 为独立结构表目的。句中 defined by surface mapping 是过去分词短语表示动作与逻辑主语 the well 的被动关系，充当 the well 的后置定语。

4. The Suez rift trends in a north – northwest – south – southeast direction, separating the African plate from the Sinai microplate.

（参考译文：苏伊士湾裂谷走向北北西—南南东，将非洲板块和西奈（Sinai）微板块分开。）

本句为简单句，separating the African plate from the Sinai microplate 是由现在分词做伴随状语。

5. Both reached the same conclusion, namely that the general movement of the Arabian plate relative to the African plate was toward the northeast。

（参考译文：测得的板块运动方向与 Abd El – Gawad（1970）的研究结果完全相同：阿拉伯板块的总体运动方向为相对于非洲板块向东北方向运动。）

本句主句为 Both reached the same conclusion，从句是由 that 引导的同位语从句 the general movement of the Arabian plate relative to the African plate was toward the northeast，是对 conclusion 的解释说明。namely 为副词，表示即，也就是"的意思。

Reinforced Learning

Ⅰ. Answer the following questions for a comprehension of the text.

1. Where is the area that forms the scope of this study?

2. Why does the author indicate "the study area has an excellent potential for hydrocarbon accumulation"?

3. What are the purposes of this study?

4. What are the two megasequences of the stratigraphic section of the northwestern Red Sea?

5. Who made the first reconnaissance survey in the study area?

Ⅱ. Multiple choice: choose the correct one from the alternative answers to give the exact meaning of the words.

1. A landing on Mars is within the <u>scope</u> of current physical theory.

A. scheme B. range C. scrap D. scale

2. Across time and space, food has always been used to <u>delineate</u> social distinctions, whether in Roman dinning rooms or modern gourmet supermarkets.

A. decline B. delicate C. designate D. describe

3. This job calls for a man with a great deal of <u>maturity</u>.

A. matureness B. maturate C. mature D. maturation

4. He has <u>magnetic</u> personality.

A. magnet B. attractive C. magnificent D. magnify

5. He is <u>adverse</u> to going abroad.

A. harmful B. Absurd C. opposed D. addictive

6. Curator <u>conducted</u> the visitors round the museum.

A. leaded B. producted C. reducted D. adducted

7. Prices <u>range</u> from £ 6 to £ 10.

A. frame B. control C. vary D. scale

8. Your problem <u>lies in</u> lacking efficient methods.

A. stays up late B. dwells in

C. gives birth to D. lies to

9. <u>In accordance with</u> his father's wish he gave the money to the school.

A. in light of B. in spite of

C. in addition to D. in honor of

10. A single man is no more prone to be in an automobile accident than a married man.

A. likely to　　B. tend to　　C. lying to　　D. able to

Ⅲ. Multiple choice: read the four suggested translations and choose the best answer.

1. He was anxious to mend the rift between the two men.

A. 长峡谷　　B. 断裂　　C. 裂痕　　D. 友谊

2. Clastic facies pattern recognition is somewhat systematic.

A. 塑料的　　B. 风化的　　C. 分解的　　D. 碎屑岩的

3. The ranch is in the middle of a large plateau.

A. 高原　　B. 草地　　C. 稳定水平　　D. 停滞

4. The gulf between the two leaders cannot be bridged.

A. 海湾　　B. 吞没　　C. 鸿沟　　D. 漩涡

5. Hydrogen and oxygen are the constituents of water.

A. 选民　　B. 委托人　　C. 组分　　D. 宪法

Ⅳ. Put the following sentences into Chinese.

1. The area that forms the scope of this study lies in the northwestern Red Sea, Egypt, at the triple junction of the main rifts between the Red Sea, Gulf of Aqaba(亚喀巴湾), and Gulf of Suez(苏伊士湾)

2. This survey led to the discovery of several oil and gas fields (e. g., Hareed and Felefel) in the province, especially in its southernmost part where the seismic surveys are of poor quality because of the Miocene evaporite noise.

3. They constructed three representative structural cross sections and calculated 5.1, 14, and 23 km of extension and an increase of 11%, 17%, and 33% of the initial width in the northern, central, and southern parts of the Gulf of Suez, respectively..

4. The limits of the Gulf of Suez rift are defined by laterally persistent fault zones on both sides of the rift system.

5. This discovery encouraged several other companies to explore for hydrocarbons in the area, among them the African Prospecting Company, the Eastern Petroleum Company (EPC), and the Sinai Petroleum Company in the middle 1920s.

V. Put the following paragraphs into Chinese.

1. The present analyses of the structural geology in the northwestern Reel Sea are based on the interpretation of both geophysical (magnetic, gravity, and processed seismic) and geological data, including subsurface information from more than 45 wells , drilled in, and close to, the study area; surface outcrops; and aerial photograph examination of the structural configuration of the region. Construction of several cross sections of the region has also improved understanding of the basin geometry.

2. The bounding faults branch into numerous curving, interconnected extensional faults toward the north; moreover, the displacement across the fault zone progressively decreases to the north (Robertson Research Group, 1985). These bounding faults and basement exposures are clear in the study area and stand out as topographic markers outlining the rift geometry

4.2 Structural Influence on Hydrocarbon Entrapment in the Northwestern Red Sea, Egypt (Ⅱ)

Guidance to Reading

Magnetic, gravity, seismic, surface, and subsurface data from the northwestern Red Sea delineate several elongate structural highs separated by elongate troughs. Both highs and troughs have the same northwest – southeast direction as the clysmic trend. Some of the highs are dissected by cross elements that trend northeast – southwest and east – northeast – west – southwest and laterally offset these highs.

The tectonic framework of the northwestern sector of the Red Sea had a significant influence on hydrocarbon generation, migration, and accumulation. The evidence for this influence includes the following: (1) *the troughs form the main source kitchens where the Precambrian basement rocks are present at depths exceeding 4877 m* (*e. g.*, *Gemsa Trough*); (2) *the magnitude of throw on the clysmic fault is critical in the entrapment mechanisms*; (3) *the cross elements play a major role in the hydrocarbon migration and accumulation because they truncate the extension of most of the oil fields and form their bounding faults*; *and* (4) *all the discovered oil fields in the study area are structural and / or combination traps and show good matches to the magnetic anomalies.*

Text

BASIN GEOMETRY

The present analysis of the structural **geology** of the northwestern Red Sea is based on the interpretation of magnetic and seismic data and the construction of several cross sections of the area. Knowledge of the surface geology has aided the understanding of the basin geometry.

In general, the northwestern sector of the Red Sea consists of **elongated troughs** separated by elongated structural highs. Both troughs and highs follow the Red Sea – Gulf of Suez trend (northwest – southeast). The highs are **dissected** by cross elements trending northeast – southwest and east – northeast – west – south – west; these cross elements are regarded as transfer faults, which dislocated the highs.

DATA AND INTERPRETATION

Geophysical Data

The most recent seismic surveys of the area were used to delineate the basin geometry; however, the presence of a very thick Miocene evaporite sequence made it difficult to distinguish any deeper horizon structural levels on seismic reflection profiles. Because of this difficulty, we used additional geophysical tools. The available magnetic maps (reduced to pole) were very useful in detecting the regional geometry of the northwestern sector of the Red Sea. The magnetic anomalies, representing basement highs, were traced and linked longitudinally as high trends. Moreover, the cross elements were traced using shifts in the extension of these high trends.

Geological Data

All the available geological data, including **subsurface** information from more than 45 wells drilled in the area together with the surface **outcrops** data, were used to clarify the structural **configuration** of the northwestern sector of the Red Sea. **A series of schematic** structural dip and strike sections were constructed. The purpose of these sections is to **highlight** the structural high **trends** in the basin that might act as a focus for both the migration and accumulation of hydrocarbons.

Data interpretation

Both geophysical and geological data have shown that the northwestern sector of the Red Sea consists of clysmic high trends dissected by cross elements (**transfer faults**). These high trends are separated by major troughs and can be classified according to their longitudinal extension into major and minor trends. The major highs are, from east to west: the Shadwan High, the Abu Shiban – Hareed High, the Hurghada – Umm Agawish High, the southern coast highs (Dabaa, Sharm El Arab, and Abu Soma highs), the Esh Mellaha range, and the Red Sea hills. The minor high trends are, from east to west, RSOX 94 High, Felefel High, Mellaha field high, and West Hurghada high.

MAJOR HIGH TRENDS

Shadwan High Trend

The Shadwan High trend is the easternmost high trend in the study area, and is so called because it includes Shadwan Island, where the Precambrian basement rocks are exposed. This trend extends farther north to form Gubal Island, where the depth to the basement is ±300 m. The oldest **stratigraphic** unit recorded in this trend is the Rudeis Formation, indicating that this trend was a pre – Rudeis high.

Abu Shiban – Hareed High Trend

The Abu Shiban – Hareed High trend is separated from the Shadwan High by the West Shadwan, trough. This high extends for a considerable distance from its southernmost known point, the Hareed South – 3 well, through the Hareed 1 and 2, Hareed North, Estakoza – 1, and Abu Shiban – 2 wells, and still farther to the north of the study area. The depth to basement in these wells increases northward, where it measures 1684 m in the southern well, Hareed South – 3, and 2836 m at the Abu Shiban – 2 well in the north. Neither the pre – Miocene nor the early Miocene Nukhul Formation sediments were recorded in the wells drilled on this trend. The oldest unit, lying directly over the basement rocks, is the lower Miocene. Rudeis Formation, suggesting that this trend was a pre – Rudeis high.

Southern Coast High Trend

The southern coast high trend is represented by the highs along the southwestern coast of the study area. The trend consists of three separate highs **offset** from each other by cross elements. This trend includes, from north to south, the Dabaa, Sharm El Arab, and Ras Abu Soma highs. The trend tilts southward, where the depth to the Precambrian basement rocks at the Dabaa high is 556 m, whereas the depth in the Ras Abu. Soma well is 1237 m. The earliest Miocene unit recorded on this high is the Nukhul Formation.

Hurghada – Umm Agawish High Trend

The Hurghada – Umm Agawish High trend consists of three separate highs offset by some faults. The three highs are, from north to south, the Hurghada field, Abu Minqar, and Umm Agawish highs. The depth to Precambrian basement increases southward in this trend, where it attains 795 m at Hurghada field and 1513 m at the Umm Agawish High. Most of the pre – Miocene units are well preserved on this high, especially in the southern sector.

Esh Mellaha Range Trend

In the Esh Mellaha range trend, the basement is **exposed** at the surface and **plunges to** the south under a Miocene reef complex known as Gebel Abu Shaar. The basement elevation averages 427 m and decreases southward, where it is only 341 m at the southern tip (Abu El – Karamat, 1988). This trend is the only high trend in the study area on which a full sequence of the prerift (Cambrian to Eocene) units has been preserved (Figure 2).

Red Sea Hills

The Red Sea hills occupy about one fifth of the study area and are located in the southwestern corner of the study area (Figure 1). In the study area, the elevation of these hills ranges between 46 and 335 m. A full pre – Miocene sequence is recorded on their western side, outside the study area (Said, 1962, 1990).

Minor High Trends

RSOX 94 High

The RSOX 94 High is the **southernmost** offshore high in the area. The basement on this high was reached at a depth of 1313 m. Both magnetic and seismic data indicated that well RSOX 94 – 1 was drilled on a high. No pre – Miocene units were recorded in this well.

Felefel High

The Felefel High is dissected by cross elements into two parts, Abu Nigar C in the south and Felefel to the north. The average depth to the basement on this high is 914 m. A very thin pre – Miocene unit is present in the northern part, but is absent in the wells drilled in the southern part of the trend.

Mellaha Field High

Hydrocarbons are produced from the Mellaha field high. The depth to the basement in this field is about 1219 m. The Miocene **rests unconformably** on basement and no pre – Miocene sediments were recorded in this field.

INFLUENCE ON HYDROCARBONS

The structural configuration of the study area, as a part of the overall basin geometry of the rifted Red Sea, **plays a very important role** in hydrocarbon generation, migration, and accumulation.

Hydrocarbon Generation

Interpretation of the available data shows that tectonic development and the structural configuration of the area of concern play an important role in several ways. First, the rifting produced favorable conditions for the deposition of organically rich source rocks and potential reservoirs and seals. Second, the northwestern Red Sea consists of parallel longitudinal troughs separated by highs following the clysmic (northwest – southeast) trend. Some troughs are sufficiently deep to place both the **prerift** (pre – Miocene) and the **synrift** (late to middle Miocene) source rock levels within the hydrocarbon generation window (Salah, 1992). The depth to the Precambrian basement **exceeds** 5180 m in the deepest trough (Gemsa), which places the pre – Miocene source rocks in the gas generation window. Third, this part of the Red Sea is characterized by the **heterogeneity** of the crustal composition (Fichera et al. , 1992), with local high heat – flow spots helping maturation of local source kitchens even within relatively shallow depressions. The average **geothermal gradient** in the northwestern Red Sea reaches 1.9°F/m, **compared with** 1.7°F/m average for the Gulf of Suez. Finally, because the regional dip in the northwestern Red Sea is toward the southwest, the migration pathways are toward the northeast. In the case of the Esh Mellaha oil field, however, the migration pathway is from the Gemsa Trough southwestward, because no basins exist to the southwest of the field.

Hydrocarbon Sealing and Trapping

Several sealing **mechanisms** for hydrocarbon **entrapment** are recorded in the northwestern Red Sea. These include structural, stratigraphic, and combination traps, as described in detail by Meshref et al. (1988), Saoudy (1990),

Hammouda (1992), Alsharhan and Salah (1994), and Salah (1994).

The prerift Upper Cretaceous carbonates (Duwi – Sudr carbonates), the Esna shale, and the Thebes limestone formations act as seals for the Cretaceous sandstone reservoirs. Within the synrift sequence, however, the Miocene evaporites are always considered to be the ultimate seals in the Gulf of Suez (Rashed, 1990). This is particularly true in the northwestern Red Sea where they are generally thick, either on the downthrown side of major clysmic faults or on the downdip direction of uplifted tilted fault blocks. However, the magnitude of throw on the clysmic fault is critical in effective sealing (Meshref et al, 1988). A small throw will **juxtapose** the evaporites on the downthrown side of the fault against the Miocene porous section on the uplifted block (e. g., Esh Mellaha and Hareed oil fields). A large throw will bring the Miocene evaporites to juxtapose the pre – Miocene reservoirs on the uplifted block as in the Geisum and Ashrafi oil fields (just north of the study area) (Salah, 1989).

Shales within the Miocene clastic section can act as sealing agents. In such cases, **porous** intervals within the formation will act as reservoirs, whereas the shaly intervals will become vertical and / or horizontal seals, depending on the **magnitude** of the **throw** of the fault (e. g., Hurghada oil field).

CONCLUSIONS

The purpose of this research was to study the effect of structural configuration and tectonic development on the generation, migration, and accumulation of hydrocarbons in the northwestern sector of the Red Sea, Egypt. The stratigraphic sequence in the area of concern is subdivided, relative to the rifting event, into two megasequences: prerift (pre – Miocene) and synrift (Miocene to Holocene). The tectonic development of the region occurred in six stages, showing changes in structural stress, nature of sediments, and depositional environment. The six stages are: (1) Cambrian to Early Cretaceous; (2) Late Cretaceous to Oligocene; (3) early Miocene; (4) early to middle Miocene; (5) middle to late Miocene; and (6) post – Miocene. The northwestern Red Sea consists of elongated, northwest – southeast – trending depositional troughs separated by structural ridges. The structural ridges are dissected by northeast – and east – northeast – trending transfer faults.

The structural configuration and the tectonic development of the northwestern Red Sea controlled **to a great extent** the deposition of organically rich source rocks and potential reservoirs and seals, the suitable heat flow needed for hydrocarbon, and the trapping mechanism for the generated hydrocarbon.

We conclude that the northwestern Red Sea is a potential hydrocarbon exploration area and should receive more exploration activity.

Words and Expressions

geometry	几何学
geology	地质学
elongate	拉长,伸长
trough	槽,水槽,饲料槽,木钵
dissected	多裂的,解剖的,切割的,分成部分的
subsurface	表面下的,地下的
outcrop	露出地面的岩层
configuration	构造,结构,配置,外形
schematic	示意性的
highlight	加亮,使显著,突出
highs	高度,高处
trend	(海岸、河流、山脉等)走向,方向,隆起带
stratigraphic	地层学的
offset	偏移,形成分支
expose	揭露,暴露
southernmost	最南的
rest	使休息,依靠,搁在
unconformably	不相合的(不一致的,不服从的);间断面
prerift	前裂谷期
synrift	同裂谷期
exceed	超过其他
heterogeneity	异种,异质,不同成分
mechanism	机械装置,机构,机制
entrapment	诱捕的行动(过程),圈闭
juxtapose	并置,并列
porous	多孔渗水的
magnitude	大小,数量,巨大,广大,量级
throw	偏心距离,偏移度,落差,摆幅,断层垂直位移

subsurface 表面下的,地下的

Phrases and Expression

a series of 一系列
plunge to 投入,插入
play an important role in 起关键作用
compared with 与……比较
to a great extent 很大程度上

Proper Name

transfer fault 传递断层
geothermal gradient 地热梯度

Language Focus

1. The Shadwan High trend is the eastern most high trend in the study area, and is so called because it includes Shadwan Island, where the Precambrian basement rocks are exposed.

(参考译文:Shadwan 隆起带是研究区内最东边一个隆起带,因其包括 Shadwan 岛而得名,岛上前寒武系基岩出露地表。)

本句为由 and 连接的并列句。句中 and is so called 省略与前句相同的主语 Shadwan High trend, because 为连词,引导原因状语从句(二级从句),解释为什么 Shadwan High trend 这样命名。Where 引导未限定性定语从句(三级从句),修饰 Shadwan Island,进一步解释 Shadwan Island 的地理位置。

2. The oldest unit, lying directly over the basement rocks, is the lower Miocene Rudeis Formation, suggesting that this trend was a pre – Rudeis high.

(参考译文:最老的盖层直接覆盖在基岩之上,为下中新统 Rudeis 组,说明该隆起带为前 Rudeis 期的隆起。)

本句的主干是 The oldest unit is the lower Miocene Rudeis Formation。非谓语动词 lying 和 suggesting 为现在分词作定语,分别修饰 unit 和 Formation。lie 和 suggest 用现在分词表示与逻辑主语 unit 和 Formation 为主动关系。

3. This trend is the only high trend in the study area on which a full sequence of the prerift (Cambrian to Eocene) units has been preserved.

(参考译文:它是研究区唯一前裂谷期地层(寒武系到始新统)保留齐全的隆起带。)

本句中为主句+介词+关系代词引导的定语从句。其中介词 on 是由动词 be preserved 和宾语 trend 决定的,逻辑上为 prerift units has been preserved on the trend。

4. In such cases, porous intervals within the formation will act as reservoirs, whereas the shaly intervals will become vertical and / or horizontal seals, depending on the magnitude of the throw of the fault.

(参考译文:在这些情况下,碎屑岩剖面中的孔隙发育层段将作为储集层,而页岩层段将作为横向和(或)垂向的封堵层,这要视断层落差大小而定。)

本句为 whereas 连接的并列句,表转折关系。非谓语动词 depending 为现在分词作定语修饰 seals,逻辑主语 seals 和非谓语动词 depending 为主动关系。

5. The stratigraphic sequence in the area of concern is subdivided, relative to the rifting event, into two megasequences: prerift (pre – Miocene) and synrift (Miocene to Holocene).

(参考译文:根据裂谷的演化阶段,本区的地层可分为两个巨层序:前裂谷期(前中新世)层序和同裂谷期(中新世—全新世)层序。)

本句中 relative to the rifting event 为独立结构作状语。

Reinforced Learning

Ⅰ. Answer the following questions for a comprehension of the text.

1. How can we overcome the difficulty in distinguishing the deeper horizon structural levels on seismic reflection profiles?

2. What is the earliest Miocene unit recorded on this high?

3. What result can we gain by knowing that "the oldest stratigraphic unit recorded in this trend is the Rudeis Formation"?

4. What are the six stages that the tectonic development of the region occurred in?

5. What conclusion can we elicit by reading this article?

Ⅱ. Multiple choice: choose the correct one from the alternative answers to give the exact meaning of the words.

1. We plan to <u>elongate</u> the cooperation with that company in Australia.

A. ensure　　B. extend　　C. exchange　　D. confirm

2. The configuration of internal and external packet filter provides very good security.

A. shape B. form C. equipment D. sign

3. The President highlights the importance of his visit to China.

A. emphasizes B. enlightens C. lights D. names

4. He exposed the plan to the newspapers.

A. disagreed B. discounted C. disclosed D. discovered

5. If your liabilities exceed your assets, you may go bankrupt.

A. surpass B. express C. over D. succeed

6. The WTO provides a mechanism for resolving trade disputes.

A. principle B. machine C. mechanic D. example

7. I want to know the magnitude of this equipment.

A. affect B. appearance C. face D. size

8. The student always asks his teacher a series of questions.

A. a piece of B. a lot of C. a success of D. matter

9. That man plunged in the river but not to save the child.

A. put B. placed C. immersed D. input

10. Money seems unimportant when being compared with the joys of family life.

A. setting beside B. being replaced by

C. being taken away D. giving up

Ⅲ. Multiple choice: read the four suggested translations and choose the best answer.

1. The high lasted all night.

A. 高地 B. 高度 C. 身高 D. 兴奋

2. The trend at the moment is towards a more natural and less made – up look.

A. 趋势 B. 流行 C. 山脉走向 D. 通向

3. How could a country rest its security on such promises?

A. 依赖 B. 休息 C. 搁置 D. 埋葬

4. The two passages that I'm about to read juxtapose the viewpoints that I've been trying to evoke in describing Gadamer's position.

A. 并列 B. 区分 C. 阐述 D. 反驳

5. The trees threw long shadows across the lawn.

A. 落差 B. 惊忧 C. 投下 D. 发射

Ⅳ. Put the following sentences into Chinese.

1. The present analysis of the structural geology of the northwestern Red Sea is based on the interpretation of magnetic and seismic data and the construction of several cross sections of the area.

2. The most recent seismic surveys of the area were used to delineate the basin geometry; however, the presence of a very thick Miocene evaporite sequence made it difficult to distinguish any deeper horizon structural levels on seismic reflection profiles.

3. Neither the pre – Miocene nor the early Miocene Nukhul Formation sediments were recorded in the wells drilled on this trend.

4. The structural configuration of the study area, as a part of the overall basin geometry of the rifted Red Sea, plays a very important role in hydrocarbon generation, migration, and accumulation.

5. This is particularly true in the northwestern Red Sea where they are generally thick, either on the downthrown side of major clysmic faults or on the downdip direction of uplifted tilted fault blocks.

Ⅴ. Put the following paragraphs into Chinese.

1. The fault system geometry of the basin indicates an extensional setting. Generally, the Gulf of Suez is subdivided into three sub – provinces, which are in accordance with the dominant structural dip of the sedimentary cover. These sub – provinces are separated by two major transfer faults or hinge zones by most of the geologists working in the Gulf of Suez.

2. Drilling was adversely affected by World Wars Ⅰ and Ⅱ, but some wells were drilled between 1938 and 1950 on the western coast of the Red Sea in the Dishet El Dabaa and Abu Shaar areas. No discoveries were made at that time. During the last 20 years, more intensive drilling has resulted in the discovery of the Esh El Mellaha oil field in 1982.

Chapter 5 Petroleum Exploration and Production

5.1 Petroleum Exploration and Production in Fold and Thrust Belts: Ideas From a Hedberg Research Symposium (Ⅰ)

Guidance to Reading

This text reviews ideas presented at the February 1997 Hedberg Research Symposium on petroleum exploration and production in fold and thrust belts, held in Veracruz, Mexico. This was the first AAPG conference to focus on exploration and production within this structural ***domain****. This conference brought together* ***geologists*** *and* ***geophysicists*** *from around the world who are actively working in fold – thrust belts to share their experiences and to address a broad range of exploration and production concerns. Symposium topics included hydrocarbon generation, migration, entrapment and preservation, exploration methods and strategies, field development, and data acquisition. Numerous case studies were presented illustrating these topics.*

Text

INTRODUCTION

AAPG and the Asociacion Mexicana de Geologos Petroleros **cosponsored** the Hedberg Research Symposium on Oil and Gas Exploration and Production in Fold and Thrust Belts, held in Veracruz, Mexico, February 23 – 26, 1997. The conference was **convened** by Richard S. Bishop (Exxon), Bernardo Martell – Andrade (Pemex), and Rafael Sanchez – Montes de Oca (AMGP). Approximately 270 participants from 18 countries attended the conference. The purpose of the conference was to provide a **venue** to exchange experiences and highlight the application of new technologies to shared problems in exploration, production, and field operations in fold – thrust belts. The **symposium** included over 30 oral papers and nearly 50 posters.

This was a business – oriented meeting. **In addition to** the technical aspects of their papers, speakers were asked to **address** the potential business impacts of their topic. Business considerations included identifying and evaluating new opportunities, highgrading play areas, identifying and **mitigating** risk, and developing exploration and production strategies. The majority of the papers **focused on** fold and thrust belts in the Western Hemisphere, but fold – thrust belts from around the world were well represented. Two field trips were held in **conjunction with** the meeting. The pre – meeting field trip was to the northern Sierra Madre Oriental fold – thrust belt near Monterrey and Saltillo, Mexico. The post – meeting field trip was to the Zongolica fold – thrust belt, a southern extension of the Sierra Madre Oriental in the Veracruz district of Mexico. These trips provided contrasting structural styles and surface expressions and illustrated many of the exploration and production challenges within this structural domain.

The following summarizes some of the major topics presented at the meeting. With 80 talks and posters, it is impossible to summarize each. Instead we have attempted to highlight major points from each of the eight sessions. The oral sessions included (1) play elements: generation and **migration** of **hydrocarbons** in fold belts, (2) play elements, including **entrapment** and **preservation** of hydrocarbons in fold belts, (3) exploration methods and strategies in fold and thrust belts, and (4) field development in fold and thrust belts. Poster sessions included (1) data acquisition and interpretation in fold belts: geology and **remote sensing**, (2) data acquisition and interpretation in fold belts: geophysics and other methods, and (3) case histories, including techniques and examples of field development in fold belts.

Although many viewpoints and experiences were presented, several common themes were repeated throughout the symposium. First, and perhaps foremost, fold – thrust belts can contain large reserves of oil and gas, as evidenced by several recent frontier successes. This is **offset** by the complex geology, often difficult **terrain**, and environmental issues that surround this structural play. Key risks include trap **delineation**, timing of migration vs. trap formation, and fault seal. Success often relies on the intelligent application of the right technology, efficient use of all resources to reduce risk, persistence, and the willingness to take risks.

PLAY ELEMENTS—GENERATION AND MIGRATION OF HYDROCARBONS IN FOLD BELTS

The first session of the symposium focused on hydrocarbon generation and migration in fold – belt plays. The presence of hydrocarbons and the prediction of oil vs. gas are key uncertainties **due to** the complex relationship between source **maturation** and structural development; the difficulty in mapping multiple migration pathways; and the commonly narrow window between the time of source maturation, hydrocarbon migration, and trap development. It is critical in these terrains to identify the source interval (or intervals) and its characteristics, identify migration conduits and drainage areas, and constrain the timing of trap formation and source maturation. Examples were presented from Bolivia, Peru, Mexico, Colombia, Venezuela, and Canada.

Several papers presented recent techniques to better constrain the timing of hydrocarbon generation and migration, and identification of regional hydrocarbon systems. Covey et al. (Exxon) illustrated an application of **illite / smectite** analysis to date the timing of thrusting in the Western Canadian fold belt. This technique dates the timing of structuring by dating diagenetic illite produced from smectite during fault movement. Similarly, Yurewicz et al. (Exxon) illustrated the integrated use of illite / smectite analysis, **fission** track analysis, and fluid inclusion analysis to constrain thermal and **burial** history models, and geochemical characterization of hydrocarbon fluid inclusions to delineate regional hydrocarbon systems. Bachu (Alberta Geological Survey) described the interplay between hydrodynamic and geothermal regimes and how they **play important roles in** the thermal history of an area, hence influencing hydrocarbon generation, migration, and **accumulation**.

Several papers illustrated the complex relationship among structural development, source rock maturation, and hydrocarbon migration. Pepper and Daly (BP Exploration) presented an excellent case study illustrating many of the potential problems in fold – thrust belts by describing the complex maturation, migration, and fill and spill history within the El Furial trend of eastern Venezuela. Similarly, Colletta et al. (Institut Francais du Pétrol) illustrated the complex interplay between structural development and source rock maturation with examples from the French Alps. They emphasized that to reconstruct the temperature history in a fold – thrust belt; it is necessary to model the timing; sequence;

and rate of thrusting; as well as concurrent or subsequent **sedimentation**, **erosion**, and **subsidence**; and changes in the conductive properties of the, affected rocks. **Rigorous** two – dimensional forward modeling of these conditions will give the explorationist a better prediction of the type of hydrocarbon that can be expected in different parts of a **fold** and **thrust** belt.

PLAY ELEMENTS—ENTRAPMENT AND PRESERVATION OF HYDROCARBONS IN FOLD BELTS

The symposium's second oral session focused on **entrapment** and **preservation** of hydrocarbons within fold belts. Several different perspectives and **case studies** were presented. In one study, Coleman et al. (Amoco) analyzed 24 fold belts and foreland basins from around the world and evaluated 20 play elements and six possible risk levels. They concluded that the presence of high – quality source rocks severely reduces the risk of all other play elements with the exception of trap delineation. Simply put, large volumes of hydrocarbons generated from high – quality source rocks can overwhelm risks associated with migration, entrapment, and preservation.

Kluth (Chevron) evaluated trap and seal risks in fold – thrust belts. These elements control the volume of reservoir that is contained within a structure, and hydrocarbon column height; these translate into hydrocarbon volumes. Risking these elements is difficult and requires "brutal honesty." He emphasized that there is never enough data to completely constrain an interpretation and that there is always a need for more and better data or more robust models. He cautioned, however, that we have to assess the cost of more and better data against the value of the information that is acquired. Examples of "more and better data" included improved seismic data, better logs, and better test data. "More robust models" are needed to maximize interpretations from available data. The use of cross sections was cited as a method of assessing trap **geometry** that has progressed rapidly, from cross sections drawn "free – hand," to balanced cross sections, to incremental restoration of balanced cross sections. Improvements in computer analysis may eventually make it possible to construct incremental three – dimensional balanced cross sections. The utility of cross sections to test structural models was repeated throughout this symposium. Kluth also concluded that although top seal is not a common risk in fold – thrust belts, fault seal is a major risk. Although examples were provided of fault seal in several areas that hold back large hydrocarbon columns, we still lack the ability to predict the presence or effectiveness of fault seal.

Pottorf et al. closed this session with additional examples of Exxon's use of fluid inclusions to unravel complex fill and spill histories. In an example from Trinidad, fluid inclusions were used to unravel confusing well results and complex migration and post – emplacement processes. In a second example from Mexico, fluid inclusions were utilized to constrain regional structural geohistory and to map regional oil families.

EXPLORATION METHODS AND STRATEGIES IN FOLD AND THRUST BELTS

Fold and thrust belts present many challenges to the explorationist. One of the key problems is acquisition of high – quality seismic data. Seismic acquisition can be limited by difficult access in mountainous terrain, and processing can be complicated by rugged surface **topography**, vertical and lateral **velocity** variations, complex structures with steep dips, and near – surface effects of weathered and karsted terrain. These problems, obviously, are not unique to fold – thrust belts, but it is unusual for the explorationist to face all of them in one setting. The purpose of this session was to illustrate how different companies have coped with such adverse conditions. In general the authors did not **comment on** their exploration philosophies, but they nevertheless showed how they acquired data in this terrain.

Rodriguez et al. (Pemex) illustrated many of these problems in exploration of the Zongolica sector of the Sierra Madre Oriental. Despite numerous geologic, geochemical, and geophysical studies, exploration success in this trend has been marginal. They suggest that poor 2 – D (two – dimensional) seismic resolution may **account for** their limited success **to date**. Similarly Bentham and Serra (Amoco) cited difficulties in acquiring adequate seismic data over Opon field in central Colombia. They **extolled** the benefits of 2 – D and 3 – D (three – dimensional) forward modeling to test different structural models in structurally complex areas. Because the 2 – D seismic data over Opon field is poor, Amoco constructed 21 structural cross sections across the field from which they built a 3 – D model of the structure. The construction of the 3 – D model over the Opon gas discovery was instrumental in deciding to cancel a planned 3 – D seismic survey, in recalculating reserves, in planning development wells, and in communication among all parties in the project. Apotria et al. (Exxon and Maraven) presented a similar paper highlighting the use of 3 – D visualization tools in interpretation of fold – thrust structures in the western Maracaibo Basin, Venezuela.

Graham et al. (Monument Oil and Gas, BP, and British Gas) emphasized the importance of timing in fold – thrust belts. Although fold – thrust belts may deform preexisting passive margin and foreland basin rocks with excellent reservoirs, seals, and source rocks, the mechanics of deformation typically **result in** uplift, which halts source rock maturation and hydrocarbon generation. They concluded that fold – thrust belts with a long history of subsidence and multiple uplifts thus are more likely to be **prospective**.

FIELD OPERATIONS IN FOLD AND THRUST BELTS

The challenges in obtaining high – quality seismic data in rugged terrain typical of many fold – thrust belts were reiterated in this session. The global expansion of exploration into fold – thrust belts has **brought forward** new methods and strategies of gathering seismic data. This session included six papers that illustrate present – day challenges and solutions.

Gray et al. (Amoco) addressed problems of data acquisition and showed how they improved data quality by using a series of topographically related corrections that included (1) processing data directly from topography rather than from a flat or floating datum, (2) paying close attention to the treatment of amplitudes, (3) paying close attention to the effect of local topographic variations along the recording spread, and (4) computing the image along a crooked line, e. g. , along a “line” defined by the set of Common Mid – Point locations.

Although acquiring 3 – D seismic surveys in fold – thrust belts has many inherent problems, Villamieva et al. (PEMEX) demonstrated the benefit of acquiring 3 – D seismic in the fold belt of southeastern Mexico. A 3 – D seismic grid was acquired over Gaucho and Sfecadero fields near the Sierra de Chiapas. The improved imaging prevented Pemex from drilling what would have been a dry hole in a syncline and helped to identify three new prospects, which, if successful, will double reserves.

In a related paper, Bertelli et al. (AGIP and Western Geophysical) summarized available techniques to acquire velocity and VSP (vertical seismic profile) data while drilling. In areas of poor velocity control, this technique can provide timely data to improve seismic data quality and update structural models and well **trajectory** while drilling.

Two papers (Barker et al. ,Amoco; and Fauria,Triton) also addressed issues of operating in remote, environmentally and politically sensitive areas. Examples were given from recent exploration programs in Ecuador, Peru, Venezuela,Guatemala,and Colombia. Effective programs in these areas require a business Strategy that includes (1) identification of environmental issues prior to acquiring new acreage,(2) development of a business plan that is committed to minimizing environmental and cultural impacts,and (3) development of public affairs,communications and outreach programs to build and foster local support.

Words and Expressions

domain	领地,领域
geologist	地质学家
geophysicist	地球物理学家
migration	运移
cosponsor	共同倡议
convene	召集,召开
venue	会场,聚集地点
symposium	专题讨论会
hydrocarbon	烃;碳氢化合物
entrapment	圈闭
preservation	储藏,保存
offset	补偿,抵消
terrain	地貌
delineation	圈定,描绘
maturation	成熟
illite	伊利石
smectite	蒙皂石
fission	核裂变
burial	埋藏
accumulation	累积
sedimentation	沉积

erosion	侵蚀
subsidence	下沉
rigorous	严格的,精确的
fold	褶皱
thrust	冲断层,逆断层
geometry	几何学
topography	地形,地形学
acquisition	探测,采集
velocity	速度
extoll	称赞
prospective	远景的,有希望的
trajectory	轨迹
address	致辞

Phrases and Expression

in addition to	除……以外
focus on	集中于
in conjunction with	与……协力;共同
due to	因为,由于
play important roles in	在……中发挥重要作用
comment on	对……评论
account for	说明(原因)
to date	迄今
result in	导致
bring forward	提出

Proper Name

remote sensing	遥感
case study	实例研究

Language Focus

1. It is critical in these terrains to identify the source interval (or intervals) and its characteristics, identify migration conduits and drainage areas, and constrain the timing of trap formation and source maturation.

（参考译文：在该地带确定源岩层段（或多个层段）及其特征，确定运移通道和泄油面积，并限定圈闭形成时间和源岩成熟的时间是其关键所在。）

本句是由 it 作为形式主语构成的主系表结构的简单句，It is critical...。真正的主语是之后的三个并列不定式结构 to identify...，identify...，and constrain...。

2. They emphasized that to reconstruct the temperature history in a fold – thrust belt, it is necessary to model the timing; sequence; and rate of thrusting; as well as concurrent or subsequent sedimentation, erosion, and subsidence; and changes in the conductive properties of the affected rocks.

（参考译文：他们强调，要重建褶皱和冲断带的温度史，必须建立时间、层序和冲断速度模型，同时或后来的沉积、剥蚀和沉降模型，并分析受影响岩层的输导性的变化。）

本句的主干是 They emphasized that... 主谓宾结构。在 that 引导的宾语从句中，to reconstruct the temperature history in a fold – thrust belt 是不定式充当从句中的目的状语。从句的主干是 it is necessary to model...，it 为形式主语，不定式 to model... 结构是真正的主语。

3. Simply put, large volumes of hydrocarbons generated from high – quality source rocks can overwhelm risks associated with migration, entrapment, and preservation.

（参考译文：简而言之，从高品质生油岩中生成的大量油气可抵消与运移、圈闭和保存有关的风险。）

本句的主干是 large volumes of hydrocarbons can overwhelm risks。过去分词短语 generated from high – quality source rocks 是主语的后置定语；过去分词短语 associated with migration, entrapment, and preservation 是宾语的后置定语。

4. Improvements in computer analysis may eventually make it possible to construct incremental three – dimensional balanced cross sections.

（参考译文：计算机分析能力的提高可能最终建立增量式三维平衡剖面。）

本句的主干是 Improvements make it possible。不定式短语 to construct incremental three – dimensional balanced cross sections 是真正的宾语，it 作为形式宾语。

Reinforced Learning

Ⅰ. Answer the following questions for a comprehension of the text.

1. What is the purpose of the conference held in Veracruz, Mexico, February 23 – 26, 1997?

2. What did the first session of the symposium focus on?

3. What did the second session focus on?

4. In an example from Trinidad, what were fluid inclusions used to show?

5. According to Rodriguez et al. (Pemex), what is the possible reason for their limited success in exploration of the Zongolica sector of the Sierra Madre Oriental.

Ⅱ. Multiple choice: choose the correct one from the alternative answers to give the exact meaning of the words.

1. The conference was convened by Richard S. Bishop (Exxon), Bernardo Martell – Andrade (Pemex), and Rafael Sanchez – Montes de Oca (AMGP).

A. converted　　B. gathered
C. dismissed　　D. convinced

2. Speakers were asked to address the potential business impacts of their topic.

A. live　　B. add　　C. home　　D. explain

3. The following summarizes some of the major topics presented at the meeting.

A. concluds　　B. assumes　　C. consumes　　D. conducts

4. This is offset by the complex geology, often difficult terrain, and environmental issues.

A. outset　　B. compensated
C. offloaded　　D. combined

5. They extolled the benefits of 2 – D and 3 – D (three – dimensional) forward modeling to test different structural models in structurally complex areas.

A. exaggerated　B. extended　　C. examined　　D. exalted

6. Apotria et al. (Exxon and Maraven) presented a similar paper highlighting the use of 3 – D visualization tools in interpretation of fold – thrust structures in the western Maracaibo Basin, Venezuela.

A. involving　　B. describing　　C. emphasizing　　D. illustrating

7. They concluded that fold – thrust belts with a long history of subsidence and multiple uplifts thus are more likely to be prospective.

A. interesting B. exciting C. promising D. ravishing

8. This session included six papers that illustrate present – day challenges and solutions.

A. talk B. involve C. praise D. explain

9. The improved imaging prevented Pemex from drilling what would have been a dry hole in a syncline and helped to identify three new prospects, which, if successful, will double reserves.

A. establish B. draw C. classify D. ascertain

10. Effective programs in these areas require a business Strategy that includes development of a business plan that is committed to minimizing environmental and cultural impacts.

A. shock B. influence C. factor D. heritage

Ⅲ. Multiple choice: read the four suggested translations and choose the best answer.

1. AAPG and the Asociacion Mexicana de Geologos Petroleros cosponsored the Hedberg Research Symposium on Oil and Gas Exploration and Production in Fold and Thrust Belts, held in Veracruz, Mexico, February 23 – 26, 1997.

A. 圈闭 B. 褶皱 C. 沉积 D. 结晶

2. Key risks include trap delineation, timing of migration vs. trap formation, and fault seal.

A. 圈定 B. 描绘 C. 上移 D. 勘探

3. It is critical in these terrains to identify the source interval (or intervals) and its characteristics, identify migration conduits and drainage areas, and constrain the timing of trap formation and source maturation.

A. 沉积 B. 融合 C. 排泄 D. 采集

4. It is necessary to model the timing; sequence; and rate of thrusting; as well as concurrent or subsequent sedimentation, erosion, and subsidence.

A. 抬升 B. 沉降 C. 成熟 D. 断裂

5. Although fold – thrust belts may deform preexisting passive margin and foreland basin rocks with excellent reservoirs, seals, and source rocks, the mechanics of deformation typically result in uplift, which halts source rock maturation and hydrocarbon generation.

A. 裂缝 B. 断层 C. 河床 D. 封层

Ⅳ. Put the following sentences into Chinese.

1. In addition to the technical aspects of their papers, speakers were asked to address the potential business impacts of their topic.

2. Several papers illustrated the complex relationship among structural development, source rock maturation, and hydrocarbon migration.

3. Simply put, large volumes of hydrocarbons generated from high – quality source rocks can overwhelm risks associated with migration, entrapment, and preservation.

4. These problems, obviously, are not unique to fold – thrust belts, but it is unusual for the explorationist to face all of them in one setting.

5. Despite numerous geologic, geochemical, and geophysical studies, exploration success in this trend has been marginal.

Ⅴ. Put the following paragraphs into Chinese.

1. A petroleum reservoir consists of a suitably shaped porous stratum of rock that is capped with an impervious rock. The shape of the structure must be such that the oil (or gas) can collect in one zone to form an accumulation, and the cap rock is essential to prevent the further upward migration of the contents.

2. Stratigraphically, the petroleum system includes the following rock units or essential elements within the geographic extent: a petroleum source rock, reservoir rock, seal rock, and overburden rock at the critical moment. The functions of the first three rock units are obvious, however, the function of the overburden rock is subtler because, in addition to providing the overburden necessary to thermally mature the source rock, it can also have considerable impact on the geometry of the underlying migration path and trap.

5.2 Petroleum Exploration and Production in Fold and Thrust Belts: Ideas From a Hedberg Research Symposium (Ⅱ)

Guidance to Reading

This paper reviews ideas presented at the February 1997 *Hedberg Research Symposium on petroleum exploration and production in fold and thrust belts, held in Veracruz, Mexico. This was the first AAPG conference to focus on explo-*

ration and production within this structural domain. This conference brought together geologists and geophysicists from around the world who are actively working in fold – thrust belts to share their experiences and to address a broad range of exploration and production concerns. Symposium topics included hydrocarbon generation, migration, entrapment and preservation, exploration methods and strategies, field development, and data acquisition. Numerous case studies were presented illustrating these topics.

Text

FIELD DEVELOPMENT IN FOLD AND THRUST BELTS

New technologies useful to our industry are, of course, not limited to subsurface imaging, but include new ways to drill wells and to manage **reservoirs**. The purpose of this session was to illustrate present – day methods of field development, using case histories presented from fields with different development challenges. Examples were presented from Papua New Guinea; Campeche Sound, Mexico; Neuquen basin, Argentina; Canadian Rockies; U. S. Rockies; and the Llanos foothills, Colombia. Common themes included the need to manage costs effectively, to obtain the maximum benefit from subsurface data, to integrate that data with reservoir engineering models, and to continually learn and adapt plans as field development progresses. A key contribution of this session was to show that development costs typically decline rapidly as an operator gains experience in a field. Thus, the costly early wells, which one hears so much about, may mislead us about the true, much lower development costs.

One of the more challenging examples of field development was Cupiagua field in the Llanos foothills by Dupree (BP Exploration). Drilling of Cupiagua field is "the most severe they have experienced anywhere In the world." The first three wells experienced hole instability, high horizontal stresses, **borehole deterioration** with time and difficulty maintaining the well trajectory. The first well cost $45 million and took 1. 5 year to complete. BP has learned to drill subsequent wells more efficiently, in less time, and at a lower cost. The ninth well at Ctipiagua cost $13 million and took only 118 days to drill.

Several problems **contribute to** the difficulty in drilling wells at Cupiagua. The area is technically active, and borehole instability is a major issue. The main problem occurs in the thick Carbonera Formation, which **consists of** shale and fractured sandstone that develop **ledges** in the well bore. It was difficult to log, the drill bit would stick, and cavings were measured in truckloads. Considerable time and money were lost in sidetracking early wells. BP **circumvented** these problems by learning to directionally drill in shallower formations and then allow the drill bit to "walk" through the Carbonera Formation. They can now drill three wells from a single pad, substantially reducing costs, and are working on scenarios to drill up to five wells from one pad. Mie Mirador reservoir also presented problems. It is a hard tight rock and initially required numerous bit runs. Improvements in bit technology have significantly improved drilling efficiency in the Mirador and saved additional drilling time and costs.

Hebberger and Franklin (Chevron) presented another case study of dramatic cost reduction in Iagiuf – Hedinia field, Papua New Guinea. The Papuan fold – thrust belt is one of the most challenging environments in which to work, due to the rugged terrain, intensely karsted outcrops, the wet tropical climate, dense vegetation, and little **infrastructure**. Seismic data in this setting are of poor quality and exploration **is dependent on** field mapping, remote sensing, potential field surveys, and careful integration of all data. The Iagiuf – Hedinia field was discovered just after the collapse of global crude oil prices in 1986. Because of lower crude oil prices and uncertainties in discovered reserves, the project was judged to be feasible only if project costs could be reduced substantially. The key to success was the early commitment to active reservoir management, aggressive acquisition of reservoir data, use of the latest technology, and creation of a **multidisciplinary** reservoir management team, coupled with development of a close and effective working relationship with the host government and local landowners.

A poster session also included a broad sampling of field development case studies in fold – thrust belts. Field examples were presented from the Apennines, Italy; Aquitaine basin, France; Maracaibo basin, Venezuela; Monagas area, Venezuela; Sabinas basin, Mexico; Veracruz district, Mexico; Chiapas – Tabasco province, Mexico; Sound of Campeche, Mexico; foothills of British Colombia, Canada; Trinidad; and the Neuquen basin, Argentina. These examples illustrated a variety of trap styles, field sizes, reservoirs, hydrocarbon types, and development issues. The two studies discussed in the following paragraphs are a representative sample of these papers.

Le Vot et al. (Elf) described production problems and their solutions in the Meillon gas field in France. This field is situated under the leading edge of the Pyrenean foothills. The field produced gas from tight fractured **dolomites** for 13 years, but then began to experience water breakthroughs that dropped production by 50%. Water was thought to travel along faults, thus necessitating a detailed structural model of the field. Older 2 – D seismic data were of poor quality, so a 3 – D seismic program was acquired over the area. This improved subsurface data permitted the construction of detailed reservoir models and a field model that delineated water circulation pathways. **Armed with** these data, additional development wells were drilled, significantly improving field production and adding reserves.

Cooper et al. (Pan – Canadian and Shell Canada) described Boulder field in the foothills of northeastern British Colombia, Canada, to illustrate difficulties common to drilling in fractured fold – thrust plays. The reservoir consists of tight fractured Triassic dolomites in a tight **asymmetric anticline**. Despite mapping based on a 3 – D seismic survey, a 1994 well penetrated the **backlimb** of the structure, rather than the anticipated crestal position. The reservoir was highly fractured, but the fractures were small and tight. Consequently, initial flow rates were only 14 mmcf/d (million cubic feet per day), far below the expected rate of 40 mmcf/d. The well was sidetracked as a subhorizontal well in an attempt to encounter more highly fractured reservoir facies in a more crestal position. The sidetrack successfully encountered the reservoir in a crestal position and on testing flow rates more than doubled to 32 mmcf/d with increased flow pressures. Despite this success, two subsequent wells flowed at noncommercial rates and the pool will be produced from the two initial wells.

DATA ACQUISITION AND INTERPRETATION IN FOLD BELTS: GEOLOGY AND REMOTE SENSING

Rugged terrain, dense vegetation, lack of bedrock exposures, and poor seismic data **hamper** exploration and development activities in many fold – thrust belts. In these areas geologic interpretation is heavily dependent on the use of remote sensing data, including Landsat MSS, Landsat TM, SPOT, SAR, and RADARSAT. These data, combined with surface information, help define surface fold and fault patterns. When combined with gravity and magnetics, seismic reflection and well data, and fault – related folding models, they can be used to infer subsurface structural styles and to map buried structural traps. The application of these tools were illustrated in studies from Mexico, Colombia, Peru, Trinidad, Cuba, Papua New Guinea, Canada, Switzerland, Alaska, China, Pakistan, and Italy.

As pointed out by Snedden et al. (Texaco), remote – sensing images cost only a fraction of seismic and well data and can be useful throughout the life of an exploration and development project. Properly geo – referenced, these data can serve as a base for mapping and can be used for preparation of environmental baseline studies, to plan the location of seismic lines and gravity surveys, for environmental document preparation, to lead delineation, for well site selection, for selection of confirmation well sites, and as "before" images for site remediation.

DATA ACQUISITION AND INTERPRETATION IN FOLD BELTS: GEOPHYSICS AND OTHER METHODS

As reiterated in many of the oral presentations, acquisition of high – quality seismic data is a major challenge in fold – thrust belts and a significant limitation to viable exploration and development programs. This poster session presented **a broad array of** new methods of geophysical data acquisition and processing. A common thread through many of the posters was the recognized need to design specific acquisition and processing programs to fit the local geologic conditions. Test lines that vary energy source, charge size and depth, shot – hole patterns, and fold are essential to design the **optimal** acquisition **parameters**. Rapid field processing allows in – field adjustments and a continuous quality check of acquired data. Examples were presented from Peru, Bolivia, Colombia, Argentina, Papua New Guinea, Mexico, and Austria. Chevron's strategy for improving mountain – front data was to use large charges and deep holes, maintain high fold, and as recommended, use field processing during acquisition to maintain quality control.

Rigorous attention to data processing is essential in acquiring high – quality seismic images in fold – thrust belts and, as with data acquisition, processing streams must be tailored to the local geology. As pointed out by Mitchel and Tilander (Chevron), the cost of processing is only a fraction of the cost of acquisition in many fold – thrust belts, so every effort should be made to find the best processing stream. They recommended careful quality control during processing, using interpretive methods during processing, incorporating geologic models, and processing the data more than once using different methods and different shops or processors. In a field example from Colombia they demonstrated how processing corrections had to be made for near - surface weathering profiles. A seismically defined weathering layer was used for statics corrections. It was discovered in the course of the program that this layer is thicker and has faster interval velocities than that used in previous models; consequently, the velocity of the weathering layer was determined from refraction statics and deep uphole tests. The resulting seismic line showed significant improvement. In an example from eastern Venezuela, Uzcategui and De Almeida (Intervep and Corpoven) emphasized that building velocity models as key to obtaining good depth - migrated sections.

SUMMARY

Judging from the stated purpose of this research symposium, the quality and diversity of papers and posters that were presented; the field trips that accompanied the meeting; and the numerous discussions held throughout the meeting rooms, hallways, vans, and on the outcrops; this meeting was a noted success. The discussion below is a summary of some key observations from this meeting.

Although fold and thrust belts contain a modest percentage of the world's discovered petroleum, they have significant potential for large discoveries as evidenced by recent successes in Colombia and Venezuela. Although exploration and production within this structural setting must address many of the same issues as other plays, there are additional challenges. These can include complex geology (complex trap geometry, migration pathways, and geohistory), difficult terrain, poor seismic quality, higher cost of field operations, environmental considerations, and drilling problems. Success in this setting requires efficient application of available tools to mitigate risk and costs. Given the complex geology and poor imageability, explorationists must be willing to be persistent in the face of initial failures. As a corollary, they must also recognize those play elements that can make or break a play and have a contingent withdrawal strategy.

Historically, one of the main limitations to exploration and field development in many fold and thrust belts has been the moderate to poor quality of seismic data. Many of the papers demonstrated that seismic quality can be improved in a number of ways. The first steps should include custom design of acquisition programs specific to the local geology, and rapid field processing to quality check acquired data and to adjust acquisition parameters. The cost of processing is only a fraction of the cost of acquisition, so every effort should be made to design the optimal acquisition parameters to assure that the maximum data is recorded in the field. Once the data are acquired, numerous processing streams can be evaluated. This includes careful quality control during processing, use of interpretive methods during processing, incorporating geo; logic models, and processing the data more than once using different methods and different processors. In all cases, seismic interpretations should **be integrated with** outcrop data, well data, satellite and **radar** images, and gravity and magnetics. Multiple interpretations should be tested with rigorous 2 – D and 3 – D balanced cross sections.

Large hydrocarbon accumulations can occur in **a wide variety of** structural styles and a wide variety of reservoir rocks. Key limiting play elements in this setting include trap and migration timing. Source rock maturation commonly is driven by rapid structural burial followed by uplift that halts further maturation and hydrocarbon generation. Because hydrocarbon charge and trap formation commonly are only partly **synchronous**, only a portion of the total yield is available to fill traps. It is critical, therefore, to constrain the geohistory in fold – thrust belts using all available data. Several techniques were described at the symposium that help to constrain the timing of structuring, migration, and entrapment. These include the application of illite age analysis, **apatite** fission track analysis, and use of fluid inclusions. Fault seal was identified as another key risk in this structural domain and as a topic requiring additional research. Given these risks, it was suggested that the most favorable fold belts in which to explore include those with high – quality source rocks, an active charge, and an extended history of structuring.

Words and Expressions

reservoir	储层
borehole	井眼
deterioration	恶化,退化
ledge	台肩

circumvent	绕行,设法避开
infrastructure	基础设施
multidisciplinary	多学科的
dolomite	白云岩
asymmetric	非对称的
anticline	背斜
backlimb	缓翼
hamper	阻碍
optimal	最佳的
parameter	参数
radar	雷达
synchronous	同步的,同期的
apatite	磷灰石

Phrases and Expression

contribute to	促成,有助于
consist of	由……组成
be dependent on	依赖
arm with	用……武装
a broad array of	广泛的,多的
be integrated with	与……结合
a wide variety of	种种,多种多样

Language Focus

1. Thus, the costly early wells, which one hears so much about, may mislead us about the true, much lower development costs.

(参考译文:于是,昂贵的早期钻井成本,听起来非常之高,可能会使我们对非常低的实际开发费用感到迷惑不解。)

本句中 which one hears so much about 为非限定性定语从句修饰 early wells。主句的句子主干为 early wells may mislead us about costs。句中 true, much lower development 做定语限定 costs。

2. The main problem occurs in the thick Carbonera Formation, which consists of shale and fractured sandstone that develop ledges in the well bore.

(参考译文:这个重要的问题存在于厚厚的 Carbonera 组,而 Carbonera

组由页岩和裂缝性砂岩构成,在井中形成台肩。)

本句包含两个定语从句,其中 which consists of shale and fractured sandstone 为非限定性定语从句修饰 Carbonera Formation。句中 that develop ledges in the well bore 为限定性定语从句修饰 shale and fractured sandstone。

3. Properly geo – referenced, these data can serve as a base for mapping and can be used for preparation of environmental baseline studies, to plan the location of seismic lines and gravity surveys, for environmental document preparation, to lead delineation, for well site selection, for selection of confirmation well sites, to aid as "before" images for site remediation.

(参考译文:经过恰当的地理标定之后,这些资料可作为绘图的基础并作为环境基础研究及环境文件的准备,以确定进行地震测线和重力勘探的位置,引导圈定井位;且可用于选择并确定选中的井位,还可作为进行现场抢修的"前"成像。)

本句的结构简单来说是这样的:these data can serve as a base for mapping and can be used for... to..., (can be used) for... to..., (can be used) for... to... 。重复部分省略的多并列谓语结构。

4. Chevron's strategy for improving mountain – front data was to use large charges and deep holes, maintain high fold, and as recommended, use field processing during acquisition to maintain quality control.

(参考译文:雪佛龙公司改进山前数据的策略是使用大炸药量和深井、坚持高覆盖次数,且在采集时按照建议,采用现场处理系统进行质量控制。)

本句是主系表结构,to use... to maintain... to use 是并列的三个不定式结构充当表语,as recommended 做状语。

5. They recommended careful quality control during processing, using interpretive methods during processing, incorporating geologic models, and processing the data more than once using different methods and different shops or processors.

(参考译文:他们建议在进行处理时认真做好质量监控,处理过程中采用解释方法,与地质模型相结合,用不同的方法和不同的处理队伍(即处理员)对数据进行处理。)

本句主干为 They recommended careful quality control during processing。句中 using interpretive methods during processing, incorporating geologic models, and processing the data more than once 为并列的分词结构做伴随状语。

句中 using different methods and different shops or processors 这个分词结构是做 processing the data 的状语。

Reinforced Learning

Ⅰ. Answer the following questions for a comprehension of the text.

1. What was the common theme of the February 1997 Hedberg Research Symposium?

2. According to Venezuela, Uzcategui and De Almeida, what was the key to obtaining good depth – migrated sections?

3. Although exploration and production within fold and thrust belts must address many of the same issues as other plays, there are additional challenges. What are they?

4. What is one of the main limitations to exploration and field development in many fold and thrust belts?

5. Given all the risks, what was suggested to be the most favorable fold belts to explore?

Ⅱ. Multiple choice: choose the correct one from the alternative answers to give the exact meaning of the words.

1. The purpose of this session was to illustrate present – day methods of field development.

A. decorate B. adorn C. picture D. demonstrate

2. This arrangement will be of great benefit to you both.

A. importance B. harm C. profit D. significance

3. The government misled the public about the road's environmental impact.

A. confused B. led C. clarified D. guided

4. Several problems contribute to the difficulty in drilling wells at Cupiagu.

A. encourage B. manage C. donate D. attribute

5. All effects are dependent on their causes.

A. determined by B. reliable as C. combined with D. relative to

6. The team have shown enthusiasm and commitment.

A. pledge B. dedication C. duty D. passion

7. Gambling is always coupled with degradation.

A. related to B. in addition to C. affected by D. cupped with

8. Their work is hampered by lack of funds.

A. helped B. suspended C. accelerated D. hindered

9. It is important to define these terms accurately.

A. clarify B. understand C. regulate D. bound

10. The program is designed for general application.

A. completion B. repetition C. competition D. use

Ⅲ. Multiple choice: read the four suggested translations and choose the best answer.

1. New technologies useful to our industry are, of course, not limited to subsurface imaging, but include new ways to drill wells and to manage reservoirs.

A. 储藏 B. 汇集 C. 储层 D. 水库

2. The field produced gas from tight fractured dolomites.

A. 石灰石 B. 云母 C. 断层 D. 白云石

3. The first three wells experienced hole instability, high horizontal stresses, borehole deterioration with time and difficulty maintaining the well trajectory.

A. 地洞 B. 蛀孔 C. 虫洞 D. 井眼

4. The main problem occurs in the thick Carbonera Formation, which consists of shale and fractured sandstone that develop ledges in the well bore.

A. 台肩 B. 边缘 C. 窗台 D. 矿脉

5. The reservoir consists of tight fractured Triassic dolomites in a tight asymmetric anticline.

A. 向斜 B. 倾斜 C. 背斜 D. 倾角

Ⅳ. Put the following sentences into Chinese.

1. BP has learned to drill subsequent wells more efficiently, in less time, and at a lower cost.

2. Despite mapping based on a 3 – D seismic survey, a 1994 well penetrated the backlimb of the structure, rather than the anticipated crestal position.

3. Rugged terrain, dense vegetation, lack of bedrock exposures, and poor seismic data hamper exploration and development activities in many fold – thrust belts.

4. Rapid field processing allows in – field adjustments and a continuous

quality check of acquired data.

5. Historically, one of the main limitations to exploration and field development in many fold and thrust belts has been the moderate to poor quality of seismic data.

V. Put the following paragraphs into Chinese.

1. Although exploration and production in fold – thrust belts must address many of the same issues as in other structural plays, there are additional challenges. Fold and thrust belts, for example, are characterized by complex trap geometry; a complex burial and thermal history; a narrow time line between the onset of petroleum generation, migration, and trap development; and a complex history of fill and spill. Other challenges can include difficult terrain, poor seismic quality, high cost of field operations, environmental constraints, and drilling problems related to active tectonic stress regimes.

2. Rugged terrain, dense vegetation, lack of bedrock exposures, and poor seismic data hamper exploration and development activities in many fold – thrust belts. In these areas geologic interpretation is heavily dependent on the use of remote sensing data, including Landsat MSS, Landsat TM, SPOT, SAR, and RADARSAT. These data, combined with surface information, help define surface fold and fault patterns.

Chinese Translation and Key to Exercises

第 1 章　石油地质勘探技术

1.1　Palacios 油田:一个三维勘探史例

导语

1992 年下半年,Mitchell 能源公司在得克萨斯湾海岸做了首次三维地震测量,其目的是揭示由断距为 30 ~ 100ft 的隐蔽断层所组成的断层组合,这对 Matagorda 县的 Palacios 油田的油气生产影响极大。成功的三维地震勘探使我们能重建整个地区的地质发展史。本课文着重介绍了 Palacios 油田的三方面内容:三维地震勘探结果,地质历史,二维和三维勘探结果的差异性。

课文

1992 年下半年,Mitchell 能源公司在得克萨斯湾海岸做了首次三维地震测量,其目的是揭示由断距为 30 ~ 100ft 的隐蔽断层所组成的断层组合,这对 Matagorda 县的 Palacios 油田的油气生产影响极大。这次成功的三维地震勘探发现了与依据二维地震资料所做的完全不同的断层组合形式,使我们能重建整个地区的地质发展史。虽然这地区的油气开发已相当成熟(该油田发现于 1937 年),但仍有许多事情要研究(即使对 1953 年就已经在这里进行勘探的 Mitchell 公司也是如此)。三维地震测量则是最好的研究手段。

Palacios 油田位于县城西南部,滨海城镇 Palacios 位于 Tres Palacios 海湾油田的正南部。已产气 2.3×10^{11} ft^3 以上,油和凝析油 7×10^6bbl,产层埋深为 7500 ~ 15200ft,其构造为大的生长断层下降盘的滚动背斜。我们以最初的起源地为名,将这个断层称为 Palacios 断层。

本文主要研究 F - 1 和 G 砂层带。

多年以来,Mitchell 能源公司在油田范围内购买了覆盖 200 多英里的地震资料,虽然大多数资料是在 20 年前采集的,但对地震资料进行再处理,使之在一段时间内还可使用。1983 年,利用井控和这些资料做了 F - 1 砂层的构造图。该图的断层组合与当时资料闭合很好。同时,它还保持着得克萨斯湾海岸简单而古老的模型，即局部断层平行于主生长断层（Palacios 断层）和海岸线。这些断层应是平行的并有相似的生成时间。简而言之，这个模型认为构造应属于时间、空间上一致的地应力状态。或如我们的一位高级副总裁所说“还是这样简单，笨蛋”。为什么不呢？数据拟合相当好。可是，仍存在一些令人烦恼的生产异常现象，而这张构造图也解释不了。

1990 年，我们又做了 F-1 砂层构造图。这张图用了更多的二维数据，有些还是最近得到的 40 次覆盖专用资料。该图与 1983 年的构造图有所不同，但总的来说，它仍保持着 1983 年得到的简单构造模型，即断层组仍平行于西北方向。1983 年和 1990 年的构造图仅仅是多年来所做许多图中的 2 张；虽然每张图都有它自身的断层组合，但所有的图都遵循着简单平行的思想。

虽然油田中这些断层不大（断距很少超过 100ft），但是确定排水系统和预测储层质量时，将这些断层正确成图却是至关重要的。这些断层是封闭的，且砂层沉积与断层的活动是同时发生的。我们曾准备用手头上现有的 1990 年的构造图钻一口新的开发井，但为了油田的长期利益——因为我们想进一步开发它——我们做了一次三维地震测量，这有助于把断层组合敲定下来（同时，我们公司的创始人 George Mitchell 说我们需要对油田做三维地震测量，我们力图按照他所说的去做）。1992 年底，Tide Lines 地球物理公司采集了 7.5mi^2（1mile = 1.609km）的资料。

3D 地震勘探结果

红色的同相轴是 F-1 砂层的顶。在处理的初始阶段，我们将 3D 初叠数据体加载到一个工作站，以观察时间切片的早期构造形态。当我们看过时间切片后，立刻惊呆了！我们立即从时间切片上认识到 Palacios 断层的组合与我们预想的差异很大，我们曾预计，三维地震勘探将使断层位置发生某些小的变化，但没有想到会发生断层大的重新组合。有些断层走向东北，有些断层走向西，有些向南延伸时就消失了。

在三维地震勘探的基础上，1993 年我们又作了 F-1 砂层的新构造图。三维地震勘探范围用虚线框在图上标出，其他图上也用虚线框出。在图上存在三种截然不同的断层系统，呈现为红色、蓝色和橙色。

蓝色断层是东掉断层，并以 60°角与 Palacios 断层相接。蓝色断层下降盘的构造等值线平行于断层的走向，因此断层系统形成这个沉积构造。下降盘的断层改善了 F-1 砂层的质量。

红色断层是比较复杂的，但它们都是南掉断层，并以 30°角与 Palacios 断层相连。它们与蓝色断层有相似的发育时间。除了一条红色断层外，其余都终止于与蓝色断层系统交会处,对 F-1 砂层质量有不利影响。

第三个断裂系统为橘色断层系统,在更深的 G 砂层构造图上可以看得更清楚。这个断层系统平行于 Palacios 断层。实际上它是消失在位于 F 和 G 砂层之间的角度不整合面上的一个老的断层系统。不整合面为 *Nod. blan.* 古标志层,它是强地应力的顶。橙色断层对于圈闭 G 砂层中的气是至关重要的。

一条横测线(或走向测线)显示出这三种断层系统。红色和蓝色断层是发育时间相似、差异明显的断层系统,而橙色断层因平行于这条地震测线所以很难见到。需要重点指出的是,所有三维地震断层拾取是很精细的,且很明显,并与井中发现的所有断层吻合得严丝合缝。

地质历史

现在我们已认识到 Palacios 油田断层组合的错综复杂性是由 Palacios 断层的发育史和在其下降盘沉积物的沉积史所造成的。已观测到的断层组合形式是与刺穿构造有关的放射状分布断层,但在 Palacios 油田存在的刺穿既不是盐岩又不是页岩。造成断层系统发散的原因在于较深的 Frio 段。

第一次重要的沉积是下 Frio *Anomalina bilateralis* 段和 *Tex. miss.* 段。在下 Frio 段中的砂泥岩比率为最高。偏泥相的中 Frio *Discorbis D* 段和 *Nod. blun.* 段接着沉积,而在 *Discorbis D* 期间以超过 100:1的生长率沉积在 Palacios 断层上。可以证明 *Discorbis D* 层在上升盘仅有 35ft,而在下降盘可达近 6000ft 厚,在 F 和 G 砂层之间的 *Nod. blan.* 层的顶部生长率大大降低了。平行于 Palacios 断层的橘色断层是在这段时间产生的,Palacios 断层强烈地控制着造成该断层的应力。同时,让 Palacios 断层的滑动面生长和运动,使砂质下 Frio 层段向盆地方向倾斜和位移,倾斜度达 40°的这个层段,它是相对不可压缩的,成为上 Frio 沉积期间的支撑体。

在晚 Frio 期间,大多数产层 Frio 砂以小的生长率沉积在 Palacios 断层上,支撑砂体翼部的差异压实作用造成的坍塌使红色和蓝色断层系统十分活跃。没有三维勘探,我们不可能这样可靠地重建这个地区的地质发展史,那么为什么我们在二维地震资料上见不到这种断层组合呢?

二维与三维地震勘探对比

二维和三维地震构造图存在差异的一个原因是二维地震覆盖面不够。将二维地震测线突出标在 1990 年(三维以前)的构造图上,根据剖面最初解释的断层称为“01”。在几条二维地震剖面上,“01”断层是模糊可疑的。绿色圆圈突出用来解释“01”断层所使用的关键断层交点。根据三维地震勘探的结果,我们发现“01”断层的截点实际上是几种不同断层与二维地震测线的交点。我们错误地把地震测线上的断点给连成一条断层,为了尽力使在二维地震构造图上保持简单的断层组合形式,所以对其余断层也重复这个错误。只有用三维地震所提供的数据密度,我们才能发现一个准确的断层组合。

二维地震的另一个缺陷是不可能对小断层成像。我们购买的一条40次覆盖专用剖面是穿过测区中部的一条倾向测线,其覆盖次数是三维勘探最高覆盖次数的2倍,道间距为82.5ft,而相应的三维大小为110ft×110ft。根据三维数据体,用三维断层解释这条二维测线,两条剖面的水平和垂直比例尺相同,其断层位置和断层条数的差异是惊人的,我们从来没有在二维地震剖面上这样高精度、高准确度地解释出目前的断层组合。

一个明显的问题是"三维地震勘探帮助我们在Palacios油田上找到了新的储量了吗"? 回答是没有。在三维测量以前作的构造图指出,存在的断块都是未钻井的,且现有的井位都不在上面。不幸的是,实际上存在的放射状分布断层向我们指明,多数Palacios断层特性是与排液系统相通的,且从这里许多已钻的井来看,油层压力都已在递减。现在我们感到这里存在的潜力是有限的,对现今的天然气价格是无商业意义的。

虽然三维勘探没有为我们增加油气储量,但却为我们节省了钱。正如我们前面所指出的,在我们实施三维测量之前,我们已经准备好在老构造图的基础上钻一口井,而三维的测量结果使我们避免去钻那口井。因为三维勘探费用大约是钻一口开发井费用的1/3,这样可以节约的经费就将近100万美元。

进一步,我们已认识到小断层对这个油田和其他油田是至关重要的。目前,我们已在附近做一块三维勘探,上面有许多小的、以前构造图上没有的断层组成封闭断块,许多断块上还未钻过井。在这里我们希望能赚到钱,而不是仅节省钱。

当我们在Palacios油田上开始做三维勘探时,我们只想简单地确认一下断层组合,使一些开发井位置更加牢靠,没想到却以一个完全不同的断层组合而告终。其原因为:

(1)二维地震测线覆盖面不够以及隐蔽断层显示不出或错误成像,使得不可能准确和精细地解释正确的断层组合;

(2)二维地震勘探仅可提供简单的断层组合,而实际地壳的复杂性只能用三维地震数据来理解。

一位高级副总裁曾说"还是这样简单,笨蛋",又对我们说"思想还是这样顽固不化"。地球物理解释人员用二维资料,致使他们的解释方案太简单又错误百出,这已经太久了。现在用三维地震资料则可以认识到我们所勘探的真实构造和地层特征,并且我们可以以常规的,并以比原有期待更大的范围去阐述重要而且全新的有关构造地质和地层地质的概念。确实,有了三维资料以后,我们现在能够稳如泰山地思考了。

Key to Exercises

Ⅰ.

1. The purpose was to unravel a fault pattern consisting of subtle faults — with throws of 30 – 100 ft — that significantly influence oil and gas production from Palacios Field in Matagorda County.

2. Because they realized that the fault pattern at Palacios was much different than expected.

3. It was in Upper Frio time.

4. No. But, although we did not add reserves as a result of the 3 – D survey, we did save money.

5. No. The former means to think or act slowly and inflexibly; and the latter means to think calmly and reasonably.

Ⅱ. 1 ~ 5　ACBAB　6 ~ 10　CBABD

Ⅲ. 1 ~ 5　DCBAC

Ⅳ.

1. 1992 年下半年,Mitchell 能源公司在得克萨斯湾沿岸做了首次三维地震测量。

2. 但是,依然存在一些令人烦恼的生产异常现象,而这张构造图也解释不了。

3. 在晚 Frio 期间,大多数产层 Frio 砂以小的生长率沉积在 Palacios 断层上。

4. 没有三维勘探,我们不可能这样可靠地重建这个地区的地质发展史。

5. 只有用三维地震所提供的数据密度,我们才能发现一个准确的断层组合。

Ⅴ.

1. 在石油地质中,将物理应用到岩石研究(地球物理)中很重要。地球物理的广泛应用对于了解地壳,尤其是应用了现代板块构造理论后,对于了解沉积盆地的成因和潜在石油资源作出了重要贡献。更为特别的是,在理解褶皱、断层和底辟以及它们在石油圈闭过程中的作用时需要物理概念。

2. 地震学是地质学的一门分科，研究通过地球的波的运动。对由地震仪记录到的地震以及波形的研究，已经成为了解地球内部结构的主要资料来源。借助于某种专用地震仪或地震检波器，通过记录由人工爆炸所产生的地面运动，地震勘探就可以探查地下沉积带的地质构造。

1.2 堪萨斯州芬妮县斯图尔特油田薄层河道储集层的地震识别

导语

在科罗拉多、堪萨斯、得克萨斯及俄克拉荷马的部分地区，早宾夕法尼亚世（莫罗期）的河道砂体含有区域性储层。在堪萨斯州的西南部，这些储层埋深一般为4000～5000ft（1200～1500m），并且每口井约有（0.15～0.2）×10^6bbl原油的控制储量，经济效益很高。储集砂层构成了海进期河谷充填层序的一部分，该层序沉积于切入下伏密西西比纪碳酸盐岩的河道内。充填厚度最大达60ft（18m），一般为10～30ft（3～9m），沿河道厚度变化剧烈。因此。精细勾绘河道走向是很困难的。位于堪萨斯州芬妮县的斯图尔特油田就是这种储集类型的典型实例。最好的储集层存在于由潮汐改造作用形成的极细—细粒河道砂岩中。由于现有的二维地震及钻井资料无助于准确地确定河道的方位，因此早期试图使油田向东扩展的努力失败了。在注水驱油开始之前进行的三维地震调查，有助于：（1）查明现存干井之间河道的位置；（2）确定钻探能够成功的远景目标区。三维地震资料的进一步外推导致了一口干井，证实本区解释的局限性。因此，斯图尔特油田提供了勘探井间远景区时三维地震资料的能力及其局限性的一个重要实例研究。

课文

介绍

在得克萨斯、俄克拉荷马、堪萨斯和科罗拉多的巨大Hugoton海湾内，下宾夕法尼亚统莫罗河道砂为油气产层。这样的河道发育于海退期古盆地的内部及边缘。切入下伏上密西西比统的石灰岩侵蚀谷后来被冲积物、河口砂及海相泥岩所充填。产油的就是那些含河道砂岩的河道，它们或者沉积于高能环境中，或者受潮汐改造和筛选作用影响。

莫罗河道砂的分布通常是很复杂的，彼此相互交错。单个河道包含的不是一个而是数个处于不同地层层位和不同保存阶段的峡谷充填层序。晚期层序常常切入早期层序中。并不是所有的充填层序中都含有储集性质的砂岩体。此外，沿着大多数河道的净砂岩厚度及特征经常是突变的。因此，运用传统的地下方法预测储层就很困难。河道砂体平均厚度为 25 ~ 30ft (7.5 ~9.0m)，用二维地震资料解释来分辨潜在的储层就有很大的局限性。最近三维地震资料的认真应用使得分辨率有了明显提高。

位于堪萨斯州芬妮县的斯图尔特油田提供了研究该应用的很好范例。1956 年时将该油田作为浅层密西西比油藏进行勘探和开发，后来由于在 4700 ~4800ft(1430 ~1460m)深的上覆莫罗地层中有了意外的发现使油田得到扩展。有几口井钻遇了薄层产油砂层[15ft(4m)或更薄]。但作业人员不能确定相关砂岩较厚部分的位置。后来，在 1985 年由 Sharon 资源公司钻探的一口井(Sherman 3 井)钻遇了净厚 36.5ft(11m)的储集砂岩，分布于三个峡谷充填层序之中。根据后来采集的二维地震资料，到 1994 年，钻了 30 多口生产井，仅有 5 口干井。尽管取得了这样大的成功，但后来的钻探表明，厚达 55ft(16.6m)的最厚的河道砂仍未被钻到，而且不能通过二维地震资料对产油与不产油的河道亚相分布的细微差别作出恰当的解释。人们认识到这种解释的缺乏是联合开发和水驱研究的一个潜在的困难。

1994 年，在约 1.5mi^2(3.2km^2)的小范围内做了三维地震勘探，这对于加深对储层的认识是必要的，还表明了相关资料对研究其他地区薄储层的价值。河道边界的更好圈定及储层分布预测能力的提高是此次三维勘探的重要成果。根据获得的资料，Sharon 资源公司认为以前据二维地震异常所打的三口干井，可能刚好没有打在储集砂岩上，而是钻遇了主充填期形成的河道粉砂岩和泥岩。假如当时有三维资料，就不会钻这些干井。花 42000 美元的三维勘探费用将会节省 50 万美元的钻探费用。此外，对斯图尔特油田的进一步开发，包括二次采油，将因对莫罗河道相定位和特征描述能力的提高而大大受益。

下面是对有关斯图尔特油田三维地震资料再表征的地质和地球物理信息的总结。我们认为这些资料对于薄砂岩储层，尤其是对分布不规则或极复杂的砂岩储层的分析具有极大的潜在意义。

区域背景

斯图尔特油田位于 Hugoton 海湾的东北部，沿着巨大的 Hugoton 产气区边缘分布。它处于科罗拉多东南部、堪萨斯东部及俄克拉荷马西北部几个地区的中间部位，产油层位于下宾夕法尼亚统(莫罗)河道砂之中。这些河道砂是由于海进—海退旋回形成的。这种旋回是那时 Hugoton 海湾的特征。密西西比纪与宾夕法尼亚纪沉积层边界以区域性不整合面和由石灰岩到碎屑岩明显的沉积变化为标记，对应重要海退事件。海岸上超模式表明在连续的莫罗剖面上有最多达6～7个海进—海退旋回。这些旋回的保存情况随相对于Hugoton海湾边及周边隆起区限制的位置而变化。

早宾夕法尼亚世海进期间的Hugoton海湾是范围广阔的、以数个大型隆起区为界的北西向展布的臂状海湾。这些隆起区包括：延伸到东北部的中央堪萨斯隆起；延伸到北部的横大陆弯隆；延伸到西北部的Las Animas隆起/Ancestral前缘隆起和延伸到西部的Sierra Grande隆起。所有这些构造区域表明那时的构造活动都和早期古北美与南美大陆的碰撞有关（Kluth，1986；Rigo和Kanes，1986）。板块重建表明堪萨斯西南部地区处于赤道位置（Kluth，1986）。

在莫罗期，发源于中央堪萨斯隆起的向西南方向泄出的河流体系横穿此区。在高水位期间，海水侵没高地并向北扩展到内布拉斯加南部。在最低水位期间，海水几乎从堪萨斯东南部全部退出。在这时，堪萨斯中央隆起成为主要的碎屑供给区。形成的河流体系以在出露的海相陆架上的低梯度及强烈的季节性泄流为特征，这有助于快速下切作用及后期的加积作用（Krystinik和Blakeney，1990）。这些河流体系注入Anadarko盆地，在那里为三角洲复合体提供物源（Swanson，1979）。

莫罗初期的海退产生使密西西比地层出露向北逐渐变老的剥蚀面。早期河道切入到向北包括St. Louis和Spergen层段及向南包括Ste. Genevieve段（Wheeler等，1990）的碳酸盐岩中。河道发育可能局部受与基底断裂带有关的地形细微变化的影响（Sonnenherg，1985）。

莫罗河道的沉积模式

曾有几位作者（例如Sonnenberg，1985；Clark，1987；Krystinik和Blakeney，1990；Wheeler等，1990）展示了科罗拉多东部及堪萨斯西南部地区莫罗河道的详细沉积模式：

——最大海退引起了早期河道切入到下伏台地架碳酸盐岩中；

——海进早期，在冲刷面上形成了底部滞留沉积及粗砂岩；

——海进中期，产生进一步的河流加积作用，包括在叠置层序中主要为细—中粒的河道砂沉积，并多次与更细的泛滥平原粉砂和泥岩互层；

——海进晚期，产生了细粒的受潮汐影响（港湾的）的砂体，向上递变为潮坪和港湾/海湾泥（这时也以因海水侵蚀加宽峡谷为标志）；

——最大海进期，产生了海相泥岩沉积，并覆盖在河道充填层序上。

位于堪萨斯中央隆起西南翼的斯图尔特油田区发育了三套明显的峡谷充填层序（Clark和Steinhauser，1996）。该地区比科罗拉多的最东部海拔稍高一些，在科罗拉多，沿着Hugoton海湾的古轴线，有7个这样的层序已被识别，并已绘图(Blakeney 等，1990)。地震和钻井资料的证据表明斯图尔特油田的河道体系高度线性展布，并且在构造上受断层或与地垒—地堑发育有关的地形特性控制(C. Clark，1996，私人通讯)。

在任何一个特定的峡谷充填层序中，滞留沉积物、河道沉积物和海湾沉积物所占比例似乎与下列三种可能的因素有关：(1)Hugoton 海湾内的河道位置；(2)河道几何形态；(3)海平面上升的相对速率。沿着科罗拉多和堪萨斯州界之间的河道呈线状几何形态，并含有较大比例的粗粒下部河道沉积和底部滞留沉积。在更靠近海湾边缘的位置，例如堪萨斯州西南部芬妮县常发育低能河流体系。这些地区粗粒峡谷充填层序并不发育，而细粒河流相和海湾相沉积在整个层段中占有较大的比例。在这些地区线性形态的河道似乎通过“上涌水锥”强化了潮汐作用，从而形成了大量的再改造和筛选的河流碎屑物质。

但是，Krystinik 和 Blakeney(1990)根据他们在州边界区研究的结果，认为较大数量的河道粗碎屑物质反映了海水以相对固定速率逐渐海进。相反的是，这些作者将峡谷更快速的水淹解释为产生了充填层序，这些层序的特征为递增的上河道和受潮汐影响(河口湾)的沉积物，这些沉积物是较粗粒物质。

两幅解释性图件都被应用于斯图尔特油田。这个油田包含一个沿着 Hugoton 海湾东北边缘展布的线状河流体系。古海拔使得该区只是在莫罗较大海侵事件期间有渐进的海泛作用。这种海泛作用导致了海湾的形成及受潮汐影响的砂岩的沉积，包括再改造的河流相。在斯图尔特油田这种砂体尤其丰富，并且成为高质量的储层。

在堪萨斯的西南部，沿着 Hugoton 海湾的东翼，莫罗沉积层厚度变化范围为 0～300ft(0～90m)。在斯图尔特油田，莫罗层相当于整个的河道充填层序，厚达 53.5ft(24.0m)，一般为 10～35ft(3～11m)。粗碎屑岩及底部滞留沉积罕见或缺失；河流物质主要由极细—细砂岩、粉砂岩和页岩组成。在峡谷充填层段之上为莫罗组或阿托坎组的最下部，由海相页岩组成。这一整体组合构成了包括生、储、盖在内的很好的油气系统。

斯图尔特油田的莫罗储集层

在对大量钻井资料分析的基础上，在斯图尔特油田具有产能的莫罗河道复合体内识别出三个相互叠置的峡谷充填砂岩体。这些产层是由潮汐作用再改造和筛选形成的极细—细粒的、中等——较好分选的岩层。孔隙度和渗透率分别为 8%～20% 和 5～250mD。孔隙度低于 12% 的被认为是无效产层。最好的储层位于最早期的峡谷充填砂中(VF－3)，最差的储层为放射性较强的中部砂岩段(VF-2)。

整个河道复合体的几何形态、规模及方位可由净产层等厚图表示。这个河道长大于5mi(8km),宽度范围为0.25~0.40mi(0.40~0.65km)。沿河道延伸方向有几处净砂岩最大厚度达45~55ft(14~17m)。在这些地方峡谷方向由东西向突变为北西—南东向。这些地方的河道深度加大(等厚图上厚度最大),可能与下伏密西西比统碳酸盐岩的断裂活动引起的强烈冲刷有关。

Rader(1990)讨论了莫罗河道砂的成岩作用。早期成岩产物包括了绿泥石、次生加大石英和碳酸盐胶结物。碳酸盐胶结物在烃类进入前已溶解运移掉,成岩作用于烃类进入时停止。埋藏史资料表明烃类进入发生在晚白垩世(Rader,1990;Sonnenberg 等,1990)。

油气生产

斯图尔特油田的储量估算值为(5~7)$\times 10^6$bbl。

莫罗层单井预计可生产原油(0.15~0.20)$\times 10^6$bbl,包括初次平均采收0.1$\times 10^6$bbl 和注水再次采收(0.05~0.1)$\times 10^6$bbl。

产率从完井时的75~120bbl/d,下降到第一年内的30~50bbl/d,尔后下降很少或不下降。井在4750~4850ft(1440~1470m)深度范围内生产,完井是没有问题的。这使得油田开发有了更高的经济效益。

三维地震勘探的优势及局限性

为了帮助查明油田的东部边界,在1994年进行了三维地震勘探。此项勘探主要是提高储层特征的描述能力,从而使油田持续发展和为注水作业服务。此项勘探的覆盖面积为1.5mi^2(3.2km^2),中心位于Sec.7,T23S,R30W。1987年钻的三口干井似乎限定了该区莫罗产能的边界。这三口井(7-6 Bulger,7-7 Bulger 和 7-9 Bulger)都是据二维地震资料在Sec.7定的井位。二维资料显示了与莫罗河道有关的振幅异常。正如地震模型所示的,这种异常为复合波(波谷与波峰),对应于河道充填与下伏密西西比碳酸盐岩的接触面。尤其在厚度大于25ft(7.6m)时,莫罗波谷很明显。在7-6 Bulger 井和7-7 Bulger 井情况下,这种异常与致密的粉砂岩和河道充填的页岩有关。

三维资料的解释表明,这些井实际上钻到了含砂充填层的两侧。如果将7-6井和7-7井分别向东北和西南方向偏移几百英尺(约100m),它们都应该是产油的。

在钻探成功的基础上,根据二维地震资料中振幅的异常,1995年在东边又做了一块三维地震勘探,范围是Sec.8,Sec.9,Sec.16 和 Sec.17(T23S,

R30W)，面积约 1.5mi^2(3.2km^2)。在这个地区，两口钻遇莫罗产层的井已经完钻，但产能很低，然而有足够的储层压力表明附近有更高质量的砂岩。

三维地震资料表明莫罗峡谷在本区变宽，而总的充填层序减薄。根据三维资料的振幅异常所钻的一口井(8－6 Hafhch)位于边缘生产井东南方向300ft(91m)处，此处测井解释了18ft(5.5m)的莫罗砂层。8－6 Haflch 井未钻遇砂体，而钻遇了8ft(2.4m)细粒碎屑岩和下伏高孔隙度的 Ste Genevieve 灰岩，其声波时差为67s/ft(221s/m)。经辨认，该井位置紧靠 Ste. Genevieve 灰岩的隐伏露头边缘。三维地震剖面上的异常反映了与该层段侵蚀作用有关的孔隙度增大。

后来的地震模型部分地证明了这一点。相同厚度的莫罗砂岩和孔隙性好的 Ste. Genevieve 灰岩也会产生同样的响应。唯一的区别是莫罗砂层可能产生稍强的振幅，这要求精细调制莫罗层地震模型并确定该区三维解释的界限。这将会给堪萨斯州西南部其他地区的莫罗储层的勘探和开发提供基本的指导。

结论

具有高质量储集性能砂体的莫罗河道在科罗拉多州和堪萨斯州的 Hugoton 海湾内分布广泛。另外，特别在科罗拉多的东部地区，许多这样的河道已被勘探和开发，在堪萨斯的西部和西南部肯定存在仍未勘探的这类河道。本文所展示的资料对在这些尚未勘探的区域勘查莫罗砂岩有指导作用。

斯图尔特油田在应用三维地震资料圈定薄河道砂体时所导致的优缺点方面也提供了一个范例。这类储层在包括墨西哥湾沿岸在内的北美许多地区都存在，通常是河流相、三角洲相、潮汐、障壁沙坝、海底河道及其他岩相。由于不能精确地描述这些储层的分布并绘图，因此极大地制约着这类储层的开发(包括强化开采作用)。因此，薄砂岩储层构成了未来钻探的重要井间目标。正像斯图尔特油田实践证明的那样，三维勘探对于开发未知区是一个重要的新工具，但不能解决由于地质情况的复杂性而产生的所有困难。

Key to Exercises

Ⅰ.

1. Lower Pennsylvanian Morrowan channels are productive of oil and gas within the greater Hugoton embayment of Texas, Oklahoma, Kansas, and Colorado.

2. Evidence from seismic and well – log data indicates that the channel system at Stewart field is highly linear and was structurally controlled by faulting or by local topographic features related to horst – graben development.

3. The relative percentage of lag, channel, and estuarine material in any specific valley – fill sequence appears related to three possible factors: (1) location of the channel within the Hugoton embayment, (2) channel geometry, apt (3) relative rate of sea level rise.

4. Channels with linear geometries ill these areas seem to have enhanced tidal action through "fun – neling," thereby resulting in a larger amount of reworked and winnowed fluvial material.

5. No. Several wells encountered a thin, oil – productive sandstone (15ft (4m) or less), but operators were unable to locate the thicker part of the relevant sandstone.

Ⅱ. 1 ~ 5　BCBAD　6 ~ 10　AACBA

Ⅲ. 1 ~ 5　BCABA

Ⅳ.

1. 河道发育可能局部受与基底断裂带有关的地形细微变化的影响。

2. 这时也以因海水侵蚀加宽峡谷为标志。

3. 地震和钻井资料的证据表明斯图尔特油田的河道体系高度线性展布,并且在构造上受断层或与地垒—地堑发育有关的地形特性控制。

4. 孔隙度和渗透率分别为8% ~20% 和5 ~250mD。

5. 这将会给堪萨斯州西南部其他地区的莫罗储层的勘探和开发提供基本的指导。

Ⅴ.

1. 完整层序常常不能保存。这主要由于在后来的海退事件期间发育的河流产生了部分侵蚀作用。许多河道部分在莫罗沉积期间似乎保留在地形低洼部位,因此这实际上促使后续的河流体系再次占据其位置。大多数主河道显示了多幕峡谷充填的沉积作用影响。

2. Montgomery(1992)展示的沿科罗拉多与堪萨斯州界的莫罗储集层的信息表明,一口井的产率可能影响到其最终采收率。模型研究表明,对于一定的井距,若每天生产速率降至自流量或泵能的50% ,则最终采收率能稍有增加(最大到10%)。这可能是与河道储层有些欠压有关。未发现井距和最终采收率之间有任何关系。

1.3 复杂地形陆上数据的叠前处理

导语

本课提出一个新的以波动方程为基础的叠前地震处理方法。该方法仅有两个关键环节:速度分析和深度偏移。不管地表高程多高、如何变化及近地表速度变化多大,该方法均采用真正地表一致性静校正。它利用层析法估算浅层速度细节,求取双程波动方程有限差分解,以计算成像时间并在偏移过程中进行数据外推。文中列举了一组野外数据,由于高程剧烈变化及近地表速度的变化而不能满足常规共中心点(CMP)处理中的绝大多数假设条件,但用本文的方法成功地进行了处理。最终深度剖面上明显显示一复杂褶皱冲断层,这种特征在原来 CMP 处理后都是看不到的。

课文

引言

构造变形地区的多数地震测线都具有复杂的地形。没有什么文章论述过叠前偏移过程中的复杂地形问题。Rajasekaran 和 McMechan 提出过一个新的叠前处理方法,该方法对陆上和海上数据的处理都很便利,是一个用逆时偏移以波动方程为基础的处理方法。该方法的独特之处是,对地形剧烈变化的静校正不是作为一个直接的独立步骤,而是在偏移过程中隐含地进行的。本文的目的是简要介绍该叠前处理方法的要点。并把它应用到地表高程及表层速度变化剧烈的野外数据中,以证实该方法的可行性。

野外数据采集及特点

下面实例使用的野外数据来自南美洲西部的安第斯造山带。区域构造主要是挤压形成的。褶皱带呈西北走向,其轴线平行于现代峡谷。古老的、成熟岩石掩冲在年轻的非成熟岩石之上,岩性复杂多样,有盐岩、砂岩、石灰岩、碳酸盐岩以及火山岩。进行数据处理的测线部分,地表高程变化超过 1km。如此剧烈变化的地形导致最大静校正量(对垂向传播的波)高达 1700ms。处理了 500 炮,其野外采集参数为:炮间距 25m,道距 25m,240 道中间放炮排列,最小炮检距为 37.5m,最大炮检距为 3012.5m。时间采样间隔为 2ms,总记录长度 8s。数据信噪比低,地滚波强且沿测线特征变化不定。一般来说,较高高程的炮信号质量比较低高程的炮要好。反射相干性强。因在所有炮的记录上 3s 以下看不到任何相干同相轴,因此,数据只处理到 4s。对于常规和叠前处理,我们假设构造是二维的,与测线相垂直的方向上构造不变。当测线近似垂直构造走向时，这个假设基本上是正确的，但下面讨论的某些三维影响仍然存在。噪声压制在该区数据的常规和叠前处理中都非常关键。

常规处理

由于缺乏辅助的地质资料和解释，也没有必要的测井资料，因此数据处理是作为盲目试验进行的。这项工作未经人工合成数据，而是在野外数据上以 Marmousi 模式进行，且在无约束条件下用于实验。为了提供构造几何形状及速度的初始估计值，进行了常规处理。

为了增强信号，在评价预处理技术上花费了大量的时间和精力。认真检查了各炮的噪声道及强振幅随机噪声，许多噪声用人工方法剔除。处理中采用浮动基准面。最终处理流程中包括求取振幅均衡的扩散校正、反褶积及滤波。迭代地进行叠加速度分析和剩余静校正。在包括主反射（500 ~ 2000ms）的一个时窗内用求叠加能量极大法估算剩余静校正量。

叠前波动方程方法

综述

叠前处理有两个关系密切的目标：一是产生最佳偏移成像；二是准确地估算偏移速度。各共炮点道集的逆时偏移产生的图像作为偏移速度的函数，由叠加时产生最大图像的相干性进行对比。成像及速度估算是以迭代方式进行的。

输入数据单元是共炮集记录。仅估算一种速度分布，即层速度。利用初至波旅行时的透射层析法估算近地表速度分布；用迭代反射层析法或相干/聚焦分析可估算深层速度。用近地表层析速度分布及波场外推时的实际炮点和接收点位置巧妙地解决了静校正问题，简化了地滚波的压制。此时处理步骤大大简化；NMO、DMO 和静校正可完全不用，或者不作为一个独立步骤，而是在偏移的过程中隐含地进行。

常用的叠前波场处理流程建议如下：(1)将测量的观测系统信息加入道头以及对噪声道编辑和滤波；(2)用层析法估算近地表速度；(3)偏移前数据处理，包括各共炮集边道进行斜坡处理及时间轴倒转；(4)各炮集依次进行深度偏移、聚焦深度分析或反射层析成像后重新偏移；(5)将偏移后的各个共炮集叠加产生深度剖面。

预处理

现有数据集内的信息受到噪声的干扰，必须作一些预处理以增强信号能量。在叠前深度偏移前，对每个共炮集作了振幅均衡以补偿炮间能量大小差异和耦合变化，剔除了噪声道和噪声炮，在滤波器通带范围内作了带通滤波((8－12－40－50Hz)和谱均衡。谱均衡增强高频信号(Pritchett,个人通讯),并通过增加有用带宽改善偏移的分辨率。第一轮处理并不打算消除直达波或地滚坡。为了尽可能地减小外推的边界效应,各共炮集在时间上和空间上进行斜坡处理,并且在偏移前作了时间倒转。对数据在时间上进行了重采样,精确度达1ms,空间进行内插,精确度达12.5m,从而满足了有限差分稳定性和网格频散的要求。

近地表速度的层析法

偏移对所用的速度是很敏感的。这种现实开拓了利用偏移的可能性,它不仅是一个成像手段,还可以用来估算叠前速度。偏移可以与层析法相结合进行速度分析。

叠前处理中的关键一步是用于偏移的速度模型的近地表部分的层析成像(隐含速度静校正)。这一点通过将拾取的初至波的时间当作数据来实现。

偏移速度分析

偏移对速度的敏感性可用来估算深层构造的速度。较高的速度将同相轴偏移至更大的深度;较低的速度则将同相轴偏移到更浅的深度。用不同的恒速对数炮记录偏移,并观察成像结果的深度和空间排齐状况进行近地表以下的构造偏移速度分析。我们不仅可以通过观察偏移后的共地面位置道集中的反射是否排列成行来判断聚焦,还可以通过各深度偏移剖面叠加中的同相轴的相干性来判别聚焦。

叠前偏移

对每个共炮集单独地进行叠前逆时偏移。这既可用声学方式进行,也可用弹性方式进行。对本套数据,我们采用了根据双程波动方程的一个4阶有限差分解的型式。逆时偏移以波动方程的完全可逆性为基础。该方法对于有效、准确地处理速度垂直及横向变化是很理想的。由实际的炮点位置,用同样的波动方程可以计算每一炮记录成像条件的旅行时。由炮点至二维地下各深度点的直达波时间是偏移成像条件。对于复杂速度模型,与以射线为基础的方法相比,这种波动方程方法计算成像时间更精确,因为可以选择最小旅行时间和最大振幅的波动。为便于陡倾同相轴的偏移,在外推过程中使用了很大的偏移孔径(10km)。

偏移后处理和解释

为了减小输入数据中噪声的一些影响,我们进行了偏移后处理,甚至在单张共炮集记录上看不到信号的地方也通过道混波增强相干性。我们在62.5m范围内采用了5道倾斜混波,并采用了一个高通波数滤波器衰减近地表假象，改善剖面的相干性。在最终叠前剖面上看到的构造与叠加剖面或叠后偏移剖面上所看到的构造相比要相对地完整一些。叠前偏移剖面上的同相轴相干性更好、更连续。剖面具有掩冲断层的特征，山下解释有数个断裂地层特征。推测山谷有一向斜，但该地段构造不如山下构造连续，也许被断层切割。还有两个强同相轴，对角切割剖面，被解释为冲断层。

讨论

常规处理与叠前处理的比较

该项目的目标是在不规则地形的野外数据上进行叠前逆时处理试验。首先进行常规处理以提供一个近似成果，并为比较评价提供一个基础。

考虑到野外数据的质量，常规处理还是得到了一张较好的剖面，进一步做工作也许可能改进叠加剖面的质量，但我们叠加的成果似乎与分析前专业处理员的处理结果类似。标准处理步骤如静校正、NMO 和 DMO 是假定一个平的或缓慢变化的参考基准面计算静校正、动校正。这种假设对于大多数高程变化不大或浮动基准面随地下构造形态变化的情况是有效的。而对于像在这里处理的地形变化剧烈的数据，这种假设则不够准确。

当正常时差为双曲线型并且速度横向上有变化时，NMO 和 DMO 是有缺陷的，并会产生错误的结果。常规静校正仅对垂直传播才完全正确。如果叠加速度估算不正确，虽然它可能是相干的，但却不再是零炮检距剖面的准确的近似，即使偏移速度不是由叠加速度推导出来的，也得不到一个准确的地下界面图像。最佳叠加速度函数指的是产生相干性最好的叠加剖面的速度，它与偏移中使用的层速度无任何明显关系。这样，用叠加来提高信噪比是一种不以实际速度为基础的主观（虽然为正的）效应，并且，后继的叠后偏移不可避免地将相应的近似包括在偏移速度中。

在叠前处理方法中，数据被看做是由介质的物理特性改造过的一个波场。关于地下构造、介质速度、炮点及接收点高程或传播角度无任何限制性的假设。只需少量预处理工作，以求振幅均衡及信号增强。由于采用双程波动方程进行外推，因此陡倾角（甚至超过 90°）的构造也可以成像，无任何畸变。静校正的运用是隐含的。叠加的优越性（提高信噪比）依然存在。现在，偏移速度是实际的（层）速度，偏移后叠加成像的相干性对它们很敏感。这是因为叠加相干性和偏移聚焦现在都是一种（而不是两种）速度分布的结果。正是这种敏感性才是所有速度分析深度聚集算法的物理基础。调整指速度估算和偏移变成迭代方式。质量控制在叠前处理中更困难，因为为了获得可解释的成像需要处理大量数据。

静校正

偏移后的共炮集数据的最终叠加剖面上呈现良好的相干性,说明偏移过程中隐含地进行了静校正。这一点是用层析法估算近地表速度分析,从地面实际观测位置对各炮数据进行波场外推,应用由实际炮点位置计算成像时间条件来实现的。采用地面实际的炮点和接收点位置,高程静校正就是以真实地表一致性的方式进行的。速度静校正(由近地表速度变化引起的旅行时异常)通过估算速度时的偏移、初至波层析成像和根据数据本身来处理。对于所有传播角度的短、长波长静校正是在偏移过程中自动进行的。这样,无须用任何非实际的或昂贵的近似办法进行静校正来对付复杂地形。就估算长波长静校正而言,层析法一般比常规的静校正方法好。除此而外,也不涉及任何分层假设。通过初至波旅行时层析法获取的静校正信息的深度约等于最大炮检距的10%(这里约300m)。如果将反射数据以及折射数据包括在内,层析法就能用于估算较深层的速度。

限制和未来方向

要成功地估算静校正的变化就必须准确地估算近地表速度的分布。在有噪声的数据中获取可靠的时间拾取是很困难的。在使用层析法之前应认真评价旅行时拾取的一致性。当近地表不太复杂时,用准确的近地表速度进行逆时偏移可以把水平传播的面波与垂直传播的反射波分离,并在震源附近将这些面波作为一种强振幅异常成像。偏移后的高通波数滤波器可以消除这些异常。但在本文列举的实例中,深度滤波器未能完全消除这种近地表异常。初至切除后重新处理是比较成功的。

在存在复杂构造时,从信噪比达不到要求的数据中得到偏移所能接受的速度模型是非常困难的。叠前偏移只能估算一个地下宏观速度模型,需要增加地质约束条件才能得到详细的构造和速度。

在叠前处理时,当构造复杂和速度未知时,对处理进行质量控制的唯一办法是在可能有收益的地区选择一些炮记录,进行迭代偏移和叠加。每次迭代时,改变预处理的方式或用新的参数(如速度)。简而言之,在缺少解释过的剖面或没有区域地质家协助的情况下,质量控制是非常困难的,需要进行多次的深度偏移。

用不同的技术处理复杂地区的数据,并比较其结果,可加深对地下情况的认识。这是评价未勘探地区数据构造成像的一种有效方法。通过层析成像估算复杂地形地区数据的静校正是可行的。这也许是计算三维静校正最有效的方法。

在一个CRAY-YMP处理机上完成一炮数据的偏移需400cpu秒。尽管费用昂贵,但必须牢记这是总费用,因为不再需要许多中间步骤,而且这种方法可处理相当困难的数据,而用不太精确的方法处理这些数据则不能给出满意的结果。这使得该方法不仅对二维是可行的,而且对三维也是可行的。三维数据管理用单炮/偏移方法来进行简化。

只有当采集到足够空间采样的全三维、三分量地震数据时,才可能进行波场处理。此时才可以在附加的地质和地球物理约束条件的指引下使用一种有优良的信号增强的方法和准确的波场成像方法的混合处理技术。

结论

Marmousi 试验揭示了目前构造复杂地区成像和估算速度的可能性,并且认识到成像的关键并非在于成像本身而是成像速度的估算。当涉及复杂地形时,这一问题将更为复杂。旅行时异常需要以地表一致性方式进行校正。什么时候和如何进行这些校正,将决定整个处理流程的成败。目前已提出许多解决复杂地形问题的方法,但有关在叠前对陆上数据应用这些方法的报告以前尚未发表过。

我们提出了一种简单的方法去进行真正的波场处理,其中静校正是在偏移过程中,以真正地表一致性的方式隐含地进行的。对于这种棘手的问题,我们还未听说有一种更简单的、或更巧妙的解决办法。我们已向前迈了一步,成功地把叠前偏移运用于复杂陆上数据,并证实该方法确实可行,效果比常规处理有明显改进。

Key to Exercises

Ⅰ.

1. A typical prestack wavefield processing sequence is suggested as follows: (1) addition of survey geometry to trace headers, and editing and filtering noisy traces; (2) estimation of near – surface velocities by tomography; (3) data conditioning prior to migration, which includes tapering of the edges and reversal of time axis of each common – shot gather; (4) depth migration of each shot gather in turn, with an option to remigrate after focusing depth analysis or reflection tomography; and (5) stacking over the individual migrated source gathers to produce a depth section.

2. A key step in this implementation of prestack processing is tomographic imaging of the near – surface part of the velocity model for use in migration (which implicitly includes velocity statics).

3. Reverse – time migration is based on the complete reversibility of wave

-equation. It is ideal for handling both vertical and lateral velocity variations efficiently and accurately

4. Yes, it is. Because arrivals with minimum traveltimes and / or maximum amplitudes can be selected (Geoltrain and Brae, 1993) for the image conditions.

5. The goal of the project was to test prestack reverse-time processing on field data with irregular topography.

Ⅱ. 1~5　ABCBA　6~10　ADABC

Ⅲ. 1~5　ADBAD

Ⅳ.

1. 一般来说,较高高程的炮信号质量比较低高程的炮要好,反射相干性强。

2. 这种现实开拓了利用偏移的可能性,即它不仅是一个成像手段,还可以用来估算叠前速度。

3. 在最终叠前剖面上看见的构造与叠加剖面或叠后偏移剖面上所看见的构造相比要相对地完整一些。

4. 最佳叠加速度函数指的是产生相干性最好的叠加剖面的速度,它与偏移中使用的层速度无任何明显关系。

5. 就估算长波长静校正而言,层析法一般比常规的静校正方法好。

Ⅴ.

1. 常规处理的目的是产生近似零炮检距的剖面(至少从运动学角度看)成像。只要关于地层(平直)、正常时差(双曲线)、反射(临界角前)和速度横向变化(无)等大多数假设条件得到满足,便会实现上述成像。也允许存在某些偏差,但应足够小。更令人满意的解决办法是把数据看作一个完整的波场。

2. 高程的剧烈变化意味着三维块状构造的存在,并且还会产生附加的侧面噪声,这是在二维测线上很难识别与消除的。垂直检波器只记录波场的垂直分量,当存在高角度的大型构造时,反射的纵波将是不垂直的。构造引起的噪声只有用三维采集和处理才能正确地体现出来。

第2章 油藏特征

2.1 Vacuum 油田的动态油藏特征

导语

延时多组分地震测量使动态油藏特征和动态油藏模型的建立成为可能。也就是说,它有助于做出经济上和技术上的综合决策。这种决策能够延长油藏的开采期限,并能提高采收率,同时降低风险和环境影响。

本课简要叙述了在 Mines 的科罗拉多研究所利用油藏特征工程(RCP),四维三分量地震技术在新墨西哥州 Vacuum 油田的研究应用。这种技术能够为有效的油藏特征提供所需的最为全面的信息,本文将讨论这种技术测定各向异性及渗透率的可能性,并用一个在新墨西哥州 Vacuum 油田的研究实例得出结论。

课文

四维三分量地震

延时(或四维)地震最简单的定义不过是用一个重复的测量或以后在同一地理位置进行的测量与原来的测量进行对比。这些测量最佳测定时间的确定应与油藏模型和经济情况结合起来。

多分量(或三维)地震学包括记录两个水平分量和一个垂直分量。这种记录地震数据的方法比单独的常规纵波地震测量能够提供更加全面的有关油藏岩石流体特性及其变化的信息。比较传播时间或速度测量,振幅及纵、横波的频率,使岩石和流体特性及其随时间变化的测定成为可能。

当把多分量地震学组合成延时多分量地震学时,综合的方法是一种体积变化方法。也就是说,这种方法提供了测定油藏大块岩石/流体特性随时间变化的性能,速度和衰减系数的测量包含了油藏岩石内流体状态及其分布的信息,特别在低宽高比(裂缝性孔隙或裂缝)的岩石内更是如此。

各向异性

比起常规地震,横波的各向异性能够提供更为精细的分辨率。各向异性是岩石和油藏岩组内微观结构的度量。它把地震资料的体分辨率与包括孔隙度、渗透率、流体及流动通道等重要油藏描述特征的地震测定结合起来。通过地震横波各向异性与油藏参数的结合，就能进行较好的油藏管理。例如，分离横波在各向异性介质的衰减和地震波各向异性的特性使我们对储层渗透率进行测定成为可能。定向渗透率校正类似于高速横波的定向。低速分离横波受孔隙结构的可塑性影响，并且它是渗透率的主要标志，而高速分离横波则受孔隙或裂缝中流体状态的影响。

通过各向异性结构与储层渗透性结构的结合，我们就能基于地震使油藏模拟的渗透率和流动模拟的渗透率标准化。这种技术有助于在油藏开采的各个阶段进行油藏管理。油藏特性的预测主要由渗透率和渗透率结构所确定。如果能够提高面积波及效率，并能有效地处理油藏低渗透率的未波及区，那么油藏开采效果就能得到提高。借助于四维三分量地震测量和动态油藏特征，我们就能预测和监测油层波及系数。

渗透率

利用四维三分量地震技术检测大块岩石/流体特性的能力使最重要的储层传导特性描述——即渗透率的描述成为可能。为了得到精确的流动模拟，必须对井之间的渗透率进行定义，并在油藏模拟中把渗透率网格化。由于四维三分量地震有高的体分辨率，我们就能更加精确地描述油藏流体空间及它们随时间的变化情况。

因此，我们能够监测开采过程中的波及效率，以便利用围绕油藏低渗透区的沟道作用了解储层是否未被波及以及发生沟道作用的地方的储层波及比例。为了做到这一点，我们可以改变注入方法以便使油藏的波及更为有效。我们不但能够监测油藏特性，而且还能对其进行超前预测。对于预测油藏特性和指导油藏管理来说，这种技术的最大经济效益是把大块岩石/流体性质变化从地震到地质细胞油藏模拟结合到一起。

实例研究

在新墨西哥州 Lea 地区的 Vacuum 油田实施了一次延时四维多分量的试验研究，这里圣安德罗斯碳酸盐岩油层的平均开采深度为 4300ft。这是一个壮年期油田，自从 1978 年就通过注水把压力维持在饱和压力以上，并且现在已经处于 CO_2 驱替的早期阶段。

相隔八个星期采集了两次三维三分量的测量。在这两次测量期间，把 $50000000ft^3$ 的 CO_2 注入了 CVU－97 井。在后来的地震采集中，CO_2 被从同一井中抽出。

利用油藏特征工程进行的研究说明，储层的非均质性比预想的要普遍得多。实施油藏流体流动预测非常困难，并且必须进 CO_2 驱替监测。在这次研究过程中，研究尚未完成而新的资料就已采集出来。从测井、岩心数据和先前采集的区域性三维数据集着手,形成了一个划分复杂的油藏模型。1996 年可用于解释的多分量资料的第一次迭代就得到了对空间中不同岩石特性具有较高分辨率的图像。三维三分量资料的第二次迭代得到了 CO_2 层带沿着高渗透裂缝带流出井筒的延时图像。

三维解释

从三维数据集中得到的不同纵波属性说明了圣安德罗斯层段储层的非均质性,最具有说服力并使人信服的属性是相干性。储层中断裂作用存在的证据是受到了构造活动性的改造,这种构造活动性到二叠系瓜达鲁普阶段,圣安德罗斯碳酸岩沉积时已经大大减弱了。从三维纵波资料中得出的相干属性被用于确定一旦注入 CO_2 时,断层是否对 CO_2 通过的通道产生影响。

区分由断层引起的地震不连续面和其他与噪声和倾斜反射层有关的不连续面的主要辨别特征是倾角。为了突出断层描述,把从地震数据中计算出的相干属性进行频率—波数域扇形滤波,以切除倾角小于每道 4ms(大约 0°~20°)的同相轴。

把相同的相干性变形应用于三维纵波测量。在 CVU—97 的 CO_2 注入井的南部和西部,是第三条断层,呈现出弯曲形态,它向北弯曲,与大的东北向断层交汇。

四维三分量解释

在这次研究中,解释的目的是对油藏进行描述,并试图描述与 CO_2 注入相联系的动态油藏生产中圣安德罗斯层段所发生的任何变化。提取出从全部数据集中得到的大量属性,并朝这一目的对其进行分析研究。横波速度的各向异性提供了较高级别的体分辨率,并且这种各向异性也是检测与 CO_2 注入相联系的油藏动态特征的标志。

从圣安德罗斯层顶到其底层,利用不同低速和高速横波等时线实施了这些测量。利用高速横波(S1)等时线消除来自于圣安德罗斯储层上部浅层的各向异性影响就可以校正这种差异。在初始的和复测的各向异性图之间明显地存在差异。利用产生于不同测量之间的油藏附加压力可以预测这种差异。可以看出这种差异大部分存在于测量区域的西北部分,此处的井呈现出较好的开采/注入特性。

初始各向异性值减去复测的各向异性值而得到的差异图表明,在 CVU—97 的 CO_2 注入井上倾方向南 600ft 处有一较大的异常。差异图放大 100 倍为接近于百分之一的差异。这种异常说明,在两次测量之间大约有 12% 的差异(大于加上或减去的 6% 的差异背景值)。

初始各向异性图显示出在四维异常的范围内有一个近于零各向异性的区域,说明存在以下两种可能:(1)岩石没有开放性裂缝;(2)开放性裂缝存在于两个共扼的方向上。

异常区域内的差异说明初始测量和重复测量之间高速横波速度增加了17%。通过改变低宽高比裂缝的几何形态,利用库斯特—图克兹模拟对这种影响进行模拟试验。横波受孔隙的宽高比或由 CO_2 注入而导致的微裂缝选择性开启的变化控制。随着低宽高比裂缝孔隙度的最终变化,高速横波(S1)速度衰减较少。高速横波和低速横波都受到 CO_2 注入的影响,但各向异性异常的特征证实了高速横波的变化量最大。裂缝中流体的黏度或饱和度的变化可能影响裂缝系统的稳定性,从而导致高速横波速度的增加,然而定量的变化还没有模拟出。根据应力场的统一性,通过对油藏和注入 CO_2 的试压分析,证实了在 CO_2 注入点附近与最大应力场方向相垂直的微裂缝的选择性闭合。

库斯特—图克兹模型也能预测纵波速度的变化。如果模型正确的话,纵波速度增加 7% 就能得出结果(大大低于高速横波速度变化的 17%)。在注入层段中计算出地层四维解释的纵波时差,正如所预测的那样,揭示出速度增加了 7%。

油藏特征工程和这项工程的工业合作者正在同一位置继续开展这项研究,监测全面的水气交替注入的 CO_2 驱替。在多井注入方案中至少要采集三次附加的三维三分量测量值,在这个方案中一年注入的 CO_2 体积大约是这次研究中的 40 倍。

结论

延时多分量技术(四维三分量)为经济高效的烃类开采提供了当前可用的最为全面的信息。利用这种技术,对比分析及计算机模拟的模型可以揭示油藏动态特性的变化。不同测量之间的差异可以指示出油藏开采中的变化,而且通过油藏模型校正之后,这些变化还能预测油藏的性能。

不用大量增加作业成本,动态油藏特征就能最大限度地提高油藏采收率,在工程项目操作周期的早期使用这种技术具有经济潜力,因此能够指导开发。例如,渗透率的测定和非对称性流体流动的监测有助于死油的开采。

对于包括注水开发的其他强化开采作业,动态油藏特征是变化的。通过使用这种技术指导加密钻井或水平钻井,能够节省相当大的费用,而且并不妨碍开发钻井。我们认为进一步研究将体现出这种研究方法在开发的全阶段(从发现到衰竭)有着广泛的应用,并有助于勘探阶段烃类的直接检测。

Key to Exercises

Ⅰ.

1. Multicomponent (or 3 – C) seismology involves recording two horizontal components and one vertical component.

2. Anisotropy is a measure of fine – scale structure within rock and reservoir fabric.

3. By linking anisotropy structure to permeability structure of the reservoir, we can seismically calibrate permeability for reservoir modeling and flow simulation.

4. Yes, it can.

5. Economically efficient hydrocarbon exploitation.

Ⅱ. 1 ~ 5 BADCC 6 ~ 10 ACDBB

Ⅲ. 1 – 5 ADDBC

Ⅳ.

1. 相对于单独的常规纵波地震测量,这种记录地震数据的方法能够提供更加全面的有关油藏岩石流体特性及其变化的信息。

2. 例如,分离横波在各向异性介质的衰减和地震波各向异性的特性使我们对储层渗透率进行测定成为可能。

3. 因此,我们能够监测开采过程中的波及效率,以便利用围绕油藏低渗透区的沟道作用了解储层是否未被波及以及发生沟道作用的地方的储层波及比例。

4. 从三维纵波资料中得出的相干属性被用于确定一旦注入 CO_2 时,断层是否对 CO_2 通过的通道产生影响。

5. 可以看出这种差异大部分存在于测量区域的西北部分,此处的井呈现出较好的开采/注入特性。

Ⅴ.

1. 渗透率是岩层传导流体的能力。从用法上讲,渗透率就是岩层传导流体能力的术语。它是多孔介质的一个特性,是对介质传导流体能力的量度。因此渗透率的测量是对特定物质流体传递能力的测量。

2. 虽然油层是具有一定孔隙度和渗透率的多孔介质,但它绝不是性质稳定的均质岩层。通常情况下,油层是由很多性质不同的岩层所组成。在提高采收率试验中,油层渗透率的差异是一个很重要的因素。

2.2 油藏描述中的挑战(Ⅰ)

导语

尽管目前有关油藏描述的实施和技术非常活跃且最近取得了许多明显的进展,但油田的平均采收率并没有显著提高,实际生产经常与预测不符。石油公司中日常用于油藏特性的模拟、作图、网格化、可视化以及预测的地学和(或)工程方法在最近5年中也没有明显改变。本文总结了油藏描述实践和研究中的最新技术和趋向,提出并讨论了油藏描述今后的发展方向和重点。

课文

引言

油藏描述方面的论文、参考文献、学术讨论会和讲座逐年明显增加。事实上,上述活动使世界上一切石油公司和开发机构能够立即获得所有新的进展、想法和成果。因此,这一技术缺乏明显效果这一事实有些让人难以理解。可能是为时太早,还不到可以看出成果的时候;也许那些于1987年至1992年间投产的油气田以及那些开发设计得益于三维地震数据、多学科研究方法、良好的露头类比对地质模型的控制、精细的模拟网格系统、由露头控制和地震数据作为条件的“数值岩石模拟”、井中观测结果、其他信息(诸如提供侧向变化的水平井取心技术等的油气田)将会证明,储层描述的研究和发展因预测的正确和采收率的不断提高确确实实地得到了回报;或者是我们正面临一个典型的实施问题,也可能是我们在自己的油田并不实施我们在会议上所鼓吹的一切;或是那些写论文和参加会议的人(包括我们自己)只在某些特定的油藏利用这一新的工具、技术和方法,而不是解决油藏描述研究和发展方面遇到的普遍问题。这样,油田的采收率能够实际上得到提高吗?说到底,每一个油田都是一个新的“研究”项目。

即使在许多盆地中发现和开发了大的、“容易”的油藏,但我们并没有驱使自然界献出比以前更多的石油。甚至近来的生产预测曲线令人吃惊地与实际不符。我们能够做些什么?什么是油藏描述的主要挑战?我们怎样抓住重点?谁应该进行这项研究?哪些是可能收效最大的领域?

本文提出了许多对于将来研究和发展的建议,但我们相信,为了驱使自然界献出更多的石油,你必须了解她。因此,由已知技术(如地震)或尚未发现的技术得到详细的储层的层析成像。这种层析成像能够以1m的分辨率产生所有断层的图像、正确的构造图、地质结构中的流通单元和屏障的细节,因而应摆在油藏描述研究与开发进程表的首位。

目标

油藏描述的主要目的是在下列方面帮助油田开发和油藏管理部门:(1)足够详细地描述油藏(详细的程度取决于开发机制);(2)对已知的油藏通过最优化,以较好的位置上的较少的井、最小的投资得到更多的油气;(3)尽可能地减少生产预测的不确定性。

地质家和工程师以前达到的程度是将来在这一地区进行研究和发展需要作什么工作的良好标志。

已经过去的、或者事后的认识是准确的科学?

近来,通过对一些于20世纪70年代发现和评价,20世纪70和80年代生产的英国北海水驱油田的检查发现,开发中存在大量的超支现象,平均超支为95%,最大达97.4%!操作和维护费用比计划平均高出140%,首批原油生产比计划落后1~3年。平均只实现了65%的高峰产量,由于油井见水时间比预计的大大提前,石油回收的时间滞后。水及其他液体的总体处理能力总是被低估,因此大多数平台在很短时间后就显得能力不足。水的回注率也经常被高估。在计划阶段出了什么毛病?为什么出现这么多不准确的预测?所有的油田都是用数值模拟进行过评价和优化的啊!那么是资料不足,资料质量差,还是资料应用得不好?

当英国大陆架的发展史最终完稿后,预测不准确的理由可能有以下几点:(1)只有二维资料、检测的断层少,构造图不准确;(2)模拟模型太均质化,所有的参数都被平均化了,参数变化范围不足,对相变影响考虑不足(即缺乏详细的地质模型);(3)模拟网格太粗,由于没有空间分辨率,不能准确地模拟驱动机制;(4)在模拟模型中夸大了储层的纵向联系,不允许有流失层;(5)模拟模型中的侧向联系被夸大,所有的油层都是连续的,模型中断层太少。

根据上述分析可以预计:在最不均质的油田中,实际生产情况与预计的最不符合。根据Corrigan最近的论文,这一规律与大多数情况符合。上述分析仅适用于北海大陆架的一些特定油田。但是我们相信,对于其他油田开发史的类似分析会得出同样的结论。

过去的地质研究工作没有多少可以吹嘘的!在这方面受责难最多的是油藏描述做得不够,用粗网格块来表示油藏不够准确。但公正地说,由于通常只有二维资料,限制了预测的准确性。

为了使将来的研究和发展走上正确的道路,现在就必须:(1)完成可能有收益的地区的项目分析工作(在这些地区,油田是根据沉积环境和采收机制等来划分的);(2)对油田某一实际特性的估计和预测进行综合的事后研究,提出可能会对石油工业非常有益的结论和建议;(3)制作一份工作上碰到的最典型问题和陷阱以及由油田开发小组设计的最聪明的解决办法的表格;(4)从地质学家手里得到一份"我已做了什么和我希望我能够做什么"的表格,用来提供研究方向;(5)提出减少不确定性的建议,包括应急计划和灵活安排。

这种分析能够提供将来面临的主要的挑战,而且会形成市场需要(如短期解决问题的研究)和技术推动(如高风险和长期研究)之间的平衡。

当前:典型公司的现行做法

在过去的5~10年中,在油田地质、物探、测井和油藏工程方面都取得了很大进展。可是,我们要声明,迄今为止,这些进展对典型油气公司的日常工作并没有发生多大影响,尽管某些公司例外。大部分成果仍在学院和研究中心的实验室里或在油气公司的研究和发展部门中,等待着被用于实践。下面,我们简单地介绍一下各种专业对开发重要油田的作用。

地球物理学:构造模型和其他

地震资料通常能发现油田,揭示它们的纵向和横向分布,提供油藏表面形态(如储层顶面的深度图和油藏内其他层位的深度图),提供一些重要的参数(圈闭面积和闭合高度)用于进行石油储量计算,并指明重要断层的位置,这在建立油藏模型时是必须知道的有用资料。

现在,任何东西都代替不了高质量的三维地震解释,根据二维资料做出的构造图质量是很差的,因为二维资料和三维资料解释的构造实际上是完全不同的。原油产量随时间的变化不是由于净/总比、孔隙度和含水饱和度的变化,而是由于地震解释的变化,例如当三维地震结束后,或者是在发现新的气/油界面和(或)油/水界面位置时,或者根据生产资料做出新的地质模型时。

多年来,地震采集、处理和解释技术一直在发展。过去10年内,在地下科学的各学科中,地球物理学经历了最深刻的技术变化。我们相信,这个领域持续的发展和技术进步是油藏描述取得重要改善的先决条件。地震分辨率和灵敏度一直在提高,它是否会以同样的速度发展是一个等待回答的问题。使用属性分析技术、VSP资料、定期地震监视技术等,地震解释已经对下述方面起了作用:(1)油藏结构图,因为追踪河道砂和区分砂、泥岩有时已成为可能;(2)油藏性质图,如净/总比、孔隙度和水饱和度;(3)确定油水界面;(4)监视流体前缘。现在可以迅速而方便地在强大的计算机工作站上综合利用测井曲线、岩心、VSP和三维地震资料。数据库方面的改善和地震资料的数字化储存已经使工作效率大大提高。

井间地震解释可能不久就会用于生产前预测油层和非油层的连续性。使用安装在北海海底的永久性检波器进行的定期地震监测能够定期提供生产过程中流体前缘的位置图。这一技术将会有重要的突破,并极大地加强油藏管理。

许多油气公司都没有充分利用三维地震资料和使用反演及其他技术。三维地震资料能够揭示基本的地质特征和重要的不均匀性。此外,我们建议,让一些有经验的、甚至是不同公司的地球物理专家分析相同的资料,做一些不同的解释。当考虑了一些不同的解释后,评价井就可能定在不确定性最多的位置,而把生产井放在风险最小的位置。

石油物理学:测井分析

第一口井完钻并测井后,石油物理学家开始工作。根据一系列测井曲线和理论及经验公式,测井分析者求出重要的岩石物性参数。通常,孔隙度、渗透率、油和(或)含水饱和度及净/总比是其中最重要的。

过去的5至10年里,测井工具已大大改善。开发了一些新的工具和随钻测井,旧的工具得到改善。这就提供了更多的资料、更高的精度和更高的分辨率。分析方法上的改进并不很显著。数据库、更快的计算机和高质量的绘图仪大大地减少了手工作业并提高了成果质量,但基本的技术仍是相同的。井中所遇到的岩相、天然断裂以及地层倾角的可视化现在已是常用技术。

采油地质学:描述油藏

在开发队伍里,通常由采油或油藏地质家相互合作,利用所有相关的资料做出各种地质图件。

这项工作是进行定量的、足够详细的并且与所有资料相吻合的油藏描述。输入的资料有:构造模式和地质学家提供的其他资料、岩石物理学家提供的静态的井资料(如岩心资料和测井得出的物性资料)、油藏工程师提供的动态测试资料,还包括地球科学家在建立和修改油藏模型过程中得出的所有认识。

利用岩心资料和测井曲线(如果有的话),分析者能够沿井迹确定沉积建造、流体单元和岩相,进行井间对比。今天,这种工作主要是由手工完成的,尽管有一些软件可有所帮助。用二维剖面或栅状图进行井间对比,这种任务需要地质学家的技术和想象力,因为结果需要承受检验。现已有一些二维和三维软件可帮助进行这些工作。

当基本地质构造被建立后，油藏通常被划分为一系列的层、一般为5～20层。界面可以根据地震资料的构造解释确定，或者它们是仅仅根据在有限井之间的内插技术求出的简单的层面。在各层中，赋予岩石物理学家所提供的物性参数，可以是常数，也可以根据不同的等值线赋值。这种图件可由地质学家利用沉积相的知识手工作出，或者由计算机根据井间的内插作出。

当算出油藏的总体积和基本物性后，就可以计算油气产量，这个量值实际上是由不确定性分析所获得的一个体积参数确定的；因而有必要把基本的地质模型——包括会影响生产的地质特征、主要不确定性因素（如水层大小、隔层大小，断层封闭能力和可能未发现的断层的数量等）一并交给油藏工程师，以进行灵敏性分析。

油藏工程：动态分析

虽然以数值模拟网格表示的更先进的地质模型正被逐渐应用，但目前大部分油藏模拟仍然是使用较稀测网的简单的层状模式，且每一层使用常数的或计算机内插得物性值。

众所周知，模拟中输入的数据是不确定的，因此对输入的各种参数进行敏感性分析是非常重要的。模拟模型是发现各种不确定性的影响的主要工具。通常的做法是只改变一个参数，其他参数保持不变，这样来评价这个参数的影响。用这样的方法把各个参数评价完后，就知道了某一个参数变化时最后结果的可能变化范围。但是，当某些参数同时变化时，用这种方法就不能发现它们对最后结果的影响。

近来，统计学上的一些思想被用于设计和分析敏感性。这一成果会大大减少模拟的次数，或更多地获得信息。用这一技术可以评价各种参数之间的相互作用。

优化生产战略通常也是油藏工程师的责任。确定合适的生产井数、合适的位置、最佳的射孔层位，选择优化的高峰产量和生产能力并设计合适的采油方案，考虑各种动态和静态的不确定性，这些都是油藏工程师责无旁贷的任务。

最后一个步骤是生产史谐配。在经过一段时间的生产或长时间的试油后，可以得到最初的生产曲线，通常这些生产曲线与预测的生产模拟是不符合的。油藏工程师要对模拟模型进行一些调整（例如，引进新的封闭断层、把页岩层的长度加大或调整相对渗透率）使模型与实际曲线相符合，这一工作在油田生产过程中重复多次。尽管已出版了20多篇关于自动自适应谐配的文章，但仍然缺乏减少这种工作量的实际工具，而且当地质资料变化时，地球科学家必须占据控制地位。这种工作永远不会完全自动化,非唯一性总是在所难免。

作业队

石油工业的一个趋势是把上述所有的学科综合到一个作业队中,它还包括设备工程师和经济师。这支队伍坐在一起,把地质桌放在中间,在工作中紧密结合。队伍中的各个成员必须互相理解相互尊重并保持相互联系。重点是通过团队作业方法进行革新和创造,形成一个面向用户的工作方法。

Key to Exercises

Ⅰ.

1. The main goals of reservoir characterization research are to aid field – development and reservoir – management teams in (1) describing the reservoir in sufficient detail (the detail required depends on the recovery mechanism), (2) outsmarting Nature to obtain higher recoveries with fewer wells in better positions at minimum cost through optimization, for a given reservoir description, and (3) reducing to a minimum uncertainty in production forecasts.

2. Geophysics: the structural model and a lot more; petrophysics: the log analysis production; geology: describing the reservoir; the team.

3. Continued advancement and technological gains in geophysics.

4. Porosity, permeability, water and / or oil saturation, and the net – to – gross ratio are usually the most important.

5. Play the leading role or dominate.

Ⅱ. 1 ~ 5 AABBB 6 ~ 10 CCCDD

Ⅲ. 1 ~ 5 ABACB

Ⅳ.

1. 本文提出了许多将来研究和发展的建议,但我们相信,为了驱使自然界献出更多石油,你必须了解她。

2. 地质家和工程师以前达到的程度是将来在这一地区进行研究和发展需要作什么工作的良好标志。

3. 现在,任何东西都代替不了高质量的三维地震解释。

4. 井中所遇到的岩相、天然断裂以及地层倾角的可视化现在已是常用技术。

5. 近来,统计学上的一些思想被用于设计和敏感性分析。

V.

1. 过去的地质研究工作没有多少可以吹嘘的！在这方面受责难最多的是油藏描述做得不够，用粗网格块来表示油藏不够准确。但是，公正地说，由于通常只有二维资料，限制了预测的准确性。

2. 地震资料通常能发现油田，揭示它们的纵向和横向分布，提供油藏表面形态（如储层顶面的深度图和油藏内其他层位的深度图），提供一些重要的参数（圈闭面积和闭合高度）用于进行石油储量计算，并指明重要断层的位置，这在建立油藏模型时是必须知道的有用资料。

2.3 油藏描述中的挑战（Ⅱ）

导语

尽管目前有关油藏描述的实践和有关油藏描述的技术非常活跃，而且近期还取得了许多明显的进展，但油田的平均采收率并没有显著提高，实际生产经常与预测不符。石油公司中日常用于油藏特性的模拟、制图、网格化、可视化以及预测的地学和（或）工程方法在最近5年中也没有明显改变。本课总结了油藏描述实践和研究中的最新技术和趋势，提出并讨论了油藏描述今后的发展方向和重点。

课文

油藏非均质性的数值模拟

大部分油藏预测工具只能处理那些在空间上以一个确定规律变化的物理性质，空间变化的确定性又由于网格的数目受到约束。如果我们想调查不确定性对生产预测的影响，我们就会面临大量的实际生产模拟、大量的敏感性分析和“如果……，怎样”，因为油藏描述每一次都必须是确定性的。

由于新的工具、技术、资料和更多的网格的获得（特别是在接近注水井和生产井的地方），近年来，在油藏描述方面最重要的一个发展是详细描述地质模型的非均质性（以确定性的和随机的方法）。几年前，我们给出了关于随机模拟的一般看法和一个参考文献表，下面的概念主要来自那些看法。

确定性油藏模拟

在前一节中描述了传统的确定性油藏模拟方法。根据井所做的详细分带和井间对比来模拟油藏的主要几何结构。假定每个带中油藏的物性是常数或根据内插的等值线图侧向变化。这些等值线图可以捕捉到大规模的侧向变化，但它们总是平滑的，不会给出变化性的实际描述。

随机油藏模拟

使用随机油藏模拟的理由是:(1)资料不全;(2)油藏结构的空间分布复杂;(3)岩石物性变化;(4)物性值和平均值之间的关系未知;(5)油藏静态资料比动态资料丰富;(6)方便和迅速。

在当前的地球科学、油藏工程和水文文献中,随机模拟是指从一维、二维和三维方式产生与实际相符合并有一系列期待地质特征的合成地质剖面。它的根本目标是揭示油藏描述中的不确定性对未开发的、正在开发的和即将开发的油藏的影响。

为了接近真实,在这种研究中必须引进较小规模的不均一性,因为不均一性是控制流体流动的最重要因素之一。但是,各种不同的采收方法对油藏描述有不同的要求。对油藏不均一性的描述也有许多办法。它的选择取决于研究的目的、规模,研究人员的水平和现有的软件,而且最重要的是用于研究的现有资料和对于所研究的油藏的地质知识。

很容易区别两种主要的随机模型:离散模型和连续模型。

离散模型

离散模型是为描述离散的地质特征而建立的。这些特征包括:冲积相中砂岩体的位置和形态;砂岩体中页岩夹层的分布和大小;裂隙和断层的分布、方向、长度以及相模式。

在上述所有情况中,空间中的一个点属于某一等级中的一个数值,随机模型展示各点上的等级值的互相作用。例如,一个模型可以控制一个砂岩体是怎样侵入到另一个砂岩体中,断层是否通过或怎样通过;不同的岩相是怎样互相吸引或排斥的。可以通过计算机计算一些重要的参数,如易受影响的砂岩部分和水淹的砂岩部分,可以不必做实际的流体模拟。在制作模型时,地质指导是非常重要的。

连续模型

连续模型用于描述那些连续变化的现象,如岩石物性、地震速度和几何参数(如油藏顶、油水界面等)。

对于那些研究者感兴趣的变量来说,油藏空间或油藏面积内的每一个点都有一个确定的值。随机模型描述变量平均值、可能的侧向或纵向变化趋势、变量围绕平均值的变化幅度、相邻各点的对比强度,如果研究中有多于一个变量时,还包括多个变量的协变。

除了平均值中的趋势外,大多数连续模型在油藏中假定某种类型的稳定性。也就是说,油藏的统计学性质在空间上不变化,这种假定不总是有效。在制作连续模型时,地质指导和对油藏的经验也是很重要的,但这种方法更机械一些。

混合(二阶)模型

离散模型更接近地质学家对油藏的解释,并且更适合于模拟大规模的非均一性和油藏不连续性;连续模型较适合于模拟岩石物性的空间分布,但是多多少少地需要稳定性的假定条件。因此,一个自然的想法就是把两者的优点结合在一起形成一个混合模型。大多数离散模型和连续模型也用混合方法综合在一起。在一阶中,用离散模型描述模型中大规模的非均一性;在二阶中,用不同的连续模型描述离散模型中各等级的物性参数的空间变化。

几乎任何随机技术都可用于条件随机模拟。条件随机模拟的目的是在油藏模型中以现实和实时的方法从地层观察结果引进小规模的和(或)大规模的不均一性。以系统的方式在内插表面上加入“噪声”。在观察点上噪声为零,这样就尊重了观测值。与内插相比,模型的结果给人以更实际的视觉印象。模拟的动态流动模式有希望与实际更为接近。假定所选择的随机模拟模型与总的地质经验一致且尊重所有观测到的资料,我们相信随机模型的实际选择通常是不太重要的。

Journel 指出:“目前,非常迅速地产生大量的随机模拟,这些随机模拟的规模非常之大,其能力大大超过观看相应的图像的能力和用实际的流体模拟程序进行处理的能力。系统地利用蒙特卡洛法的瓶颈不再是随机(地质)模拟,而是计算机图像和流体模拟软件运行太慢。”

计算机在油藏描述中的发展趋势

今天,计算机在石油工业的每一领域都是不可缺少的。在油藏描述、油藏管理方面以及在各种技术和商业领域中,计算机有几百种用途。总的来讲,石油公司利用计算机采集、编辑、综合、处理、解释和观察资料,然后得出计算结果和预测。这些结果和预测成为以后进行经济评价和作业决策的基础。目前所有石油公司及所有分支机构在计算机方面的发展方向是:

(1)增加计算和输入输出的速度和内存,以便处理更多的数据,作出更精确的预测,研究和优选若干地下“平行现实”的油田开发方案和(或)未来的采油策略;

(2)迅速地存取和跨学科计算(存储、共享和综合);

(3)计算结果的可视化;

(4)方便、高效和用户友好的研究工具和过程。

与地球物理学非常相似,采油地质和油藏可视化的任务正被转换为屏幕上的任务。一些公司早已经在使用综合工作台技术了。在所有学科数据库中检索所有的资料,用特殊的软件和工具进行制图、交互编辑、显示、旋转、剪切和切片等。几年以后,大部分公司将拥有油藏可视化工作站,这将是作业队中各学科的重点。尽管如此,其目标必须是:油藏可视化软件和硬件应易于操作,以便使新工具和新技术从实验室迅速普及到开发队伍中去。当这些综合平台被广泛应用时,我们将会看到效率、学科综合、数据一致性和总的质量方面的重大改善。如果采油地质家在这项技术的发展中占据控制地位,那么大学里的地质课中将会包括更多的计算机科学、图形学、数学和统计学。

在计算领域中,未来油藏描述的挑战直接转向未来的硬件、软件和改善应用等方面。我们已经简单讨论了计算机在各种石油工程方面的发展趋势,可能导致更好的油藏描述和管理的"地质科学幻想"。进一步的发展趋势包括:

(1)改善的数据库和检索系统,地震数据的数字储存;

(2)各学科都包括在作业队中,并都在信息高速公路上;

(3)面向用户:我的输出是他的输入,接收格式对吗?我怎样改善我的产品?

(4)"地质桌"[大的,比如说2m×1m的可倾斜的、彩色的液晶屏幕,在这个屏幕上可显示各种地质平面和剖面图,并可进行交互编辑]和地质笔(像笔一样的地质桌编辑工具);

(5)与现有各种资料相吻合的物性变化的随机模型;

(6)地质仿真,可对油藏进行访问和调查;

(7)巨型并行超级计算机。

软件(而不是硬件)在不久的将来是发展的关键。单凭计算机将不能解决我们的所有问题。它们只是帮助我们达到目的的非常方便的工具。

将来的挑战

虽然油藏描述的一些设想已经实现(至少在实验室里),但仍然存在许多挑战!除非地震分辨率(可检测性)提高到几米或其他技术能够产生油藏的清晰图像,我们相信油藏描述的趋势将会沿着上述的综合方向发展。而且,像地震资料这样的静态资料只能给出有关油藏动态流动性质的间接的信息(例如,孔隙度与渗透率、净/总比、岩相类型、与渗透率有关的变化趋势、随时间变化的流体前缘位置信息)。将来这一工作要面对的挑战是:

(1)得到足够的无量纲形式的控制资料(如露头资料)和传统的地质知识以保证产生的结果是可信的。

(2)能够迅速地产生结构形态和各点的值,且均与岩心、测井、VSP、地震等资料吻合。

(3)新的结果能方便地网格化,不久之后,10^6 的网格将是常见的,压力分析仪结合计算机辅助设计(CAD)可能会被证明是一种可靠的方法。

(4)把所有结果搬上屏幕,如生产潜力、连通性、体积与驱扫、水驱能力和最终采收率,然后进行(关于盈利率或净现值的)最差、平均和最好结果的计算。

(5)使用整体和前缘追踪模型优化油井位置和采收方案,这些模型价格便宜、建立迅速,而且几乎总是正确的。

(6)以 $10^6 \sim 10^9$ 的网格进行三维三相模拟将能优化所需的设备并在预测的生产曲线上估算误差的大小。

(7)显示三维地质现实,动画演示流体流动的计算结果。

(8)如果有压力、油水界面、流体前缘等资料,能够迅速地进行谐配史模拟,且能实时模拟。

把未来划分为两个阶段可能是有益的,即层析成像期前阶段和层析成像期后阶段。在第一阶段,以各种比例进行随机模拟,用 CAD 进行网格化处理,众多现实的数值模拟将发展成为一种艺术;第二阶段,将会了解大规模的地质结构,随机模拟的重点会朝着产生小规模三维特性方面发展。可是,这并不意味着我们所知的小于 1m 的结构的预测误差就会消除;这在注水井和生产井上更为明显,以致于不需要用试验方法和纠错程序优化布井。

有关地质结构的知识将大大改善,但某些重要的方面仍然是不确定的。例如,假定所有的断层已找出并作图,这些断层是开放的还是封闭的?我们应该使用稳定状态还是不稳定状态的相对渗透率(两种数据都有,并且相当不同)?因此,除了详细的确定性油藏外,必须能获得其他的研究和开发成果,例如现场测量的相对渗透率和残余饱和度,并用带有压力记录程序的评价程序来计算的断层封闭能力等。

假定知道了油藏的一切细节(包括结构特性),那么主要的挑战是什么呢?一个足够详细的网格允许在驱动力、采油过程、不均一性和用来选择优化位置上的优化井数和采油策略的无穷尽的优化作业等之间进行重要的交互作业。这样,一个完全已知的小于 1m 网格化的油藏描述意味着重点将从地质上的“如果……怎样”转化为作业和优化上的“如果……怎样”。因此,必须用目标函数提供廉价的、可进行大量重复模拟的能力,这种模拟既针对实时控制采油作业(“智能模拟器”),也依照结果的吸引程度将“如果……怎样”进行分类。

总而言之,将来在油藏描述中的主要挑战是:

(1)在油田开发队伍中实践我们在会议中提倡的东西。

(2)从过去的油田开发中学习,为什么预测和实际的油藏动态不同?

(3)重点放在你的油田业务中最有关和最迫切的特定问题和机遇上,以及具有较高风险和较高潜力的长期技术工艺上。

(4)开展一种100%可信的烃类直接标志,不用昂贵的探井和评价井来找油。

(5)在地震分辨率上有重大改善(石油工业希望,20世纪末北海油田的油层深度方向的分辨率能达到1m)。

(6)发展震源、接收器、采集、处理和解释技术,使所有的断层图、大规模的地质结构、油田范围、流体接触面、流体前缘、沉积相类型和其他物性能够直接从地震资料中得到。

(7)发展和经常使用永久压力记录仪,以便在生产前和生产中来评价断层的封闭能力。

(8)更多地使用压力取心来获得正确的未浸染的相对渗透率和残余饱和度,因为相对渗透率和残余饱和度是大部分EOR项目的起点。

(9)从长期生产试验中确定冲积层的结构。

(10)从最重要的油田类型的类比中收集地层露头资料。

(11)将采油地质学转换成一种有效的屏示科目,提供运用于产生确定性的大规模地质结构之内的和周围的相互有关特性的三维点值,这些都取决于不同数据库中的岩心、测井、VSP和地震数据。

(12)利用一个模拟模型,经由重复试验开发出优化的方法和程序,对于每一个油田,经过周密计划的试验,通过优化采油方案、井数、井的位置、处理能力和气举等,优化不均一性、井数、生产方案、预期的结果(如高峰产量和生产期、净现值、采收率等)之间的相互关系。

这样,在将来我们可以想象:油、气、水可以直接从DHI识别,而不必用昂贵的探井来寻找石油;长1000~5000m,用大口径油管横穿整个储层的水平井或蛇形井(不管它叫做什么),地震信号产生1m的分辨力,可以识别任何地质细节(例如Gulltaks油田被网格化成40亿个网格,在计算机上进行1h的包括地面设备和所有的限制因素的模拟);在计算机上实时动画显示模拟过程;在考虑不同时间的最优采收方案时可以使用“智能模拟”,可以通过重复的地震不断地监测流体前缘;所有的井(包括探井和评价井甚至报废井)都有永久的监视产量和压力的系统。

有一个重要的问题:谁应该做研究工作,使这一切得以实现?

尽管油藏描述研究并没有什么秘密,但在这项工作中存在着巨大的重复。这一范围中的讨论并不是谁首先发明了什么,而是谁首先在实践中运用了它。几年前,许多公司派出地质家到同一个地质露头测量砂岩和页岩的长度,用便携工具测量渗透率模式。而现在,许多公司的专家以更有效的方式共同工作。

大学、公共和私人研究中心以及石油公司的研究实验室应该联合作业和专业分工。大学和研究中心具有仪器和方法,石油公司有问题和挑战。每年石油公司都应该为大家提供一个问题/挑战/机会表。"我希望我能……,我希望我已经……",如果这样做了,论文和研究报告就会针对这些挑战和问题。

所有这些研究应该使油藏描述的工具、技术和实践获得改善,以帮助我们更好地进行预测。但这些工作会使采收率提高吗?我们坚信回答是肯定的,但并不是在地震和其他技术提供油藏内部结构、流体前缘随时间变化的X射线、超声波或核磁共振图像之前。

Key to Exercises

Ⅰ.

1. There are several reasons why stochastic techniques are used to describe deterministic reservoirs: (1) incomplete information, (2) complex spatial disposition of reservoir building blocks, (3) rock property variability, (4) unknown relationships between property value and the volume used for averaging (the problem of scale), (5) relative abundance of static over dynamic reservoir data, and finally (6) convenience and speed.

2. The underlying goal of this geological quantification is to expose the effects of uncertainties in the geological description on the virgin, present, and future states of the reservoir.

3. Discrete models and continuous models.

4. The features include locations and dimensions of sand bodies in fluvial rocks; distribution and sizes of shales suspended in sands; distribution, orientations, and lengths of fractures and faults; and lithofacies modeling.

5. In the context of computing, reservoir characterization challenges for the future translate directly to future hardware, software, and improved application challenges.

Ⅱ. 1~5 DDCCA 6~10 BACAA

Ⅲ. 1~5 DACCA

Ⅳ.

1. 为了接近真实,在这种研究中必须引进较小规模的不均一性,因为不均一性是控制流体流动的最重要因素之一。

2. 可以通过计算机计算一些重要的参数,如易受影响的砂岩比例和水淹的砂岩比例,而不必做实际的流体模拟。

3. 连续模型用于描述那些连续变化的现象。

4. 除了平均值中的趋向外,大多数连续模型假定在油藏中存在某种类型的稳定性。

5. 与地球物理学非常相似,采油地质和油藏可视化的任务正被转换为屏示作业。

Ⅴ.

1. 大多数离散模型和连续模型也用混合方法综合在一起。在一阶中,用离散模型描述模型中大规模的非均一性;在二阶中,用不同的连续模型描述离散模型中各等级的物性参数的空间变化。

2. 今天,计算机在石油工业的每一领域都是不可缺少的。在油藏描述和油藏管理方面以及在各种技术和商业领域中,计算机有几百种用途。总的来讲,石油公司利用计算机采集、编辑、综合、处理、解释和观察资料,然后得出计算结果和预测。这些结果和预测成为以后进行经济评价和作业决策的基础。

第3章　储集层地质构造分析

3.1　天然裂缝性储集层的地质特征

导语

现今的大多数裂缝性储集层是偶然发现的,我们需要回顾这些裂缝性储集层的勘探情况。另外,因测试与评价不当或因在井中未钻遇天然裂缝,这些裂缝性储集层中残留有大量的油气(特别是在废弃的油气田中)。

遗憾的是,我们的经验不能很好地用于认识裂缝性储集层在某一个地区有效的工作方法,到下一个地区可能会失败。因此,对每个裂缝性储集层的勘探远景区都必然是一项独立的研究课题。

本课所讨论的裂缝地质特征大多是定性的,它们在油气生产中起重要作用。

课文

背景

Stearns 把天然裂缝定义为一个宏观的不连续面,这个面是由超过岩石破裂强度的应力造成的。Nelson 对天然裂缝的定义是岩石中因为形变或物理成岩作用,天然形成的宏观不连续面。

由此可见,天然裂缝性储集层是具有裂缝的储集层,岩石中的这些裂缝是由天然的应力差造成的,而不是人工形成的。在流体流动时,这些天然裂缝可以起正面作用,也可以不起作用或起负面作用。

例如,未胶结的开启裂缝对油气运移起正面作用,但对水与气则因锥进而造成了负面的效果。当油藏枯竭时,这些裂缝往往因垂直于裂缝的应力增加而关闭了。由于没有考虑这些裂缝封闭或部分封闭的作用,使得在储集层动态预测中做出过于乐观的估计。

因此,最重要的是:了解原地主应力的大小与方向;了解裂缝的方位、倾角、间距和裂隙大小;对裂缝孔隙度与渗透率进行合理的预测。部分被矿物充填的裂缝可以有很高的油气采收率,因为部分矿物充填可以形成一个天然的屏障,在油藏枯竭时仍可使裂缝保持开启的状态。

另外,全部矿物充填的天然裂缝对所有类型流体都可以成为一个渗透屏障。这就可能在储集层中分隔出一些小块,成为没有经济价值的储量或处于经济价值边缘的储量。

我认为,实际上所有的储集层或多或少都有天然裂缝。然而,如果这些裂缝对流体流动的作用可以忽略不计的话,这种储集层可以视为“常规”的储集层(从地质与油藏工程的角度出发)。在这一点上我同意 Nelson 的观点,即只把那些具有对流体流动起作用(正面的或负面的)的裂缝性储集层看做是天然裂缝性储集层。

根据定义,储集岩必须是多孔的和可渗透的,但是基质与裂缝对总孔隙度及渗透率的影响必须分开。于是,准确确定基质与裂缝的孔隙及油气饱和度对于准确计算原地油藏基质与裂缝中的油气分布是十分重要的。基质与裂缝的渗透率对于计算真实的流动能力是同等重要的参数。

火成岩、沉积岩和变质岩在条件适当时均可成为合格的储集岩。虽然大部分油气藏赋存于砂岩或碳酸盐岩之中,但我认为裂缝性的页岩、硬石膏、煤层、砂岩、石灰岩、白云岩、火山岩以及变质火成岩等均可作为具商业价值的储集层。在世界范围内,天然裂缝性储集层会遍布于各种类型的圈闭之中,分布在各时代的地层剖面中。

裂缝的形成和形式

裂缝的形成原因很多。Landes 与 Nelson 列举如下:

(1)与褶皱、断裂共生的构造形变作用。断裂作用往往生成沿断层线分布的裂隙,同时形成一个扩展带。扩展带是造成裂缝性储集层中油气大规模运移、聚集的主要因素。

(2)上覆岩层的快速而剧烈的侵蚀作用造成伸展、上隆和沿易碎面的断裂作用。

(3)因页岩脱水、火山岩冷却及沉积岩干缩造成的体积收缩。

(4)古岩溶作用和溶蚀塌陷。

(5)在高压沉积地层中,由于接近岩石静压力的高孔隙流体压力释放造成断裂作用。

(6)少见的陨石撞击形成复杂的强烈角砾化的裂缝性储集层。

裂缝的形态与天然裂缝表面的特征及其充填物有关。Nelson 认为裂缝的形态有开启的、变形的、矿物充填的及多孔的。

开启的裂缝未经胶结并且没有次生矿化作用,即原生的裂缝面未发生改变。裂缝的宽度通常很小,可能小于一个孔隙的直径,然而这种裂缝在平行裂缝走向的方向上明显地提高了基质的渗透率。另外,在垂直裂缝走向的方向上,开启裂缝的渗透率可忽略不计。

开启裂缝的孔隙度一般只有百分之几,虽然有时有例外。

变形的裂缝包括由裂缝泥(gouge)充填的裂缝和带擦痕的裂缝。裂缝泥是指沿易碎岩石的剪切裂缝分布的由于研磨和滑动作用而产生的细粒磨蚀物质。裂缝泥急剧地降低了裂缝的渗透能力。擦痕是沿着断层面(小断层)磨光裂缝面的滑动摩擦造成的。一个磨光的、条纹状的裂缝面可以提高平行裂缝的渗透率,但在垂直裂缝方向上,渗透率都急剧下降。擦痕和裂缝泥可以使渗透性呈明显的各向异性,从而形成并非各向同性的储集层。

矿物充填的裂缝是在裂缝形成后受到部分或全部充填,填充物一般多为石英或方解石。完全被充填的裂缝可以形成致密的渗透屏障。反之,由于裂缝的部分充填作用使次生矿物成为天然的支撑物,因此可以提高油气采收率。当油藏枯竭时,坚硬的方解石与石英防止了裂缝的关闭。我曾经在岩心上见到被矿物部分充填的裂缝,其缝隙可达1英寸。

孔洞沿着裂缝发育可以大大提高储集层的孔隙度与渗透率。由于这些裂缝是不规则的和近似圆形的,因此在油藏枯竭时,这些多孔的裂缝也不关闭。多孔的裂缝通常是因酸性水沿裂缝渗流而造成的。这样可最后导致岩溶作用发育,形成富集的油藏。

岩石的力学特性

人们一直认为,岩石的力学性质是受内在因素与环境因素双重控制的。

岩石的内在因素包括组分、颗粒大小、基质的孔隙度与渗透率、层厚以及已有的力学机制的不连续性。岩石的环境因素包括有效围压(岩石静压力和孔隙流体压力之差)、温度、时间(应变率)、差异应力,可能还有孔隙流体组分。

如果环境因素为常数,则岩石组分大体上决定了各种岩石类型的强度与可塑性。岩石组分显然影响岩石形成裂缝的难易程度。如果其他条件都相当的话,只根据岩石组分来确定裂缝发育情况,易于形成裂缝的岩石依次为石英岩、白云岩、石英胶结的砂岩、钙质胶结的砂岩、石灰岩。

岩石颗粒大小与裂缝发育程度关系的研究表明,通常由于岩石颗粒越细,岩石强度越大,其可塑性就越低,于是产生的裂缝强度较大。

同样的基质孔隙作用在实验室研究也表明,对于一给定的岩石类型,其孔隙度越低,裂缝强度越大。

层厚也影响裂缝的间距。露头与油田生产资料均表明岩层越薄,其裂缝间距越密集。

环境特性包括有效压力、温度、应变率、差异应力和孔隙流体组分。

有效压力或者围压是岩石特性中的重要因素,因此也在形成裂缝中起重要作用。实验证明,岩石的强度及可塑性随有效压力增大而加强。因此,较浅部位的岩石比上覆压力较大的同种岩石变形后产生的裂缝要多。

在出现变形情况下,应变率可能是一个重要的环境因素。通常,应变率较大时,岩石的易脆性增大。于是,作为一个重要的因素,应变率必须分成若干个级别。例如,陨石撞击的变形要比缓慢构造运动的变形产生更显著的裂缝。然而,在漫长的地质历史时期中,受到意外应变率变化影响的岩石,其裂缝的发育变化并不大。

分类

Stearns 和 Nelson 从地质角度出发,把天然裂缝分为构造裂缝、区域裂缝和成岩裂缝。

1. 构造裂缝

Stearns 和 Nelson 的描述是:“根据裂缝的方向、分布和形态,说明其成因是受局部构造事件控制的或是与之共生的裂缝。”绝大多数构造裂缝可归并到两类中的一类:褶皱作用形成的裂缝和断裂作用形成的裂缝。

与断层共生的裂缝是由形成断层的同一个远场应力差所造成的。因此,剪切裂缝被认为是断层的缩影,剪切裂缝的两个方向可由控制断层的属性确定。

就油气生产而论,构造裂缝是最重要的裂缝类型。许多储集层从构造裂缝中产油,如澳大利亚的 Palm 气田、阿根廷 Aguarague 气田以及墨西哥的海上油田。

2. 区域裂缝

Nelson 和 Steams 把区域裂缝定义为:“区域裂缝遍布于地壳上的大部分地区,裂缝方向很少变化,裂缝永远垂直于主要的层理面,破裂面两侧无明显错动。”这些裂缝的形成似乎与局部构造无关,而可能形成于表面力,常呈正交图形,几乎到处都存在。

区域裂缝的方向保持不变,长度超过 100 英里、范围在 10°~15°之间。因为破裂面两侧无错动,也就不存在对裂缝所在围岩的损害,而这种损害使得区域裂缝十分有利于流体流动。

3. 成岩裂缝

成岩裂缝是因岩石在成岩作用中的变化而形成的,最常见的是:(1)干裂;(2)脱水收缩;(3)地温梯度变化;(4)矿物相的变化。这些作用或条件的每一种都可以产生应力差异,这些应力差大到足以产生拉张或伸展运动,在成岩时体积缩小,同时生成裂缝。

这些作用或条件首先产生体内力而不是表面力;也就是始于在体内力

的作用，而不像产生构造裂缝那样始于外力。这种裂缝的实例是堪萨斯州Panoma油田二叠系Council Grove组的收缩裂缝。

没有发现天然裂缝性储集层——为什么？如何发现？

许多天然裂缝性储集层是有经济价值的，但却被废弃了。原因是：(1)压力推断错误；(2)完井方法不当；(3)井筒未钻遇天然裂缝。

如果瞬时压力测试时没有达到无穷大径流时期，则裂缝性储集层的压力可能出现推断错误，因而做出油藏枯竭的错误结论。

常规完井通常是在符合具有一定孔隙度、渗透率及含水饱和度中止准则的层段进行。这是有风险的，因为裂缝很发育的天然裂缝性储集层的孔隙度及基质的渗透率都是最低的。而且，最大密度的裂缝分布在较薄的地层中。

具有商业价值的油气不可能产自没有裂缝的致密的基岩之中，但油气却可以从致密的基岩中顺畅地流入天然裂缝。成功的关键之一是保证高陡倾角的裂缝被定向井或水平井钻穿。

钻杆试井(DSTs)和重复地层测试(RFTs)是有效的技术，但在解释时必须慎重，因为这些技术并不能全面地鉴别天然裂缝性储集层。例如，如果刚好在致密的基岩部位测试，将指出其渗透率极低，没有流动能力。即使测试到裂缝部位，也可能遇到钻井过程中进入裂缝的泥浆。

有重要经济价值的裂缝大都是垂直的或近乎垂直的。因此，在钻探天然裂缝性储集层时，垂直井不如定向斜井或水平井那样成功。

总结和结论

无疑，天然裂缝对大多数储集层和所有构造圈闭都是起作用的因素。然而在多数情况下，裂缝被忽略，最多是象征性地考虑一下。目前已建立了一个相当大的数据库用来预测裂缝的密度和方向。

另外，目前也有了以现代测井序列和/或井测试资料检测裂缝的专门技术。如果我们能把预测裂缝的方向和间距，测量裂缝性储集层特性以及控制定向钻探三者结合在一起，那么显而易见，我们必须对储集岩的天然裂缝给予更多的关注。

只有在我们开始利用所有的裂缝资料时，我们才可以从裂缝性储集层中优化利润率，且大多数储集层都是有裂缝的。

Key to Exercises

Ⅰ.

1. No. It has long been recognized that the mechanical properties of rocks

are controlled by the combined influence of intrinsic and environmental parameters.

2. If environmental parameters are constant, it basically determines the strength and ductility of various rock types.

3. Environmental properties include effective pressure, temperature, strain rate, differential stress, and pore fluid composition.

4. Stearns and Nelson, from a geologic point of view, have classified natural fractures as tectonic, regional, and diagenetic.

5. Many naturally fractured reservoirs should have been economic but were abandoned because of (1) incorrect pressure extrapolations, (2) poor completions, and / or (3) failure of the borehole to intersect the natural fractures.

Ⅱ. 1 – 5 DCABB 6 – 10 ACDDB

Ⅲ. 1 – 5 CDABB

Ⅳ.

1. 对同样的基质孔隙作用在实验室中的研究也表明，对于一给定的岩石类型，其孔隙度越低，裂缝强度越大。

2. 然而，在漫长的地质历史时期中，受到意外应变率变化影响的岩石，其裂缝的发育变化并不大。

3. 有重要经济价值的裂缝大都是垂直的或近乎垂直的。

4. 毫无疑问，天然裂缝对大多数储集层和所有构造圈闭都是起作用的因素。

5. 只有在我们开始利用所有的裂缝资料时，我们才可以从裂缝性储集层中优化利润率，而且大多数储集层都是有裂缝的。

Ⅴ.

1. 次生孔隙是沉积作用以后地质作用的产物，因此其与沉积颗粒的形成无直接关系。次生孔隙是因溶解、重结晶、白云石化或裂缝等作用形成的。

2. 文献中报道的大多数裂缝孔隙度大约在1% ~10%之间。然而，必须强调裂缝孔隙度的大小与比例有关。例如，钻遇了20ft 的放空，则在这 20ft 的井段内孔隙度为100%。

3.2 断层圈闭分析

导语

断层圈闭比简单的四向倾没圈闭风险性更大。要准确评估圈闭风险性,需要作更多的分析。可靠的断层圈闭评价始于精确的断层制图。本课重点讨论了以下 4 个问题:(1)断层制图,包括有关断层混淆问题、断层形状、三维资料、雁行断层和相干数据体的讨论;(2)断层圈闭的一般讨论;(3)并置圈闭及"Allan 剖面图"的用途;(4)断层封堵圈闭和造成断裂带毛细性质与未断裂岩石毛细性质差异的三种机理——黏土"涂抹"作用、颗粒破碎作用和成岩作用。

课文

引言

可靠的断层圈闭评价始于精确的断层制图,即使用三维数据集,精确地勾绘断层也要求绘制断面图。为了避免混淆(错误地拼接)断层,极力建议在断面图上勾绘出断距等值线或垂直间距等值线。相干处理似乎能对正确地拼接断层段提供帮助。

并置圈闭:如果断层两侧并置的岩层具有重大的毛细性质差异,或者断裂带本身的毛细性质具有封堵性,断层就可以遮挡油气。并置圈闭需要通过仔细绘制沿断面上盘和下盘地层来加以评价。

断层封堵圈闭:断层封堵圈闭依靠断裂带自身封堵。断裂带的封堵能力可以根据有关断裂波及层段的净厚和总厚之比以及位移的时间和大小来定性估算,也可以用经过当地实例标定的计算程序半定量地估算。

断层圈闭的风险性:断层圈闭具有未断裂的四向倾没圈闭所没有的两种主要类型的风险。第一种风险涉及断层的制图方法。第二种风险涉及与圈闭性断层有关的封堵性。这两种风险是独立的,任何一种都可使看来很有吸引力的远景圈闭打出一口干井。

断层作图

依据井控制或二维地震资料勾绘断层时,混淆断层的可能性很大。如果断块拼接错了,则图上的断层圈闭可能与真实的地下构造截然不同。

断层混淆问题

谈论断层混淆问题时,绘制所有的重要断面图是必不可少的。不同构造区的断层往往有其独特的形状。对构造区内具有独特形状的断层应当仔细核查,以免造成混淆。

在一种构造环境中很合理的一种断层形状,在另一构造环境中出现的可能性也许会很小。

断层形状

断层形状这个术语在此指断层面的形状,而不是构造图上断层线的形状。除了在出现垂直断层和水平层的情况下,断层线都是两个倾斜的非平面相交的结果。断层线可通过综合构造图和断面图加以确定,但不是直观的,如果断层面本身未勾绘出来,则不能轻易地确定。

断层形状虽然不在本文讨论范畴之内,但在其他方面却至关重要。断层形状控制着上升盘中的构造形状,还可以提供关于地层各部位砂/页岩比的宝贵资料。

三维资料

三维地震资料上的断层混淆问题不像井控资料和二维地震资料那样严重。断层的三维解释,不仅有密度大的地震测线,可在三维空间中进行准确的偏移,而且还可以通过解释精心选择的任意测线进行连接对比。断层解释与任意测线连接对比,大大减少了断层的混淆。

除非资料特别清楚,而且三维数据集内每条测线均已解释,否则仍有可能混淆断层,因此建议绘制断面图。大多数解释人员最初只解释 1/5 或1/10 的三维测线。在地震解释的这一阶段,要经常参照不断更新的断面图。

断面中出现扭结或意外的弯曲,表明存在解释问题,马上纠正这一问题比过后再回过头来重新解释要省事得多。幸好很多人机交互软件包使得三维地震资料解释期间绘制断面图的工作变得十分容易。

雁行断层

解释三维地震资料时,即使绘制了断面图,仍可能错误地拼接雁行(未连接、近平行的)断层。这种错误的解释造成的浪费可能特别大,因为根据那种雁行断层形式可能得出一个下降盘隆起。可惜的是,这两条雁行断层间的断口将导致油气泄漏。

关键断层解释结果的一种良好检验方法是在断面图上勾画出断距或断层垂直断距的等值线。对雁行断层解释错误会破坏断距或垂直断距等值线,这将提示解释人员应注意解释问题。根据三维地震资料手工勾绘断距或垂直断距等值线很费时间。幸好有些软件包可以大大简化绘图过程。

如果在断面上勾画断距等值线,必须注意使断距数值反映真实断距,即取垂直于断层走向的断距,而不是从相对断层走向的其他某个角度测量的视断距。视断距始终小于真实断距,勾绘视断距等值线得出的可能是没有实际意义的近乎随机的等值线。只有在绘出断面后才能确定真实断距。

相干数据体

地震处理的最新进展是相干数据体。相干处理包括指定某一数值表示每条测线相对于周边测线的连续性。相干数据区可用白色或浅灰色表示。间断区(如断层)可用深灰色表示。研究显示相干性而非振幅地震数据的时间切片似乎能真正确定断层是如何连接的。

断层圈闭

即使在断层解释为正确的情况下,与未断裂的四向倾没圈闭相比,断层圈闭封堵的风险性也很大。构造图上的断层线不是封堵层,而是图上的一条线。断层圈闭可以借助两种方式中的一种而封堵。并置圈闭是断层一侧的储层岩性与另一侧具有封堵性的岩性并置的结果。断层封堵圈闭则由断裂带自身封堵。

全面讨论封堵层超出了本文的范畴,但简单讨论一下是恰当的。封堵层是其毛细性质使得非润湿性流体(如油或气)难以进入孔隙的岩石。储集岩的毛细性质使油气进入孔隙,而且以经济开采速度被采出。

有些岩石既非盖层又非储集层。有些岩石在某些条件下是盖层,在其他条件下是储集层。有关盖层的更完整的讨论参见其他文章。

并置圈闭

并置圈闭存在于断层一侧的储集岩性与另一侧的封堵性岩性并置处。在美国墨西哥湾海岸区,通常认为并置圈闭存在于断层两侧的砂岩与泥岩并置处。但它们也可能出现(至少在理论上如此)在断层两侧具有不同毛细性质的砂岩并置处。评价并置圈闭存在可能性的最佳方法是勾绘出上盘和下盘中断面处的地层。这些图有时以推广其用途的 Urban Allan 的名字命名为"Allan 断面图"或"Allan 剖面图"。

Allan 剖面图

Allan 剖面图要求绘制远景圈闭上盘和下盘的图件。不勾画出断层两侧,不制出 Allan 剖面图就对断层圈闭开钻的话,是在冒不必要的风险。绘制精确的 Allan 剖面图要求恰当综合断面图和构造图综合断面图和构造图能确保准确地确定地层与断面交会处。未综合断面图,仅根据构造图绘制的 Allan 剖面可能不精确,可能导致对远景区风险性作出错误评估。Allan 剖面图通常可以手工绘制,或者用一些计算机软件程序绘制。

Allan 剖面图的用途

石油界已相当明确地确认 Allan 剖面图的用途。常规的 Allan 剖面图描述目前地层的并置关系。过去不同时间地层的并置关系可能很不同。在充填时间很短的地区,可能需要绘制古 Allan 剖面图和现代 Allan 剖面图。在美国墨西哥湾海岸区,目前仍有物质充填进去,古 Allan 剖面图的用途目前尚未得到确认。如已绘制出古构造图,则可手工勾绘古 Allan 剖面图。作者尚不知道有无一种能常规地用于绘制古 Allan 剖面图的计算机软件包。

断层封堵圈闭

断层封堵圈闭的作用仍然是个存在争议的问题。M. D. Downey 指出，对作为有效封堵的断裂带而言，与含油气储层接触的整个断裂带都必须具有有利的毛细性质。如果只有断面的一小段具有与墨西哥湾海岸区多孔砂岩类似的毛细性质，则从地质角度而言的较短地质时期内就可能损失大量油气。Downey 认为，可能存在断层封堵圈闭，但极其罕见。其他研究人员则提供了重要断层封堵圈闭令人信服的证据。如果断裂带的毛细性质与未断裂储层的毛细性质明显不同，则断裂带本身就可以起封堵作用。导致断裂带与未断裂岩石毛细性质不同的三种机理是黏土“涂抹”作用、颗粒破碎作用或碎裂作用和成岩作用。下面对这三种机理作更详细的探讨。

黏土“涂抹”作用

黏土涂抹作用是指塑性泥岩层沿断裂带“涂抹”于其上的作用。黏土“涂抹”作用已在实验室试验产生，在露头和岩心中观察到，并由测井解释结果中推断出。

黏土“涂抹”量主要与泥岩厚度和泥岩与研究点的距离有关。任一单个泥岩层所提供的黏土“涂抹”量均随泥岩厚度增加而增加，随泥岩与研究点的距离增大而减小。任意点的黏土“涂抹”量是通过该点的所有泥岩层所提供的“涂抹”量之和。

理论上可以认为黏土“涂抹”量不仅是泥岩厚度和泥岩距研究点的距离的函数，还是泥岩塑性、断层倾角、有效应力等参数的函数。如果说这些次级控制参数的计算并非不可能进行的话，但至少实现难度很大。黏土涂抹量需要局部地标定，这就相当于暗中假定控制泥岩涂抹量次级变量对所有局部实例而言都是相似的。某种黏土涂抹量在一个地区（如尼日尔三角洲）可能往往具有封堵性，而在另一个不同环境（如北海）则可能一般无封堵性。

黏土“涂抹”量一般说来可以根据净厚度与总厚度之比和断层位移来估算，或者用计算机软件沿断面逐点计算。用任何一种方法求得的结果都应当用本地封堵性断层和无封堵性断层实例来标定。业已证实在计算结果经过标定的地区，这种分析能成功地用于评估断层圈闭的风险性。

颗粒破碎作用

与断层有关的颗粒破碎作用或碎裂作用会导致断裂带中颗粒粒级和渗透率大大减小。这种碎裂带比未变化的岩石毛细压力可能高 1 ~ 2 个数量级，具有圈闭油气藏高度达几百英尺的油气潜力。在硬化岩石中和更高的围压下，可以预计碎裂作用更为重要。断层位移增大，碎裂作用也应增强。虽然碎裂作用在理论上是一种形成断层封堵圈闭的合理方式，但与这一作用有关的油气藏的具体实例还有待资料证实。

在墨西哥湾海岸区，紧贴砂岩层水平错断开的断层似乎不具有封堵性。R. G. Gibson 确认并证实了特立尼达哥伦布盆地内两个油田中类似的关系。断层封堵失败实例表明，若非在岩化程度低的砂岩中碎裂作用不是一种重要的作用，那么这些断层的水平断错则还不足以形成大碎裂带。前种解释似乎更可取，因为在硬化岩石错位的早期会发生颗粒粒级降低的现象。

S. D. Knott 提到了储层内断层起到封堵作用的许多北海油藏的实例。这些断层中有些封堵作用可能归因于断裂带中的碎裂变形作用，但缺乏单独阐述的实例。Knott 分析的断层大多为沉积期后断层，可以预料像这样的断层更易碎裂。

成岩作用

成岩作用被普遍认为是一种影响断裂带附近岩石物性的作用。沿断层的胶结作用可使岩石的孔隙度和渗透率比远离断裂带的岩石的孔隙度和渗透率降低一个数量级。

成岩作用和断裂作用相结合可以增强断层的封堵能力。碎裂岩的胶结作用可急剧降低其孔隙度和渗透率。碎裂作用造成的颗粒粒级的减小增大了粒级的表面积，从而强化了扩散物质的传递作用（如压溶作用）。即使断裂带内未发生流体流动的现象，由于这些受扩散控制的作用，断裂带也可能优先被胶结。

虽然成岩作用具有形成不渗透岩石的潜力，但成岩过程往往不规则，常常导致致密岩石与渗透性岩石交错。由于封堵的有效性对岩石连续性的依赖程度比对平均毛细性质的依赖程度更强，因此，因成岩特性而封堵的断层圈闭很可能少有。

本文重点讨论了断层的封堵性。断层还可以作为流体流动的通道，与断层有关的断裂可使原本致密的岩石成为极好的储层。有关断裂带内流体流动的控制的详细讨论超出了本文的范畴，但在断层运动期间更容易产生流体流动的现象。因断层运动期间存在流体流动的可能性，所以隐伏断层或稳定断层比显示出近期有活动迹象的断层更容易形成圈闭。

Key to Exercises

Ⅰ.

1. Mapping of either fault throw or vertical separation contours on fault surface maps is highly recommended to help avoid aliasing (incorrectly connecting) faults.

2. Fault traps have two major types of risks which unfaulted four – way – dip closures do not share. The first risk involves how the faults are mapped. The second risk involves the sealing behavior associated with trapping fault.

3. Three mechanisms which can cause the capillary properties of the fault zone to differ from the unfaulted rock are clay smear, grain crushing or cataclasis, and diagenesis.

4. Diagenesis and cataclasis can be combined to increase the sealing potential of a fault.

5. This article has focused on the sealing potential of faults.

Ⅱ. 1 – 5　BCABA　6 – 10　DDCBB

Ⅲ. 1 – 5　DCBAB

Ⅳ.

1. 为了避免混淆(错误地拼接)断层,研究者极力建议在断面图上勾绘出断距等值线或垂直间距等值线。

2. 断层圈闭具有未断裂的四向倾没圈闭所没有的两种主要类型的风险。

3. 断面中出现扭结或意外的弯曲表明存在解释问题,马上纠正这一问题比过后再回过头来重新解释要省事得多。

4. 如果在断面上勾画断距等值线,必须注意使断距数值反映真实断距,即取垂直于断层走向的断距,而不是从相对断层走向的其他某个角度测量的视断距。

5. 并置圈闭存在于断层一侧的储集岩性与另一侧的封堵性岩性并置处。

Ⅴ.

1. 当断层两边的地层不断互相移动,在某一位置恰好可以阻止石油进一步运移时,就形成了断层圈闭。例如,断层一侧的不渗透地层可能向断层另一侧的含油地层运动,结果不渗透地层使得石油不能再运移了。在断层圈闭中,渗透性岩层被不渗透岩层覆盖着,在断裂处又与不渗透岩层相接。

2. 断层圈闭也是很常见的。断层圈闭同样也必须具有多孔可渗透储集层和相对来说渗透性较差的细粒盖层。但真正的圈闭是由断层所形成的。由于产生了断层,存在于断层中的一些细粒物质会使石油不能再继续向上运移(这些细粒物质就是断层面发生断裂时出现的所谓“断层泥”);另外当断层切过储油层时,断层另一侧不渗透细粒物质层也会在储层被切断的地方将油层封住,使石油无法继续向上运移。

3.3 智利南部麦哲伦前陆冲断褶皱带前缘区的形态及其演化

导语

麦哲伦(Magallnnes)前陆冲断褶皱带是古新世至渐新世时期形成的一种薄皮状前陆冲断褶皱带,致使智利安第斯山脉南部麦哲伦盆地内的上侏罗统至新近系的火山岩、火山碎屑岩和硅质碎屑岩地层发生形变。本文中详细描述了该逆冲带前缘[火地岛(Tierra del Fuego)南部的 Vicuna 地区]的地质情况和构造演化,应用的资料包括地震反射、钻井资料和 1∶50000 地质图。

课文

引言

火地岛(Tierra del Fuego)的达尔文(Darwin)山脉和麦哲伦冲断褶皱带构成了南美洲南端安第斯山脉的最南部分。白垩纪中期 Rocas Verdes 边缘海盆地封闭,导致安第斯山脉的这一部分开始形成。该冲断带的南界是达尔文山脉结晶岩体,北界是未变形的麦哲伦前陆盆地。麦哲伦盆地是阿根廷和智利两国的主要油气区。本文将对麦哲伦冲断褶皱带,尤其是对位于智利南部火地岛的冲断带前缘上的 Vicuna 地区进行详细的描述和分析。渐新世至中新世时期的向北挤压形变把该地区的侏罗系和白垩系火山碎屑岩及碎屑岩推覆到麦哲伦盆地的古近系—新近系硅质碎屑沉积之上。Vicuna 地区所发现的构造是典型的冲断前缘构造。构造类型包括断传褶皱、复式断块和三角带,它们是该区潜在的烃类圈闭。对本文中首次分析的这些构造的几何形态、运动学及动力学演化过程的理解,是未来成功地勘探和开发该区油气资源的基础。尽管在 Vicuna 地区的浅井中已见到油气显示,但生产井却位于该区的极北端。冲断前缘构造均发育在未变形的前陆造山带附近的薄皮前陆褶皱和冲断带形变终止之处。这些冲断前缘构造通常产生背形构造,它们形成了诸如加拿大洛基山、怀俄明冲断带以及安第斯山前带的 Neuquen 盆地等油气区内的主要油气圈闭。

本文描述了 Vicuna 地区的地质和构造情况,并提出了麦哲伦冲断褶皱带这一部分演化的一种构造模式。确定了前缘构造与前陆区构造的关系以及山前带构造的具体几何形态与运动学演化。在山前带,地震反射剖面揭示,构造样式由冲断带至前陆盆地发生突然变化。根据深转换的地震剖面和1∶50000的地面地质图，编制了三条面积平衡构造横剖面。为检验平衡并计算缩短量，对各剖面进行了复原。为了约束构造解释，根据平衡过的剖面建立了逐渐演变的运动学模式。

区域地质

在现今称为达尔文山脉的地区，达尔文(1846)首次对火地岛做了地质描述。Harambour 等在安第斯山脉的南支中确定了三个主要构造区域。

(1)南部结晶岩区是由古生代至中生代早期多重变形和变质的基岩形成的。影响这些岩石的主要变形幕是以该构造带内部的褶皱所代表的阿尔布期至柯尼亚克期的安第斯变形幕。古生代岩石形成大的叠置推覆体，并于古近纪抬升。基岩的南界为残留的 Rocas Verdes 边缘海盆地基岩，向北推覆在麦哲伦盆地侏罗系和白垩系之上。

(2)中区主要是由北东东向的麦哲伦冲断褶皱带内的白垩系碎屑岩构成。该带的基底冲断层看来位于侏罗系内，接近古生界基岩顶面。

(3)第三个区形成于北部的前陆区，是麦哲伦盆地广袤而平缓的相对未变形区。该前陆区内的地层包括中、上侏罗统的火山岩和火山碎屑岩以及白垩系至新近系的硅质碎屑岩。

麦哲伦盆地的演化

关于该盆地前侏罗系的地史目前尚缺乏足够的认识。Herve 等认为上古生界基岩是作为与冈瓦纳古陆太平洋边缘俯冲带有关的增生楔锥体而渐形成的。

中晚侏罗世至早白垩世期间，麦哲伦盆地才成为一个拉张盆地。Tobifera 组的侏罗系岩层直接覆盖在基岩之上，它是由沉积于地堑和半地堑内的硅质火山碎屑和火山岩以及海相和非海相的硅质碎屑岩组成的一个非均质单元。岩层厚度变化大，在基岩隆起区缺失，在地堑区厚度可大于2000m。Vicuna 区以北，侏罗系火山岩和火山碎屑岩不整合下伏于 Springhill 组的下白垩统河流—三角洲相和海相砂岩、页岩之上。Springhill 组砂岩是海进的浅海至河流—滨海相砂岩。它是麦哲伦盆地中的主要储集层。Vicuna 地区是否存在 Springhill 砂岩尚未证实。地表出露的相当于 Vicuna 组的最古老岩系以及本研究中所用的地下资料尚不足以解决这一问题。

白垩系为向北海进的碎屑沉积层序，厚度向南增大。随着时间的推移，深水相向北后退。这些地层沉积于麦哲伦盆地北部的稳定边缘上。早白垩世时期的盆地沉降被认为是与侏罗纪扩展有关的热异常滞后的结果。相反，晚白垩世和古近系—新近系时期的沉降则是由来自南部的侵位冲断带所致的构造负载引起的。

阿尔布期至古近纪时期侏罗系裂谷体系收缩,以致产生了麦哲伦前陆冲断褶皱带,并形成了麦哲伦前陆盆地。前陆盆地内的古近系—新近系由厚达5000m的硅质碎屑楔状体组成,它们向北上超在白垩系之上。区域展布的下始新统—麦斯特里希特组之间的不整合可能与麦哲伦冲断褶皱带西南区的隆起所致的沉积物供给方向改变有关。

冲断体系

Vicuna地区的地质图表明,构造呈北东东向,南部的冲断褶皱带和北部的前陆盆地之间有不同的构造样式。在南部,三个较大的北北东向的推覆体构成该冲断褶皱带,这三个推覆体自南向北依次为Colo - Colo,Bahia Bell和Vicuna。这些推覆体内的地层向南变新,冲断层将老地层推覆到新地层之上。外来岩体内的褶皱轴线走向与断层平行。只有在褶皱轴横向倾没处才能见到冲断层切割褶皱。在Vicuna推覆体以北的前陆盆地内,出露的古近系—新近系剖面表明,背斜褶隆区的宽度达3 ~ 5km。这些核部有冲断层的背斜通常比相邻的向斜窄,它们的轴向与冲断褶皱带内的主要构造的轴向呈小角度斜交。

麦哲伦冲断褶皱带

Vicuna区中麦哲伦冲断褶皱带的特征是在所有地震剖面上3s以上均有两个不同反射波组,即上反射波组和下反射波组。上反射波组的特征是一组向南陡倾的反射波在深部合并为一个平缓南倾的反射波。这些反射可以与地面地质图上圈出的南倾冲断层对比。这一波组被解释为叠瓦扇。下反射波组以平缓南倾的反射为特征,它们被解释为复式断块构造。两类冲断体系均发育在侏罗系和白垩系内。

叠瓦扇体系内的边界冲断层出露地表且呈铲状形态。这类冲断层的铲状特性在地震剖面上表现为断面的反射振幅向地面变小直至消失。这一振幅减小解释为由断层倾角增大所致。某些情况下根据地震剖面有可能确定各个断块内的褶皱,但一般难以观察到其细节。

叠瓦扇系的基底断层合并成3s附近的一个平缓南倾强反射。该反射面在全部3条地震剖面上都解释为基岩与盖层的接触面,因为它标志上、下两种不同反射响应的界限。这一接触面看来被向南、北陡倾的张性断层错断。在某些情况下,冲断层断坡的位置似乎与张性断层的位置直接有关。

叠瓦扇内的褶皱规模为千米级,通常表现出有指向北的短而陡的背斜前翼。在横剖面中,不同规模的冲断层经常切过背斜的前翼,有些前翼已倒转。在冲断层附近,褶皱较窄。在多层状的白垩系地层序列中,褶皱一般呈尖顶状,然而,局部出露的圆柱状褶皱存在于较为坚硬的Vicuna组碳酸盐岩层中。褶皱的形状及其与冲断层的关系表明,叠瓦状推覆体中的褶皱作用是由断层传播所致。

复式断块构造的内部结构在地震剖面上成像极差且没有出露地表。因此,确定单个推覆体的形态及大小都是很困难的。复式断块构造的底部冲断层可能位于基岩—盖层接触面附近,并形成 Vicuna 地区麦哲伦前陆冲断褶皱带的底部滑脱面。

叠瓦扇系的前缘是一个表层楔状体,其特征与加拿大南部落基山冲断前缘构造相同。在 Vicuna 地区,叠瓦扇体系前缘发育有一个三角带,该处指向前陆的基底冲断层隐伏于地下,它在深部终止于倾向前陆而指向后陆的冲断层上。由于其在地震剖面上的成像极差,很难确定三角带内部构造的细节。在冲断楔状体前缘,原地地块内发育有倾向前陆的单斜构造。三角带之下的次级冲断作用已使上覆古近系—新近系层段发生形变。

麦哲伦冲断带的前陆

前陆区是由岩性决然不同的前陆盆地岩石组成,且展示出与上述麦哲伦冲断褶皱带完全不同的构造样式。在地震剖面的北段,以大范围的平反射和可能相当于地面背斜构造的狭窄的倾斜反射区为特征。在 Vicuna 地区以北,根据钻井资料,白垩系底面对应于基岩—盖层接触面之上的第一个强反射面。第二个强反射面相当于白垩系与古近系—新近系的分界面。在 Vicuna 地区,该界面的标志是与古近系—新近系沉积物有关的下超反射。这些下超反射表明是前积层序,可能是由来自于南部逐渐抬升的山区的沉积物形成的。前陆盆地沉积可细分为三个不同的地震地层单元。

在所有三条剖面中的前陆区地表均见到成对的背斜和向斜。地震剖面揭示深处的背斜核部为不同的冲断构造,它们的形态在纵、横向上都有变化。这些构造的形态变化被认为与滑脱层面分布和不向地层的相对强度有关。虽然与薄弱地层有关的其他次要滑脱面在地震剖面上未能成像,但在整个前陆区到处可见。

一系列压离构造(pop up)和三角带的形成是各个滑脱面向上分叉的次级铲状冲断层作用的产物。这些构造一般纵向上是叠复的,因此在主背斜的核部形成复合构造。Miraflores 背斜是前陆区内典型的构造。在地表,它是一个宽广的低幅度冲断核背斜。

结论

麦哲伦冲断褶皱带于 Vicuna 地区展现出如地面露头和地震剖面上所示的两种不同的构造样式,即冲断带本身的构造样式和前陆盆地构造样式。收缩变形发生在渐新世至中新世,褶皱和冲断构造走向为北西西—南东东。

可识别出两种明显不同的构造地层组合，即前构造楔状体和同构造楔状体，两者均向南变厚。前构造楔由上侏罗统和白垩系组成，形成了冲断褶皱带。同构造楔由上白垩统和古近系—新近系硅质碎屑岩单元组成，形成了麦哲伦前陆盆地的充填。

麦哲伦冲断褶皱带中见到了纵向叠置的两个冲断体系，即上部的叠瓦扇体系和下部的复式冲断层体系。叠瓦扇的基底冲断层形成该区南部复式冲断层的顶冲断层。叠瓦扇的前缘，发育了一个具有隐伏前缘的表层间楔状体。叠瓦扇系具有一个重要的下盘断坡，切进古近系—新近系约 3km。前陆盆地内的古近系—新近系已沿叠瓦扇系前缘三角带上的一条被动的顶部后冲断层上抬。下伏的复式冲断层由许多大小不等的断层夹块组成，形成沿其长度方向起伏的顶冲断层。它的底冲断层在接近盖层与基岩接触面处被挤离。

前陆区北部，构造样式受沉积地层内的三个上滑脱面控制。前陆区的构造指向前陆与后陆，冲断层末梢背斜为紧密褶皱，彼此由宽阔的向斜相隔。

冲断活动顺序，在麦哲伦冲断褶皱带中由后陆到前陆，在前陆区内则是山上部滑脱面到下部滑脱面。根据横剖面所计算的 Vicuna 地区的缩短量约为 60%，这与整个 Vicuna 地区内所记录到的相变及其以南地区中所得到的缩短量估算值是一致的。

Key to Exercises

Ⅰ.

1. The Springhill sandstones form the major hydrocarbon reservoir in the Magallanes basin.

2. Albian through Paleogene contraction of the Jurassic rift system gave rise to the Magallanes foreland thrust and fold belt and formation of the Magallanes foreland basin.

3. It is made up of the Colo – Colo, Bahia Bell, and Vicuna thrust sheets.

4. An imbricate fan and a duplex.

5. The Miraflores anticline is a typical example of the structural style in the foreland area.

Ⅱ. 1 – 5 CBBCC 6 – 10 CDCDA

Ⅲ. 1 – 5 DCACD

Ⅳ.

1. 构造类型包括断传褶皱、复式断块和三角带,它们是该区潜在的烃类圈闭。

2. 冲断前缘构造均发育在未变形的前陆至造山带附近的薄皮前陆褶皱和冲断带形变终止之处。

3. 白垩系为向北海进的碎屑沉积层序,厚度向南增大。

4. 前陆区是由岩性决然不同的前陆盆地岩石组成,且展示出与上述麦哲伦冲断褶皱带完全不同的构造样式。

5. 一系列压离构造和三角带的形成是各个滑脱面向上分叉的次级铲状冲断层作用的产物。

Ⅴ.

1. Vicuna 地区南部已经发现两类不同的冲断体系:上部是由变形的上侏罗统和白垩系以及较新地层构成的叠瓦扇,下部是由白垩系和可能的上侏罗统岩石构成的复式断块构造(duplex)。叠瓦扇以断传褶皱为特征,内部的铲状冲断层向下连接到可能是位于侏罗系内的基底冲断层上。叠瓦扇体系的前缘发育了一个具有三角带的表层间楔状体。叠瓦扇的基底冲断层形成下伏复式断块构造的顶冲断层面。

2. 在 Vicuna 地区北部,前渊的同构造楔状沉积体由晚白垩纪至古近纪—新近纪的硅质碎屑组成,已为三角带的被动后冲推覆作用所变形和抬升。前陆区的构造祥式表明,三个近于水平的主滑脱面位于楔状沉积体内,这是滑动由冲断带向前陆逐渐传递的结果。次级隐蔽冲断层导致重叠的压离(pop up)和三角带构造,致使背料核部形态复杂化。

第4章 结构对储层形成的影响

4.1 埃及红海西北部地区构造对油气成藏的影响(I)

导语

埃及红海西北部地区,因其位于红海、亚喀巴湾和苏伊士湾的主裂谷之间的三联点上而吸引了许多地质工作者的注意力。这一盆地地区的断裂系统的几何形态清楚地表明其为拉张背景,地层产状为区域南西倾,该区的拉张程度大于苏伊士湾的其他地区。

根据其应力史、沉积物充填以及沉积背景等方面的差别,红海西北部地区的构造运动可分为六期:(1)寒武纪到早白垩世;(2)晚白垩世到渐新世;(3)早中新世;(4)早—中中新世;(5)中—晚中新世;(6)中新世以后。

课文

前言

研究区位于埃及红海的西北部,地处红海、亚喀巴湾和苏伊士湾主裂谷之间的三联点上(图4.1.1),范围为北纬26°49′~27°32′,东经33°29′~34°05′,长57km,宽44km,面积近2508km^2。研究区内最具特色的地貌特征是前寒武系基岩在三个地方出露地表:西北部的Esh Mellaha山脉、东北部的Shadwan岛和西南部的红海丘陵(图1)。在Esh Mellaha山脉的西侧或多或少地有一套较为完整的前中新世(前裂谷期)地层,而在其南侧的Gebel Abu Shaar高原,中新统的礁复合体直接上超在基岩之上(图4.1.2)。

研究区有着良好的油气聚集潜力,因为红海裂谷活动提供了下列有利的石油地质条件:(1)同裂谷期(中新世)沉积了富含有机质、易于生成石油和(或)天然气的烃源岩;(2)有一个适合烃类生成的成熟环境;(3)前寒武系基底裂缝发育,而且从前寒武系到中新统各层系中均发育有砂岩和碳酸盐岩储层;(4)细粒碎屑岩和蒸发岩作为潜在的盖层;(5)形成了油气聚集的几种圈闭类型(Salah,1994)。目前已经发现了一些有商业性的油和(或)气田,如Hurghada油田、Esh Mellaha油田、Hareed油田和Felefel油田,最早发现的油田——Hurghada油田,是由盎格鲁埃及石油公司(Anglo Egyptian Oil Company)在1914年发现的,最近发现的Hareed油和(或)气田群是由大陆

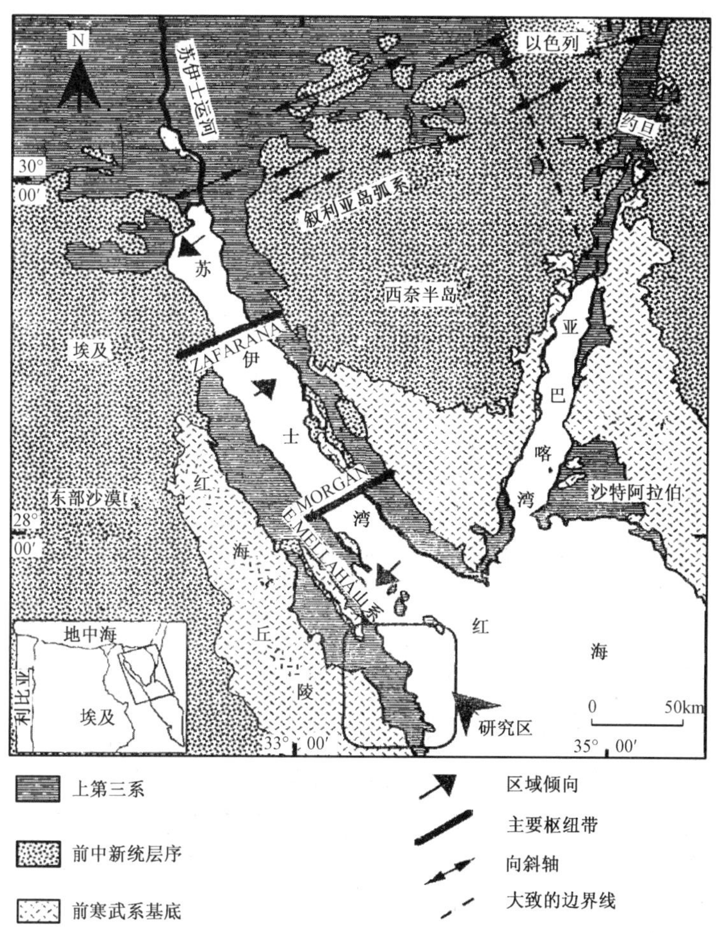

图 4.1.1　苏伊士湾地区的区域构造单元位置及形态

石油公司(Conoco)、埃索石油公司(Esso)和海湾加拿大石油公司(GulfCanada)在 1988 年发现的(图 4.1.2)。

近 90 年来,苏伊士湾和红海地区的地质情况和油气远景一直是许多研究工作的主题。该区的区域构造背景和地质演化史曾是许多研究人员感兴趣的课题,而且目前仍是许多研究课题的焦点所在。El - Tarabili(1970)、El - Ayouti(1980)、Abdine(1981)、Chenet 等(1984)、Sultan 和 Suchultz(1984)、Angelier(1985)、Richert 等(1986)、Grafunkel(1988)、Lyberis(1988)、Meshref 等(1988)、Montenat 等(1988)、Beydoun(1989)、Beydoun 和 Sikander(1992)、Cross - ley 等(1992)、Fichera 等(1992)、Hughes 和 Beydoun(1992)、Mitchell 等(1992)和 Salah(1994)等在以往和最近发表的

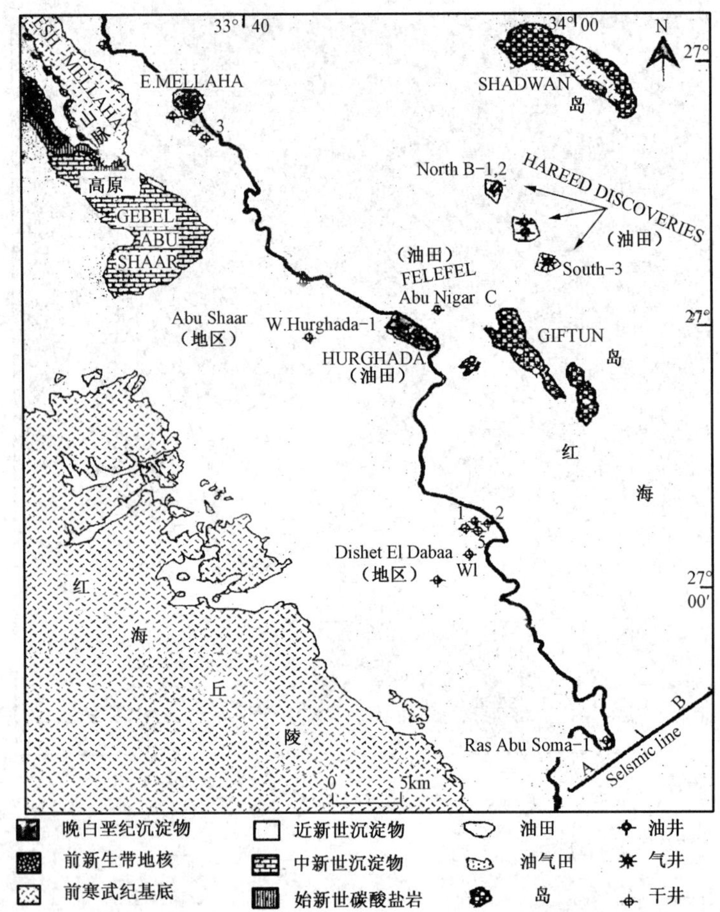

图 4.1.2　展示油气田及探井的研究区位置(改自 Salah,1994)

文章中,对研究区的不同领域感兴趣,涉及演化、发育、沉积以及油气聚集。

本次研究的目的是:(1)搞清红海西北部地区的构造格局;(2)在盆地范围内明确构造高点和低点的分布和走向,这个问题是油气运移和聚集的关键问题。

Hume(1911)、Abdallah 等(1963)、EGPC(1964,1974),Barakat 等(1986)、Darwish(1992),Darwish 和 El - Araby(1993)等对苏伊士湾和红海地区的地层进行了研究,并对该岩石地层单元进行了划分。红海西北部地区的地层从前寒武系到全新统可划分为两个巨层序:前裂谷期(中新世以前)层序和同裂谷期(中新世—全新世)层序。

勘探史

红海西北部地区的油气勘探包括地球物理勘探和钻井勘探两个方面

(EGPC,1986)。

地球物理勘探

研究区内最早的磁力和重力勘探是在第一次世界大战末期由多家石油公司完成的,包括盎格鲁埃及石油公司、美孚石油公司和东部石油公司。1964年,埃及通用石油公司(Egyptian General Petroleum Corporation)联合一些其他的石油公司[包括苏伊士湾石油公司(Gulf of Suez Petroleum Company)和通用石油公司(General Petroleum Company)]组织了在整个苏伊士湾的磁力和重力勘探。十年之后,苏伊士湾石油公司(EGPC,1986)在该区又开展了磁力勘探,由于中新统蒸发岩的影响,这一地区地震资料的品质较差,尤其是在本区的最南部。这次勘探在研究区内发现了几个油气田(如Hareed油田和Felefel油田)。

研究区内进行过多次地震勘探,最早的地震勘探是由Compagine Oriental Des Petroles d'Egypt在五十年代中期完成的。最近的海上地震勘探是在1987年由大陆石油公司(Conoco)完成的,最近的陆上地震勘探分别由Asamera埃及有限公司(Asamera Egypt Limited Company)于1990年在研究区的北部、埃索石油公司埃及子公司(Esso Egypt)于1991年在研究区的南部完成。通过对这些地震资料的解释,特别是陆上部分探区的资料的解释,确定了几口有利的探井井位。

钻井勘探

研究区内所钻的第一口井是Hurghada-1井,是在1913年由盎格鲁埃及石油公司(Anglo Egyptian Oil Company)完成的。该井位于苏伊士湾的西侧,是根据地面构造图设计的井位,钻探目标是一地垒块(图2)。通过这口井的钻探,发现了埃及红海西北部地区的第一个油田。这一发现在二十年代中期鼓舞了其他几家公司在该区勘探油气的积极性,包括非洲勘探公司、东部石油公司(EPC)和西奈(Sinai)石油公司,其中东部石油公司(EPC)在红海西北部的Giftun岛上钻探了几口井(图2),但可惜的是全是干井。尽管第一次世界大战和第二次世界大战影响了钻探,但是从1938年到1950年间,在红海西海岸的Dishet El Dabaa地区和Abu Shaar地区还是钻了一些井(图2),当时没有油气发现。在最近的二十年中,经过进一步钻探,加拿大高级石油公司(Canadian Superior Oil Company)于1982年发现了Esh El Mellaha油田;大陆石油公司(Conoco)在1987年发现了Hareed油气田,在1989年发现了Felefel凝析油田。

构造分析

为了勘探油气,研究区已做过详细的地面地质调查以及地下地质勘查和地球物理勘探。这些研究工作分别由 Said(1962,1990)、Robson(1971)、Moustafa(1976)、Bayer 等(1988), Evans(1988)、Richardson 和 Arthur(1988)、Salah(1989,1994)、Meshref 和 Khalil(1990)、Hughes 等(1991)以及 Hammouda(1992)等完成。

苏伊士湾裂谷为红海向北的延伸,裂谷形成了一个大型坳陷,该拗陷的轴部位于海平面之下。苏伊士湾裂谷走向北北西—南南东,将非洲板块和西奈(Sinai)微板块分开(图 4.1.1)。Abd El – Gawad(1970)研究了裂谷活动期板块的运动方向,提出在阿拉伯半岛和非洲的两对剪切带的横向位移与在沿亚喀巴湾断裂带观测到的位移相同。McKenzie 等(1970)为了精确地确定板块运动的方向,将阿拉伯半岛的海岸线与非洲红海的海岸线进行了对比,测得的板块运动方向与 Abd El – Gawad(1970)的研究结果完全相同:阿拉伯板块的总体运动方向为相对于非洲板块向东北方向运动。将红海裂谷北部的宽度与苏伊士湾南部的宽度作一比较,其结果说明:沿亚喀巴湾走滑带的左旋运动在红海形成的地壳拉张比在苏伊士湾形成的要强得多(Robertson 研究小组,1985)。

Meshref 和 Khalil(1990)计算了苏伊士湾北部、中部和南部的拉张量。首先在三个位置分别制作三条有代表性的构造横剖面,计算其拉张量分别为 5.1km、14km 和 23km,其拉张后的宽度比初始的宽度分别增加了 11%,17% 和 33%。上述研究结果表明红海西北部地区的拉张量大于苏伊士湾的其他地区(Meshref 和 Khalil,1990)。

苏伊士湾裂谷的边界由该裂谷系两侧横向上稳定的断裂带确定,边界断层的上升盘基岩出露地表(Robertson 研究小组,1985)。这些断裂带的走向一般为西北—东南向,但在北部不易确定。

盆地内断裂系统的几何特征指示该区为拉张构造背景。一般来说,苏伊士湾可分为三个次级构造单元,这与区内沉积盖层的主要构造倾向相一致(Moustafa,1976),许多在苏伊士湾工作的地质学家用两个主要的转换断层或枢纽带将这三个次级构造单元分开。北部的转换带为 Zafarana 枢纽带,它将苏伊士湾北部的地层产状总体为南西倾的构造单元与中部的北东倾的构造单元分开;第二转换带是 Morgan 枢纽带,它是苏伊士湾中部构造单元与南部构造单元的分界,南部构造单元的盖层产状为区域南西倾(图 1)。

构造运动对沉积作用的影响

在这一节中,我们试图将红海西北部地区的地层单元、岩相和构造演化三者之间建立某种关系。测定该区的裂谷活动期为晚渐新世到早中新世。通过测定苏伊士地区的玄武岩活动时间确定的裂谷活动时间是在距今 19 ~

24Ma 之间(Fichera 等,1992),而通过分析地层层序的岩相和生物相确定的裂谷活动期为晚渐新世到早中新世(Salah,1989,1994)。Cochran 和 Martinez(1988)认为裂谷的开始应是从红海洋壳演化的开始算起,因而应是在大约从距今 23Ma 开始,而 Moretti 等(1986)得出的结论是:主要裂谷期是在早中新世。

红海西北部地区的构造演化大致可分为六个阶段。

1. 第一阶段(寒武纪到早白垩世)

在第一阶段,主要沉积了陆相到浅海相的砂岩与薄层页岩、白云岩和灰岩的互层,形成前森诺曼期沉积。这些以前称之为 Nubia 砂岩,系红海西北部地区的储层之一,如 Hurghada 油田。

2. 第二阶段(晚白垩世到渐新世)

从晚白垩世开始,全区抬升并遭受剥蚀,之后从北向南有一次广泛海侵,人们认为这次抬升和剥蚀是由于 Tethyan 裂谷活动产生的(Said,1962)。森诺曼阶和土伦阶的层序逐步向南上超,其下部为砂岩、页岩互层(Raha 组和 Abu Qada 组),上部为碳酸盐岩(Wata 组)。在苏伊士湾的一些油田中,这些砂岩和灰岩可作为有利的储层。

在森诺曼期,下部单元以碎屑岩相为主(Matulla 组),上部单元以碳酸盐岩相为主(Duwi 和 Sudr 组),上部单元是苏伊士湾的主要烃源岩(Salah,1989)。

Esna 组是古新世的沉积,在叙利亚岛弧系隆起时部分沉积被剥蚀。由于叙利亚岛弧系的隆起,在全区范围内 Esna 组遭受剥蚀而变薄(Said,1962),局部地区甚至全部被剥蚀掉。

上覆在 Esna 组之上的是始新世广泛海侵期沉积的 Thebes 组碳酸盐岩。在苏伊士湾盆地中,这两套地层是潜在的烃源岩(Salah,1989)。局部地区,在碳酸盐岩大陆架上沉积了渐新统红色砾岩层,称之为 Tayiba 红层,这套红层可认为是渐新世裂谷活动开始的标志。

3. 第三阶段(早中新世)

第三阶段,阿拉伯板块开始与非洲板块分离,这期构造运动称之为“早 clysmic 运动”(Robertson 研究小组,1985)。张应力导致断裂活动,致使盆地内的一些地区沉降到海平面以下。早中新世沉积的 Nukhul 组具有不同的沉积相,反映其沉积背景的多相性,为独立断块在不同的构造背景下沉积的产物(Meshref 和 Khalil,1990)。其下段(Shoab Ali 段)为含砾或角砾砂岩(储集相)与薄层页岩互层,使中新统与前中新统呈不整合接触;上段(Ghara 段)由硬石膏(包括潮上带/萨布哈环境中的沉积)、浅海灰岩和页岩(浅海大陆架沉积)和陆相砂岩(代表陆上沉积)组成。

Khalil 和 Meshref(1988)将苏伊士湾裂谷的初始期分为两个发展阶段:Shoab Ali 段的沉积结构代表了裂谷初始阶段的沉积,仅局限于苏伊士湾的最南部;初始阶段之后紧接着进入第二发展阶段,整个苏伊士湾裂开,形成泛 Nukhul 盆地。裂谷停止发展有两个主要原因:(1)阿拉伯板块和西奈板块逆时针旋转与非洲板块分离,使裂谷北部岩石圈的强度增大;(2)先前存在的叙利亚岛弧系的东北东向的挤压构造地貌(Khalil 和 Meshref,1988)。

4. 第四阶段(早—中中新世)

第四阶段为构造运动最活跃期,伴随着最大的拉张应力,裂谷区发生快速沉降并形成主要的半地堑和地堑。此期沉积了 Rudeis 组,与此同时,红海的较南端开始海底扩张(Fichera 等,1992),在"中 clysmic 运动"期,断层再次活动并发生局部隆升。在中中新世,裂谷的肩部(主断层上升盘)开始上升,在沉降裂谷的边缘附近沉积了粗砂岩和砾岩(储集相)(Robertson 研究小组,1985);在较深海区,沉积了细粒沉积物(烃源岩相),并形成了一套物性较好的海底浊积岩和较粗粒级的砂岩。Khalil 和 Meshref(1988)称第四阶段为主要沉降期。

5. 第五阶段(中—晚中新世)

在第五阶段,苏伊士湾和红海西北部的气候发生了变化,沉积了 Kareem 组和 Belayim 组的泥灰质蒸发岩的韵律层(盖层相)、局部带有砂岩的富含钙质页岩(烃源岩相)和砾岩层(储集相)。晚中新世沉积了蒸发岩最发育的层系—南 Gharib 组和 Zeit 组,其主要成分为盐和硬石膏,夹有薄层页岩(盖层相)(Fawzy 和 Abdel - Aal,1984)。

6. 第六阶段(中新世以后至全新世)

从所谓的"晚 clysmic 运动"开始,裂谷演化进入第六阶段,这是由于大陆的进一步运动和亚喀巴平错断层再次活动(Robertson 研究小组,1985)的结果。断层的复活在一些地区造成了大规模的构造沉降。中新统以上的地层为不同环境的沉积,包括深海、浅海、受限海和陆相环境(Abd El - Shafy,1990)。古生物资料表明,上新世时期印度洋和红海是相通的(Abd El - Shafy,1990)。

Key to Exercises

Ⅰ.

1. The area that forms the scope of this study lies in the northwestern Red Sea, Egypt, at the triple junction of the main rifts between the Red Sea, Gulf

of Aqaba, and Gulf of Suez.

2. Because the rifting of the Red Sea produces favorable conditions for (1) synrift (Miocene) organic – rich, oil – and / or gas – prone source rock deposition; (2) a suitable maturity regime for generating hydrocarbons; (3) the development of fractures in the Precambrian basement, and the accumulation of sandstone and carbonate reservoirs, ranging in age from Precambrian to Miocene; (4) the presence of potential fine – grained clastic and evapo – rite seals; and (5) several types of traps for accumulation of hydrocarbons.

3. The purposes of this study were to (1) clarify the structural configuration of the northwestern Red Sea, and (2) highlight the distribution and trends of basinwide structural highs and lows that could act as focus for migration and accumulation of hydrocarbons.

4. The stratigraphic section of the northwestern Red Sea can be classified into two megasequences: prerift (pre – Miocene) and synrift (Miocene to Holocene)

5. The first reconnaissance survey in the study area was made in the middle 1950s by the Compagnie Oriental Des Petroles d' Egypt.

Ⅱ. 1 – 5 BDABC 6 – 10 ACBAA

Ⅲ. 1 – 5 CDACC

Ⅳ.

1. 研究区位于埃及红海的西北部,地处红海、亚喀巴湾和苏伊士湾主裂谷之间的三联点上。

2. 在该区又开展了磁力勘探,由于中新统蒸发岩的影响,这一地区地震资料的品质较差,尤其是在本区的最南部。

3. 首先在三个位置分别制作三条有代表性的构造横剖面,计算其拉张量分别为 5.1km、14km 和 23km,其拉张后的宽度比初始的宽度分别增加了 11%,17% 和 33%。

4. 苏伊士湾裂谷的边界由该裂谷系两侧横向上稳定的断裂带确定。

5. 这一发现在二十世纪二十年代中期鼓舞了其他几家公司在该区勘探油气的积极性,包括非洲勘探公司、东部石油公司(EPC)和西奈(Sinai)石油公司。

Ⅴ.

1. 目前,红海西北部地区的构造地质分析是建立在对地球物理资料(磁力、重力和处理过的地震资料)和地质资料解释的基础上的。地质资料包括取自研究区内及其附近钻探的45口井的地下资料、地面露头资料以及区内构造格局的航空照片。通过对横穿研究区的几条横剖面的解释加深了对盆地几何特征的了解。

2. 据此往北,边界断层分支成多条弯曲的、相互连接的张性断层,而且断距逐渐减小(Robertson研究小组,1985)。在研究区内,裂谷的边界断层和出露基岩的地貌特征是很明显的,可以作为裂谷几何形态的地貌标志。

4.2 埃及红海西北部地区构造对油气成藏的影响(Ⅱ)

导语

磁力、重力、地震资料、地面地质露头资料以及地下地质资料表明:红海西北部地区存在几个狭长的隆起带,隆起带之间被狭长的地堑隔开,隆起和地堑的轴向均为北西—南东向,与clysmic断层的走向一致。有些隆起带被走向东北—西南和东—东北—西—西南的横断层错断并在横向上产生位移。

红海西北部地区的构造格局对油气的生成、运移和聚集有着十分重要的影响。这种影响的证据包括以下几个方面:(1)地堑形成主要的烃源区,其前寒武系基岩的现今埋深超过4877m(如Gemsa地堑);(2)clysmic断层断距的大小是圈闭条件中的关键因素;(3)横断层对油气的运移和聚集起主要控制作用,因为这些断层圈定了大多数油田的范围并成为这些油田的边界断层;(4)研究区内已发现的所有油田均为构造油藏和(或)复合型油裁,并与区内磁异常对应较好。

课文

盆地的几何特征

目前,红海西北部地区的构造地质分析工作是以本区的磁力资料和地震资料的解释成果以及制作的几条横剖面为基础来完成的。地面地质资料有助于对盆地几何特征的理解。

从大的结构上看,红海西北部地区由多个狭长的隆起和地堑组成,隆起和地堑相间排列、相互分隔,其轴向与红海—苏伊士湾的走向一致,为西北—东南向,这些隆起被走向东北—西南和东—东北—西—西南的横断层错断。这些横断层为转换断层。

所用的资料和资料解释

地球物理资料

研究盆地的几何特征应用了区内最新的地震资料，然而，由于中新统有一套较厚的蒸发岩，使地震剖面上蒸发岩以下的反射层难以识别。鉴于这一难题，我们采用了其他的地球物理勘探方法。在红海西北部地区，用地磁图(化极后)来研究区域构造的几何特征是十分有效的方法。代表基底隆起带的磁异常，在纵向上追踪并连接成磁力高走向带，而且追踪这些磁力高走向带的偏移可解释出一些横断层。

地质资料

研究红海西北部地区的构造格局应用了区内所有可用的地质资料，包括取自区内45口井的地下资料和地面露头资料。沿区域构造的走向和倾向分别制作了一系列的剖面示意图，其目的是为了突出盆地中的隆起带，这些隆起带是油气运移和聚集的中心。

资料解释

地球物理资料和地质资料均表明：红海西北部地区由数排被横断层(转换断层)错断的clysmic隆起带组成，隆起带之间被主地堑分隔，按其长度的大小可分为大型隆起带和小型隆起带两类。自东向西大型隆起带分别是Shadwan隆起带、Abu Shiban－Hareed隆起带、Hurghada－Umm Agawish隆起带、南部海岸隆起带(Dabaa隆起、Sharm El Arab隆起和Abu Soma隆起)、Esh Mellaha山脉和红海丘陵。自东向西小型隆起带分别为RSOX94隆起带、Felefel隆起带、Mel1aha隆起带和西Hurghada隆起带。

大型隆起带

Shadwan隆起带

Shadwan隆起带是研究区内最东边一个隆起带，因其包括Shadwan岛而得名，岛上前寒武系基岩出露地表。该隆起带向北延伸到Gubal岛，岛上的基底埋深约为300m，最老的地层是Rudeis组，说明该隆起带是前Rudeis期的隆起。

Abu Shiban－Hareed隆起带

西Shadwan地堑将Abu Shiban－Hareed隆起带与Shadwan隆起带分开，该隆起带的范围从现在最南部的已知点Hareed南—3井，向北经过Hareed 1号和2号、Hareed北、Estakoza—1和Abu Shiban—2等井一直延伸到研究区较北部地区。根据这些井的钻探结果，隆起带的基底埋深由南向北加深，在南部。Hareed—3井揭示的基底埋深为1684m，而在北部的Abu Shiban—2井中埋深为2836m。在该隆起带上钻探的所有的井均未揭示有前中新统和下中新统的 Nukhul 组。最老的盖层直接覆盖在基岩之上，为下中新统 Rudeis 组，说明该隆起带为前 Rudeis 期的隆起。

南部海岸隆起带

南部海岸隆起带为研究区内沿西南部海岸展布的隆起带。它由三个独立的隆起组成，横断层的错断使三个隆起相互偏离，由北向南分别是 Dabaa 隆起、Sharm El Arab 隆起和 Ras Abu Soma 隆起。隆起向南倾没，在 Dabaa 隆起上，前寒武系基岩埋深为 556m，而在 Ras Abu Soma 隆起上为 1237m。中新统最老的地层为 Nukhul 组。

Hurghada－Umm Agawish 隆起带

Hurghada－Umm Agawish 隆起带由三个独立的、相互之间被断层错开的隆起组成，从北向南依次是 Hurghada 油田、Abu Minqar 隆起和 Umm Agawish 隆起。隆起带上前寒武系基底的埋深由北向南加深，在 Hurghada 油田为 795m。而在 Umm Agawish 隆起上为 1513m。在该隆起带上，大部分前中新统地层均保存较好，特别是在南部。

Esh Mellaha 山脉隆起带

在 Esh Mellaha 山脉隆起带中，基底出露地表，并且向南倾没在中新统 Gebel Abu Shaar 的礁复合体之下。基底的平均高程为 427m，向南降低。在南端仅为 341m（Abu El－Karamat, 1988）。它是研究区唯一前裂谷期地层（寒武系到始新统）保留齐全的隆起带（图 2）。

红海丘陵

红海丘陵位于研究区的西南角，约占研究区面积的五分之一（图 1），研究区内丘陵的高程在 46～335m 之间。在丘陵西侧的研究区以外地区，前中新统地层保留较为齐全（Said，1962，1990）。

小型隆起带

RSOX94 隆起带

RSOX94 隆起带是研究区内最南部的海上隆起带。隆起带基底埋深达 1313m，磁力和地震资料均表明 RSOX94—1 井钻在该隆起带上，但未钻遇前中新统。

Felefel 隆起带

Felefel 隆起带被横断层切割成两部分，南段为 Abu Nigar C，北段为 Felefel。隆起带基底的平均埋深为 914m。它的北部保存有很薄的前中新统，但在南部，经钻井证实该套地层缺失。

Mellaha 隆起

Mellaha 隆起上已产出原油，在该油田区基底埋深约为 1219m，基底与中新统呈不整合接触，缺失前中新统。

对油气的影响

研究区作为整个红海裂谷盆地的一部分，与整个盆地一样，其构造格局对油气的生成、运移和聚集起着十分重要的作用。

油气的生成

现有的资料解释成果表明，研究区的大地构造演化和构造格局在以下几个方面对油气的生成起着十分重要的作用。首先，裂谷活动为富含有机质的烃源岩和潜在的储层、盖层的沉积创造了良好的条件；其次，在红海西北部地区沿着 clysmic 断层的走向（西北—东南）发育有多个平行的、被隆起所分隔的狭长地堑，其中有些地堑的深度较大，足以使前裂谷期（前中新世）和同裂谷期（中—晚中新世）沉积的烃源岩处在生油窗内（Salah，1992）。在最深的地堑（Gemsa 地堑）中，前寒武系的基底埋深超过 5180m，前中新统烃源岩的埋深已经进入生气窗；第三，在红海这一地区，其地壳成分具有非均一性（Fichera 等，1992），局部高热流点有助于地堑中烃源岩成熟（即使在较浅的坳陷中），红海西北部地区的平均地温梯度达 1.9°F/m，相比之下在苏伊士湾仅为 1.7°F/m；最后，由于红海西北部地区的地层区域西南倾，油气运移的指向为北东方向，但对于 Esh Mellaha 油田，其油气是从东北部的 Gemsa 地堑向西南运移的，因为在其西南侧没有盆地。

油气的封堵和圈闭的形成

红海西北部地区的油气圈闭有几种封堵机制，包括构造圈闭、地层圈闭和复合圈闭，这些问题 Meshref 等（1988）、Saoudy （1990）、Hammouda（1992）、Alsharhan 和 Salah（1994）等均有较详细的描述。

在前裂谷期地层中，上白垩统的碳酸盐岩（Duwi - Sudr 碳酸盐岩）、Esna 页岩和 Thebes 灰岩可作为白垩系砂岩储集层的盖层，然而在同裂谷期层系中，中新统的蒸发岩一直被当作苏伊士湾的主要盖层（Rashed，1990），这在红海西北部地区的确如此，因为无论在 clysmic 主断层的下降盘还是在抬起的掀斜断块的下倾方向，蒸发岩均较厚。然而，clysmic 断层落差的大小是影响封堵的关键条件（Meshref 等，1988）。较小的落差将使断层下降盘的蒸发岩与上升盘的中新统孔隙发育段对接而形成封堵（如 Esh Mellaha 油田和 Hareed 油田）。落差较大时，将导致像 Geisum 油田和 Ashrafi 油田那样中新统蒸发岩与抬升断块中的前中新统储层对接（仅在研究区的北部）（Salah. 1989）。

中新统碎屑岩剖面中的页岩亦可作为盖层，在这些情况下，碎屑岩剖面中的孔隙发育层段将作为储集层，而页岩层段将作为横向和（或）垂向的封堵层,这要视断层落差大小而定(如 Hurghada 油田)。

结论

本课题的目的是为了研究埃及红海西北部地区的构造格局和构造演化对油气的生成、运移和聚集的影响。根据裂谷的演化阶段,本区的地层可分为两个巨层序:前裂谷期(前中新世)层序和同裂谷期(中新世—全新世)层序。构造演化可分为六个阶段,展示了各阶段在构造应力、沉积物特征和沉积环境等方面的差异,这六个阶段分别是:(1)寒武纪到早白垩世;(2)晚白垩世到渐新世;(3)早中新世;(4)早—中中新世;(5)中—晚中新世;(6)中新世以后。红海西北部地区由多个狭长的、西北—东南向的沉积地堑组成,地堑被隆起带隔开,隆起带被东北和东—东北向的转换断层错断。

红海西北部地区的构造格局和构造演化在很大程度上控制了富含有机质的烃源岩、潜在的储层和盖层的沉积,控制了适合油气生成所需的热流和油气聚集的圈闭条件。

我们得出的结论是;红海西北部地区是一个具有油气勘探远景的地区,应做更多的勘探工作。

Key to Exercises

Ⅰ.

1. The presence of a very thick Miocene evaporite sequence made it difficult to distinguish any deeper horizon structural levels on seismic reflection profiles. Because of this difficulty, we use additional geophysical tools. The available magnetic maps (reduced to pole) were very useful in detecting the regional geometry of the northwestern sector of the Red Sea. Moreover, the cross elements were traced using shifts in the extension of these high trends.

2. The earliest Miocene unit recorded on this high is the Nukhul Formation.

3. The oldest stratigraphic unit recorded in this trend is the Rudeis Formation, indicating that this trend was a pre – Rudeis high.

4. The six stages are: (1) Cambrian to Early Cretaceous; (2) Late Cretaceous to Oligocene; (3) early Miocene; (4) early to middle Miocene; (5) middle to late Miocene; and (6) post – Miocene.

5. We conclude that the northwestern Red Sea is a potential hydrocarbon exploration area and should receive more exploration activity.

Ⅱ. 1 – 5 BCACA 6 – 10 ADBCA

Ⅲ. 1 –5　DBAAC

Ⅳ.

1. 目前,红海西北部地区的构造地质分析工作是以本区的磁力资料和地震资料的解释成果,以及制作的几条横剖面为基础来完成的。

2. 研究盆地的几何特征应用了区内最新的地震资料,然而,由于中新统有一套较厚的蒸发岩,使地震剖面上蒸发岩以下的反射层难以识别。

3. 在该隆起带上钻探的所有的井均未揭示有前中新统和下中新统的 Nukhul 组。

4. 研究区作为整个红海裂谷盆地的一部分,与整个盆地一样,其构造格局对油气的生成、运移和聚集起着十分重要的作用。

5. 这在红海西北部地区的确如此,因为无论在 clysmic 主断层的下降盘还是在抬起的掀斜断块的下倾方向,蒸发岩均较厚。

Ⅴ.

1. 盆地内断裂系统的几何特征指示该区为拉张构造背景。一般来说,苏伊士湾可分为三个次级构造单元,这与区内沉积盖层的主要构造倾向相一致,许多在苏伊士湾工作的地质学家用两个主要的转换断层或枢纽带将这三个次级构造单元分开。

2. 尽管第一次世界大战和第二次世界大战影响了钻探,但是从 1938 年到 1950 年间,在红海西海岸的 Dishet El Dabaa 地区和 Abu Shaar 地区还是钻了一些井,当时未有发现。在最近的 20 年中,经过进一步钻探,1982 年发现了 Esh El Mellaha 油田。

第5章　石油勘探和开发

5.1　在褶皱和冲断带的石油勘探和开发——从 Hedberg 专题讨论会得出的观点(I)

导语

本课旨在评论于 1997 年在墨西哥 Veracruz 举行的关于在褶皱和冲断带进行石油勘探和开发的 Hedberg 专题讨论会上提出的观点。这是 AAPC 大会第一次将焦点集中在此构造领域的勘探和开发，这次大会将活跃在褶皱和冲断带研究领域的全球各地的地质学家和地球物理学家聚集一堂，交流他们的经验，并讨论范围广泛的有关勘探和开发的问题。专题讨论会的课题包括油气生成、运移、圈闭和保存、勘探方法和策略、油田开发和数据采集。会议上提出了许多的实例研究来说明这些课题。

课文

引言

AAPC 与墨西哥石油地质协会联合举办了有关褶皱和冲断带的石油天然气勘探和开发的 Hedberg 专题讨论会，此次会议是在 1997 年 2 月 23 日至 26 日在墨西哥的 Veracruz 召开的。这次大会由 Richard S. Bishop(埃克森)、Bernardo Martell – Andrade (Pemex)和 Rafael Sanchez – Montes de Oca (AMGP)召集。来自 18 个国家的约 270 名与会者出席了此次大会。大会的目的是提供一个交流经验的场所，并突出新技术的应用，以共同讨论在褶皱和冲断带进行勘探、开发和油田作业时产生的问题。这次专题讨论会包括 30 多篇发言论文和近 50 份张贴报告。

这是一次有商业意向的大会，除这些论文的技术角度之外，还要求演讲人说明他们的课题潜在的商业影响。商业方面需考虑的事项包括确定和评估新的机遇、优化远景区、确定并降低风险、提出勘探和开发策略。大部分论文集中于西半球的褶皱和冲断带，不过全球各处的褶皱和冲断带都有展示。会议安排了两次与会议相关的油田参观。会前参观的是墨西哥 Monterrey 和 Saltillo 附近的 Sierra Madre Oriental 的北部冲断带。会后参观的是 Zongolica 褶皱和冲断带，它是墨西哥 Veracruz 地区 Sierra Madre Oriental 的向南延伸带。这些参观提供了构造样式和地面显示的对比,并举例说明了此构造内勘探和开发方面遇到的许多挑战。

以下文字对在大会上提出的某些重要课题进行了总结,我们在此不可能对 80 个发言报告和张贴报告都进行总结。而是尽量阐明 8 次讨论的每一次的主要观点。发言报告包括:(1)远景区要素——在褶皱带油气的生成和运移;(2)远景区要素,包括褶皱带的油气圈闭及保存;(3)褶皱和冲断带的勘探方法和策略;(4)褶皱冲断带的油田开发。张贴报告包括:(1)褶皱带的数据采集和解释——地质和遥感;(2)褶皱带的数据采集和解释——地球物理学及其他方法;(3)实例,包括褶皱带油田开发技术和实例。

尽管会上提出了许多观点和经验,在整个专题研讨会期间仍重申了几个常见的课题。首先(也许是最主要的),像最近在几个前缘地区获得的成功所证实的那样,褶皱和冲断带内蕴藏着丰富的石油和天然气。这一优势常被构造带周围复杂的地质情况、多变的地形和环境问题所抵消。这里的核心风险包括圈闭圈定、运移与圈闭形成时间及断层封堵,而成功通常取决于明智地应用合适的技术、有效利用所有可降低风险的方法、坚持不懈和勇于承担风险。

远景区要素:褶皱带的油气生成和运移

这次专题研讨会的第一次会议着重于褶皱和冲断带的油气生成和运移。由于源岩成熟度与构造演化之间的复杂关系,绘制多次运移路径图的难度,以及源岩成熟、油气运移和圈闭形成之间普遍狭窄的时间窗口,油气的存在和油气的预测基本上是不确定的。在该地带确定源岩层段(或多个层段)及其特征,确定运移通道和泄油面积,并限定圈闭形成时间和源岩成熟的时间是其关键所在。会议中所列举的实例来自玻利维亚、秘鲁、墨西哥、哥伦比亚、委内瑞拉和加拿大。

有几篇论文提供了可更好地限定油气生成和运移时间,确定其区域性油气体系的最新技术。Covey 等人(埃克森)列举了应用伊利石/蒙皂石分析以推断西加拿大褶皱带冲断作用时间的实例。这项技术通过确定断层运动期间蒙皂石形成成岩的伊利石来判断其构造作用的时间。同样的,Yurewicz 等人(埃克森)举例说明了综合使用伊利石/蒙皂石分析、裂变径迹分析和流体包裹体分析以约束地热和埋藏史模型,以及烃类流体包裹体的地球化学特征来圈定区域性油气体系。Bachu(艾伯塔地质勘查公司)描述了水动力与地热体制之间的相互作用以及它们如何对一个地区的地热史起着重要的作用,并因此影响油气生成、运移和聚集。

有几篇论文举例说明了构造演化、生油岩成熟和油气运移之间的复杂关系。Peppe 和 Daly(BP 勘探公司)提供了一项极好的实例研究,通过描述东委内瑞拉 El Furial 走向带复杂的成熟、运移、填充和溢出史,说明了许多可能存在于褶皱一冲断带的问题。同样,Colletta 等人(法国石油研究院)通过列举法国阿尔卑斯山的例子来说明构造演化和生油岩成熟之间复杂的相互作用。他们强调,要重建褶皱和冲断带的温度史,必须建立时间、层序和冲断速度模型,同时或后来的沉积、剥蚀和沉降模型,并分析受影响岩层的输导性的变化。对这些情况进行精确的二维正演模拟将使得勘探家能更准确地预测有希望的褶皱和冲断带不同部位的油气类型。

远景区要素:褶皱带油气的圈闭和保存

专题讨论会的第二次发言会议着重于褶皱带内油气的圈闭和保存。提出了几点不同的看法和相关的实例研究。在其中的一项研究中,Coleman 等人(阿莫科)对世界各地的 24 个褶皱带和前陆盆地进行了分析,并对 20 个远景区和 6 种可能的风险水平进行了评估。他们推论出,除了圈闭确定之外,存在的高品质生油岩极大降低了远景区其他所有要素的风险。简而言之,从高品质生油岩中生成的大量油气可抵消与运移、圈闭和保存有关的风险。

Kluth(雪弗龙)对褶皱和冲断带的圈闭和盖层风险进行了评估。这些要素控制了存在于一个构造中的储量和油气柱高度;这些可换算为油气体积。对这些要素进行风险评估是困难的,并要求“绝对诚实”。他强调总是没有足够的资料能完整地进行一项解释,因而总是需要更多、更好的数据或更稳健的模型。然而,他提醒道,我们必须对更多和更好的资料的成本和采集信息的价值作出评估。“更多、更好的资料”的实例包括品质有所提高的地震资料、更优的测井数据和更好的测试数据。为对现有资料作出最佳解释,需要“更稳健的模型”。人们应用横剖面作为评估圈闭几何形态的方法,该方法已取得了极大的进步,已实现从手工画横剖面到平衡横剖面,再到平衡剖面的增量式恢复。计算机分析能力的提高可能最终建立增量式三维平衡剖面。整个专题研讨会期间一再提及采用横剖面来测试构造模型。Kluth 还总结道,尽管在褶皱和冲断带的顶部封盖不是常见风险,但断层封堵是主要的风险。尽管在维持有较大油气柱高度的几个地区列举了几个断层封堵的实例,我们仍不能预测断层封堵是否存在或其有效性。

Pottorf 等人用埃克森公司采用流体包裹体来阐明复杂的填充和溢出史的另一些例子结束了这次会议。在特立尼达的实例中,流体包裹体被用来说明极易混淆的井资料和复杂的运移与圈闭后的过程。在关于墨西哥的第二个实例中,流体包裹体被用来约束区域性构造地质史和绘制区域性油族。

褶皱和冲断带的勘探方式和策略

褶皱和冲断带向勘探家提出了更多的挑战。关键的问题是采集高质量的地震资料。进入高山地区的困难限制了地震采集，由于凹凸不平的地表、垂直和水平速度变化、较陡的复杂构造、低速带和喀斯特地形的近地表效应，使得处理变得更加复杂。显而易见，这些问题并不是褶皱—冲断带所特有的，但在一背景下，勘探家去面对所有这些问题也不是很常见的。这次会议的目的是举例说明不同的公司是如何对付如此不利的情况的。通常，这些作者没有说明他们勘探方法的特点，但他们仍然说明了他们是如何在这种地带采集资料的。

Rodriguez 等人（Pemex）举例说明了在 Sierra Madre Oriental 的 Zongolica 区块进行勘探所遇到的许多问题。尽管进行了大量的地质学、地球化学和地球物理学研究，在此走向带进行勘探的成功率还是很有限的。他们认为二维地震的低分辨率可能是导致迄今成功率有限的原因。同样，Bentham 和 Serra（阿莫科）引证了在哥伦比亚中部 Opon 油田采集足够地震数据的困难性。他们极力称赞二维和三维正演模型对测试构造复杂地区不同构造模型的好处。因为 Opon 油田的二维地震资料差，阿莫科公司绘制了贯穿油田的 21 张构造横剖面，据此创建了三维构造模型。基于 Opon 天然气发现建立的三维模型有助于决定取消一项计划好的三维地震勘探、重新计算储量、设计开发井和联系项目的各方。Apotria 等人（埃克森和 Maraven）提交了一篇类似的文章，强调在委内瑞拉的马拉开波盆地西部应用三维可视化方法解释褶皱和冲断带构造。

Graham 等人（Monument 石油和天然气公司、BP 公司和英国天然气公司）强调了确定褶皱和冲断带时间的重要性。尽管褶皱和冲断带可能会使具有极好储层、盖层和生油岩的原先的被动边缘和前陆盆地变形，但变形机制常常造成隆起，从而阻止了生油岩的成熟和油气生成。他们得出结论，经过长时间沉降和多次抬升的褶皱和冲断带更可能成为油气远景区。

褶皱和冲断带的野外作业

在这一次会议中，多次提及了在许多典型褶皱和冲断带的凹凸不平地形上获取高质量地震数据遇到的挑战。全球勘探活动向褶皱和冲断带扩展带来了采集地震数据的新方法和策略。这一次会议有 6 篇论文说明了当前面临的挑战及解决方法。

Gray 等人（阿莫科）提出了数据采集中出现的问题，并说明他们如何使用一系列地形相关校正来提高资料品质，这些方法包括：(1) 直接根据地形，而不是根据一平基准面或浮动基准面处理数据；(2) 密切关注对振幅的处理;(3)密切关注沿着记录排列的局部地形变化影响;(4)沿弯线(如沿着由一组共中心点位置确定的"测线")进行计算机成像。

尽管在褶皱和冲断带进行三维地震采集会有许多固有的问题,Villanueva 等人(Pemex 公司)论证了在墨西哥东南部的褶皱带进行三维地震采集的好处。在 Sierra de Chiapas 附近的整个 Gancho 和 Secadero 油田做了三维地震采集。这些改进的成像避免了 Pemex 公司在向斜钻一口干井,且有助于确定 3 个新的远景圈闭,如取得成功,将使储量翻一番。

在一篇相关的论文中,Bertelli 等人(阿吉普公司和西方地球物理公司)总结了应用现有技术获取随钻速度和 VSP(垂直地震剖面)资料的方法。在速度控制资料少的地区,这项技术可及时地提供数据,改进地震资料的质量,修正构造模型和井轨迹。

两篇论文(阿莫科公司的 Barker 等人和 Triton 公司的 Fauria)也提到了在偏远的、环境和政治敏感地区进行作业的情况,列举了在厄瓜多尔、秘鲁、委内瑞拉、危地马拉和哥伦比亚近期的勘探实例。在这些地区有效地实施项目需要有一套经营策略,包括:(1)获得新的区块之前考虑其环境问题;(2)制定一项经营计划减少其环境和文化的影响;(3)发展公共事务、通讯和外围项目,以获得当地的支持。

Key to Exercises

Ⅰ.

1. The purpose of the conference was to provide a venue to exchange experiences and highlight the application of new technologies to shared problems in exploration, production, and field operations in fold – thrust belts.

2. The first session of the symposium focused on hydrocarbon generation and migration in fold – belt plays.

3. The symposium's second oral session focused on entrapment and preservation of hydrocarbons within fold belts.

4. In an example from Trinidad, fluid inclusions were used to unravel confusing well results and complex migration and post – emplacement processes.

5. They suggest that poor 2 – D (two – dimensional) seismic resolution may account for their limited success to date.

Ⅱ. 1 – 5 BDABA 6 – 10 CCDDB

Ⅲ. 1 – 5 BACBD

Ⅳ.

1. 除了这些论文的技术角度之外,演讲人还被要求说明他们的课题潜在的商业影响。

2. 有几篇论文举例说明了构造演化、生油岩成熟和油气运移之间的复杂关系。

3. 简而言之,从高品质生油岩中生成的大量油气可抵消与运移、圈闭和保存有关的风险。

4. 显而易见,这些问题并不是褶皱—冲断带所特有的,但在这一背景下,勘探家去面对所有这些问题也不是很常见的。

5. 尽管进行了大量的地质学、地球化学和地球物理学研究,在此走向带进行勘探的成功率还是很有限的。

Ⅴ.

1. 油层由形状适当、顶部盖有不渗透岩石的孔隙性岩层构成。构造的形状必须适宜于油(或气)在某一层带中汇集,从而形成油气储集层,而顶部的盖层是防止油气继续向上运移所不可缺少的。

2. 从地层学角度来看,含油气系统包括所在地理分布区域内的如下岩层或基本要素:最重要时期的烃源岩、储集层、盖层以及上覆岩层。前三种岩石类型的作用是显而易见的,上覆岩层的作用较难理解,它不仅可以作为烃源岩热成熟的必备条件,而且还对其下地层中运移通道和圈闭的集合形态产生一定的影响。

5.2 在褶皱和冲断带的石油勘探和开发——从 Hedberg 专题讨论会得出的观点(Ⅱ)

导语

本课旨在评论于 1997 年在墨西哥 Veracruz 举行的关于在褶皱和冲断带进行石油勘探和开发的 Hedberg 专题讨论会上提出的观点。这是 AAPC 大会第一次将焦点集中在此构造领域的勘探和开发,这次大会将活跃在褶皱和冲断带研究领域的全球各地的地质学家和地球物理学家聚集一堂,交流他们的经验,并讨论范围广泛的有关勘探和开发的问题。专题讨论会的课题包括油气生成、运移、圈闭和保存、勘探方法和策略、油田开发和数据采集。会议上提出了许多的实例研究来说明这些课题。

课文

褶皱和冲断带的油田开发

当然,我们的行业使用新技术并不局限于地下成像,也包括钻井和管理油藏的新方法。这次会议的目的是利用所介绍的面临着不同开发挑战的油田实例,说明现今油田开发的方法。所提供的例子来自:巴布亚新几内亚、墨西哥的 Campeche Sound、阿根廷的内乌肯盆地、加拿大落基山、美国落基山和哥伦比亚 Llanos 丘陵地带。一般的议题:包括需控制效益成本,从地下资料获取最大效益,综合这些数据与油藏工程模型,随着油田开发进程不断了解和修正计划。这次会议的重要成果表明,随着作业者在油田作业获得的经验,开发费用迅速下降。于是,昂贵的早期钻井成本(听起来非常之高)可能会使我们对非常低的实际开发费用感到迷惑不解。

油田开发中比较有挑战性的实例之一是由 Dupree(BP 勘探公司)在 Llanos 丘陵地区对 Cupiagua 油田的开发。Cupiagua 油田钻井是“他们感到比在世界任何地方都困难的经历”。头 3 口井经历了井壁不稳定、较高的水平应力、随时间变化的井斜和很难保持井眼轨迹。第一口井花了 4500 万美元且花了 1 年半的时间才完成。BP 公司已学会以较短的时间和较低的成本更有效地钻随后的井。在 Cupiagua 油田钻的第 9 口井花了 1300 万美元,仅钻了 118 天。

实际存在的几个问题决定了在 Cupiagua 钻井的困难。这个地区为构造活动区,所以井壁不稳定是其主要问题。这个重要的问题存在于厚厚的 Carbonera 组,而 Carbonera 组由页岩和裂缝性砂岩构成,在井中形成台肩。因此进行测井是很困难的,钻头会被卡住,还会导致车载测井的失败。在最早进行侧钻井时,浪费了大量的时间和金钱。BP 公司学会了在浅地层中定向钻井,从而避免了这些问题的产生,使得钻头“穿过”Carbonera 组。现在,他们可用单一基座钻 3 口井,大大地降低了费用,而且正在现场用一个基座钻 5 口井。Mirador 储层也存在一些问题。这是一套坚硬且致密的岩层,需使用许多个钻头。钻头工艺的提高已显著提高了在 Mirador 钻井的效率,且节约了额外的钻井时间和成本。

Hebberger 和 Franklin(雪弗龙)提供了另一个大大降低巴布亚新几内亚的 Iagiuf – Hedinia 油田费用的实例研究。由于其凹凸不平的地形、强烈的喀斯特化露头、潮湿的热带气候、茂密的植被和基础设施的缺乏,巴布亚新几内亚褶皱和冲断带成为最具挑战性的作业环境之一。此处的地震资料品质很差,勘探主要依据野外填图、遥感、潜在的野外勘查以及各种资料的综合分析而进行。Iaginf－Hedinia 油田刚好是在 1986 年全球石油价格暴跌后发现的，由于较低的原油价格和发现储量的不确定性，只有大大降低此项目费用，才能认为此项目是可行的。项目成功的关键在于早期向现行油藏管理的承诺，积极采集油藏数据，采用最新技术并组建一支多学科油藏管理队伍，而且发展与东道国政府和地方土地所有者之间亲密的和行之有效的工作关系。

会议的张贴论文也包括在褶皱和冲断带进行油田开发的各种实例研究。所提供的油田实例来自意大利的亚平宁山脉、法国的 Aquitaine 盆地、委内瑞拉的马拉开波盆地、委内瑞拉的 Monagas 地区、墨西哥的 Sabinas 盆地、墨西哥的 Veracruz 地区、墨西哥的 Chiapas－Tabasco 地区、墨西哥的 Campeche 海峡、加拿大的不列颠哥伦比亚山麓、特立尼达和阿根廷的 Neuquen 盆地。这些实例描述了各种圈闭的类型，油田的大小，油藏，油气的类型及开发问题。在下面的段落中讨论的两项研究成果是这些论文中颇具代表性的实例。

Le Vot 等人（埃尔夫）论述了法国 Meillon 天然气田的开发问题及解决方法。这个油田位于比利牛斯山麓边缘之下。此气田已从致密的裂缝性白云岩中开采了 13 年的天然气。然后产生水窜，使产量下降了 50%。研究认为水顺着断层行进，因而必须有一个详细的油田构造模型。老的二维地震资料品质很差，因此在整个地区进行了三维地震勘探。改进后的地下资料可用来建立详细的油藏模型和油田模型以描述水道。拥有这些资料后，另钻了一些开发井，从而显著提高了油田产量，且增加了储量。

Cooper 等人（泛加拿大和加拿大壳牌公司）描述了加拿大不列颠哥伦比亚东北部山麓地区的 Boulder 油田，说明了在裂缝性褶皱和冲断带钻井时通常所遇到的困难。储层是一个紧密不对称背斜中的三叠系致密裂缝性白云岩，尽管是以三维地震勘探为基础进行成图，1994 年钻的一口井穿入这个构造的缓翼，而不是钻入预期的背斜脊部。这个油藏为高裂缝性，但裂缝小而致密。因此，初始流速仅为 $14Mft^3/d$，远远低于预期的 $40Mft^3/d$ 流速，这口井作为一口近水平侧钻井试图在更靠近背斜脊部处钻遇更高裂缝性储层相。这口侧钻井成功地钻遇了背斜脊部的储层，经过测试，随着流体压力增加，流量增加了一倍，达到 $32Mft^3/d$。尽管取得了这些成功，随后的两口的流速却为非商业性流速，只是从最初的两口井进行开采。

褶皱带的数据采集和解释：地质和遥感

凹凸不平的地形、茂密的植被、岩层露头的缺失和低质量的地震资料阻碍了在许多褶皱和冲断带的勘探和开发活动。在这些地区，地质解释强烈地依赖遥感数据,包括陆地卫星 MSS,陆地卫星 TM,SPOT,SAR 和 RADARSAT。这些数据与地面信息结合在一起,有助于确定地面褶皱和断层样式。当与重力数据、磁力数据、地震反射数据、井数据以及与断层有关的褶皱模型结合在一起时,可用来推断地下构造样式和绘制潜伏构造圈闭。在对墨西哥、哥伦比亚、秘鲁、特立尼达、古巴、巴布亚新几内亚、加拿大、瑞士、阿拉斯加、中国、巴基斯坦和意大利的研究中论述了这些方法的应用。

如 Snedden 等人(Texaco)所指出的,遥感成像的花费仅是地震和井资料费用的一小部分,但对勘探和开发项目的全过程极其有用。经过恰当的地理标定之后,这些资料可作为绘图的基础并作为环境基础研究及环境文件的准备,以确定进行地震测线和重力勘探的位置,引导圈定井位;还可用于选择并确定选中的井位,并可作为进行现场抢修的“前”成像。

褶皱带的数据采集和解释:地球物理学和其他方法

如在许多发言报告中重申的那样,在褶皱和冲断带采集高质量的地震数据是一项巨大的挑战,也是对可行的勘探和开发项目的一个重要局限。会议的张贴论文提出了一系列地球物理数据采集和处理的新方法。贯穿于许多张贴报告的一条共同的线索是认识到需要制定专门的采集和处理计划以适应当地的地质情况。必须采用不同的震源、炸药量、下药深度、井眼组合和覆盖次数试验线,用以设计最佳采集参数。快速现场处理系统可允许现场调整,并可连续对采集数据进行质量检测。所列举的实例来自于秘鲁、玻利维亚、哥伦比亚、阿根廷、巴布亚新几内亚、墨西哥和澳大利亚。雪弗龙公司改进山前数据的策略是使用大炸药量和深井、坚持高覆盖次数,且在采集时,按照建议采用现场处理系统进行质量控制。

对于在褶皱和冲断带获得高质量地震成像,对数据处理给予密切的关注很有必要,如同数据采集一样,处理流程必须符合当地的地质条件。正如 Mitchel 和 Tilander(雪弗龙)所指出的,在许多褶皱和冲断带,处理的费用仅是采集费用的一小部分,所以应尽最大努力寻找最佳的处理流程。他们建议在进行处理时认真做好质量监控,处理过程中采用解释方法,与地质模型相结合,用不同的方法和不同的处理队伍(即处理员)对数据进行处理。他们列举哥伦比亚野外实例,论证了如何不得不对近地表低速层剖面进行处理校正。一个用地震确定的低速层被用来做静校正。在此项目进程中发现相对于先前采用的模型而言,此低速层比较厚,且层速度较高;因此,低速层速度通过折射静校正和深井口测试而确定得到的地震剖面表明有重大改进。在委内瑞拉东部的实例中,Uzcategui 和 De Almeida(Intervep 和 Corpoven)强调,建立速度模型就是获取好的深度偏移剖面的关键。

总结

据此次专题研讨会所宣布的目标评估,会议所提交的论文和张贴报告具有高质量和多样性;从此次会议期间的野外考察以及自始至终在每个会议场所、走廊、车内和野外露头进行的各种讨论来看,这次会议是非常成功的。以下是对这次会议中的一些重要观测结果的总结。

尽管褶皱和冲断带只占世界石油发现的一小部分,但通过最近在哥伦比亚和委内瑞拉取得的成功证明,褶皱和冲断带具有相当大的发现大型油气田的潜力。尽管在此构造带内进行勘探和开发必然会产生像在其他远景带一样遇到许多问题,但还会有其他的挑战。这些挑战可包括复杂地质(复杂的圈闭形状、运移路径和地质史)、起伏的地形、地震资料质量低、较高的油田作业成本、需考虑的环境问题和钻井问题。要在此背景下取得成功,需有效利用现有的方法来降低风险和成本。由于复杂的地质和不可想象的情况,勘探工作者在面对初次失败时必须能坚持下去。最终的结果是,他们也必须认识那些可能构成或破坏一个远景区的因素,偶尔还必须做出撤出决策。

纵观历史,在许多褶皱和冲断带进行勘探和油田开发,遇到的一个主要难题是中至劣质地震资料。许多文章论证地震资料质量可通过多种途径得以提高。第一个步骤应为根据当地地质情况为客户专门设计的采集计划,并采用快速现场处理系统对获得的数据进行质量检验和对采集参数进行调整。处理费用仅为采集费用的一小部分,所以应尽最大努力设计最佳采集参数,以保证现场记录最大量的数据。一旦获得了数据,就应对多种处理流程进行评估。这包括处理过程中认真做好质量控制,应用解释性方法,与地质模型相结合,采用不同方法和不同处理员对数据多次处理。就一切情况而论,进行地震解释应与露头数据、井数据、卫星与雷达成像、重力和磁法数据相结合,应采用精确的二维和三维平衡剖面图对多次解释结果进行检验。

大型的油气聚集可出现在各种各样构造样式和多种多样的储集岩中,在此背景下限制远景区的主要因素包括圈闭和运移时间。生油岩成熟通常受快速的构造埋藏控制,之后是阻止使得生油岩进一步成熟和油气生成的隆起。由于油气充填和圈闭形成通常只有一部分是同时发生的,总生油量中仅有一部分会充填进圈闭。因此,采用所有可用数据来判断褶皱和冲断带的地质史是极其关键的。在专题研讨会中描述的几项技术有助于判断构造作用、运移和圈闭时间。这包括采用伊利石年代分析、磷灰石裂变径迹分析和采用流体包裹体。断层封堵是此种构造域内的另一重要风险,是另一项需要研究的课题。假如这些风险存在,则认为值得勘探的最有利的褶皱带包括具有高品质生油岩、活跃的油气充填和持续的构造作用史的那些褶皱带。

Key to Exercises

Ⅰ.

1. Common themes included the need to manage costs effectively, to obtain the maximum benefit from subsurface data, to integrate that data with reservoir engineering models, and to continually learn and adapt plans as field development progresses.

2. Building velocity models.

3. The challenges can include complex geology (complex trap geometry, migration pathways, and geohistory), difficult terrain, poor seismic quality, higher cost of field operations, environmental considerations, and drilling problems.

4. The moderate to poor quality of seismic data.

5. It was suggested that the most favorable fold belts in which to explore include those with high – quality source rocks, an active charge, and an extended history of structuring.

Ⅱ. 1 – 5　DCAAA　6 – 10　BADAD

Ⅲ. 1 – 5　CDDAC

Ⅳ.

1. BP 公司已学会以较短的时间和较低的成本更有效地钻随后的井。

2. 尽管是以 3D 地震勘探为基础进行成图,1994 年钻的一口井穿入这个构造的缓翼,而不是预期的背斜脊部。

3. 凹凸不平的地形、茂密的植被、没有岩层露头和低质量的地震资料阻碍了在许多褶皱和冲断带的勘探和开发活动。

4. 快速现场处理系统可允许现场调整,并可连续对采集数据进行质量检测。

5. 纵观历史,在许多褶皱和冲断带进行勘探和油田开发遇到的一个主要难题是中至劣质地震资料。

Ⅴ.

1. 尽管在褶皱和冲断带的勘探和开发必然会像在其他构造带那样产生相同的问题,但在这里还会遇到更多的挑战。例如:具有复杂的圈闭几何形态;复杂的埋藏和热力史;石油开始生成、运移和圈闭形成之间的窄等时线;

复杂的石油充满和溢出史。其他难题包括与活跃的构造应力体制有关的复杂地形、低质量地震数据、油田作业的高花费、环境限制和钻井问题。

2. 凹凸不平的地形、茂密的植被、没有岩层露头和低质量的地震资料阻碍了在许多褶皱和冲断带的勘探和开发活动。在这些地区,地质解释强烈地依赖遥感数据,包括陆地卫星 MSS,陆地卫星 TM,SPOT,SAR 和 RADARSAT。这些数据与地面信息结合在一起有助于确定地面褶皱和断层样式。

参考文献

[1] McWhorter R, Torguson B. Palacios 油田:一个三维勘探史例[J]. 刘玉班,译. 国外油气勘探,1996,8(5):585-592.

[2] Montgomery S L. 堪萨斯州芬妮县斯图尔特油田薄层河道储集层的地震识别[J]. 李洪革,杨红军,译. 国外油气勘探,1998,10(1):53-64.

[3] Rajasekaran S. 复杂地形陆上数据的叠前处理[J]. 李启迪,译. 国外油气勘探,1996,8(5):626-637.

[4] Talley D, Davis T. Vacuum 油田的动态油藏特征[J]. 李令喜,译. 国外油田工程,1999(9):5-9.

[5] Haldorsen H. 油藏描述中的挑战 [J]. 张申,译. 国外油气勘探,1996,8(2):177-186.

[6] Aguilera R. 天然裂缝性储集层的地质特征 [J]. 袁秉衡,译. 国外油气勘探,2000,12(2):152-156.

[7] Brenneke J C. 断层圈闭分析 [J]. 赵奇志,译. 国外油气勘探,1996,8(6):688-695.

[8] 吴洁,李茗. 北非古达米斯盆地石油地质特征及勘探方向[J]. 石油地质与工程,2014(2): 12-15,19.

[9] 柯宗强. 埃及红海西北部地区构造对油气成藏的影响 [J]. 国外油气勘探,1997,9(2):153-168.

[10] 顾莉,刘绍光. 在褶皱和冲断带的石油勘探和开发——从 Hedberg 专题讨论会得出的观点[J]. 国外油气勘探,2000,12(1):17-23.

[11] 程建,段铁军,倪春华,等. 西非科特迪瓦盆地石油地质特征及成藏规律研究[J]. 石油实验地质,2013(3): 291-295.

[12] Ron McWhorter, Bill Torguson. Palacios Field: A 3-D Case History[J]. The Leading Edge, 1995, 14(12):1225-1230.

[13] Scott L Montgomery. Stewart Field, Finney County, Kansas. Seismic Definition of Thin Channel Reservoirs [J]. AAPG Bulletin, 1996, 80(12):1833-1844.

[14] Sara Rajasekaran, George A. McMechan. Prestack Processing of Land Data with Complex Topography[J]. Geophysics, 1995, 60(6):1875-1886.

[15] Daniel J Talley, Thomas L Davis. Dynamic Reservoir Characterization of Vacuum Field [J]. The Leading Edge, 1998, 14(12):1396-1402.

[16] H H Haldorsen, E Damsleth. Challenges in Reservoir Characterization [J]. AAPG, 1993, 77(4):541-551.

[17] Roberto Aguilera. Geologic Aspects of Naturally Fractured Reservoirs [J]. The Leading Edge, 1998, 17(12):1667-1670.

[18] James C Brenneke. Analysis of Fault Traps [J]. World Oil, 1995, 216(12):63-70.

[19] J Alvarez-Marron. Geometry and Evolution of the Frontal Part of the Magallanes Fore-

land Thrust and Fold Belt (Vicuna Area), Tierra del Fuego, Southern Chile [J]. AAPG Bulletin,1993,77(11):1904 -1921.

[20] M G Salah, A S Alsharhan. Structural Influence on Hydrocarbon Entrapment in the Northwestern Red Sea, Egypt[J]. AAPG Bulletin,1996,80(1):101 -117.

[21] Javire Meneses - Rocha. Petroleum Exploration and Production in Fold and Thrust Belts: Ideas From a Hedberg Research Symposium [J]. AAPG Bulletin,1999,83(6): 889 -897.

[22] Oluwafemi S Obayori,Sunday A Adebusoye,Adams O Adewale,et al. Differential degradation of crude oil (Bonny Light) by four Pseudomonas strains[J]. Journal of Environmental Sciences,2009(2):243 -248.

[23] Xiangsheng, ZhangDejun, XuChunyan,et al. Isolation and identification of biosurfactant producing and crude oil degrading Pseudomonas aeruginosa strains[J]. Chemical Engineering Journal,2012(20):138 -146.

[24] Amy M Cecchi,William C Koskinen,H H Cheng,et al. Sorption - desorption of phenolic acids as affected by soil properties[J]. Biology and Fertility of Soils,2004 (4): 235 -242.

[25] Rengathavasi Thavasi,Singaram Jayalakshmi,Ibrahim M Banat. Effect of biosurfactant and fertilizer on biodegradation of crude oil by marine isolates of Bacillus megaterium, Corynebacterium kutscheri and Pseudomonas aeruginosa[J]. Bioresource Technology, 2011(2):772 -778.